Twenty-sixth day of June in the year One thou...

... Hughes de Wind of Singapore Esquire of the first part a...

... Rodger, Charles Dunlop and Jonas Daniel Vaughan...

... Club or Association in Singapore called the "..." all...

... dated the 1st day of November in the year 1859, ... bear...

... Esquire of the one part and the Reverend Jean Marie B...

... consideration therein mentioned did in pursuance of Act N...

... to the said Jean Marie Beurel, his executors, administrators...

... in the district of Claymore and island of Singapore as te...

... bounded on the North by Stevens Road, on the South by...

... the West by William Scott's plantation estimated to contai...

... with the appurtenances thereto belonging, (the said piece...

... Nos 28 and 29 in the Government Map of the dist...

... Government Indenture No 23 dated the 2nd day of...

... and premises comprised in the said Indenture d...

... his executors, administrators and assigns for ever...

... now vested in the said Arthur Hughes de W...

... Wind has agreed to sell and release to the par...

... piece or parcel of land and premises comprised in...

... price of Dollars six hundred ($600) but subje...

... ... of the said premises hereinafter contained...

Forty Good Men

Published by The Tanglin Club
5 Stevens Road, Singapore 1025
Copyright by The Tanglin Club, 1991

Wordmaker Design Pte. Ltd.
Typeset in Paladium
Singapore Sang Choy Colour Separation Pte. Ltd.
Printed in Singapore by Times Offset Pte. Ltd.

ISBN 981-00-2295-6

First published in 1991.

Endpapers: *Title deeds to the property of The Tanglin Club, 1866 — T.C.*
Contents: *Page 8: P & O Docks — The Straits Times Annual 1905-6, 1st Issue;*
A ladies at-home, 1913 — British Malaya, May 1939; Tanglin Club lido evening, 1932 — courtesy of Pamela Roper-Caldbeck.
Page 9: Sir John Nicoll (second from right), guest of honour at the Tanglin ball, 1954 — T.C.;
At the Max Bygraves Show, March 1989 — T.C.
Appendices: *Page 177: Malay syces — The Straits Times Annual, 1937.*
Page 178: Prisoner of war correspondence from club member — courtesy of Renée Parrish.
Page 179: Invitations to the Coronation Ball , June 3, 1953 — courtesy of Arnold Thorne.
Page 180: Cover of The Straits Calendar and Directory, 1868 — N.L.;
Menu of 1865 dinner held during the 125th anniversary celebration of the Tanglin Club, 1990 — T.C.
Page 181: Postage stamp 1922 — N.A.
Page 182: Peggy Cutler and Sue Thorne's 40th birthday party invitation, 1956 — courtesy of Arnold Thorne.
Page 183: Christmas ball tickets, 1958 — T.C.
Page 184: Invitation to the Tanglin ball, 1950 — courtesy of Arnold Thorne.
Page 185: Member's monthly account, 1948 — courtesy of Pauline Adams.

Forty Good Men

The Story Of The Tanglin Club In The Island Of Singapore
1865 ~ 1990

Text   Barbara Ann Walsh

Research   Jan and Graham Bell

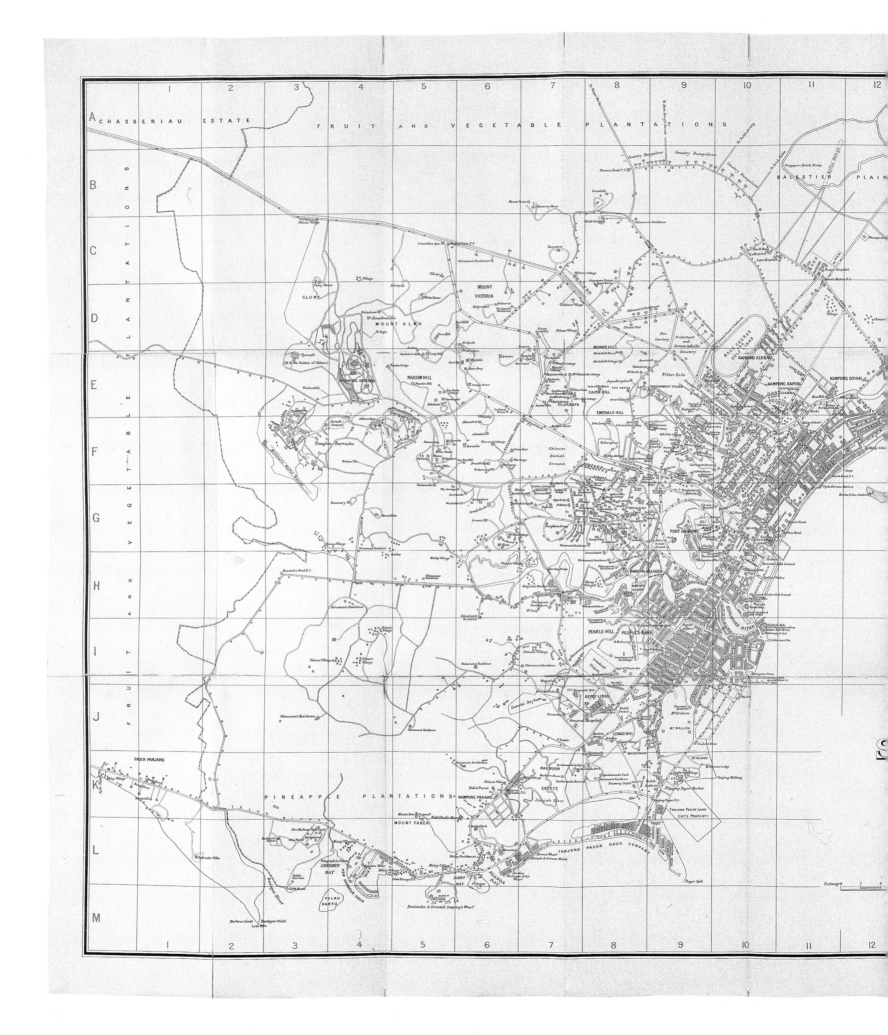

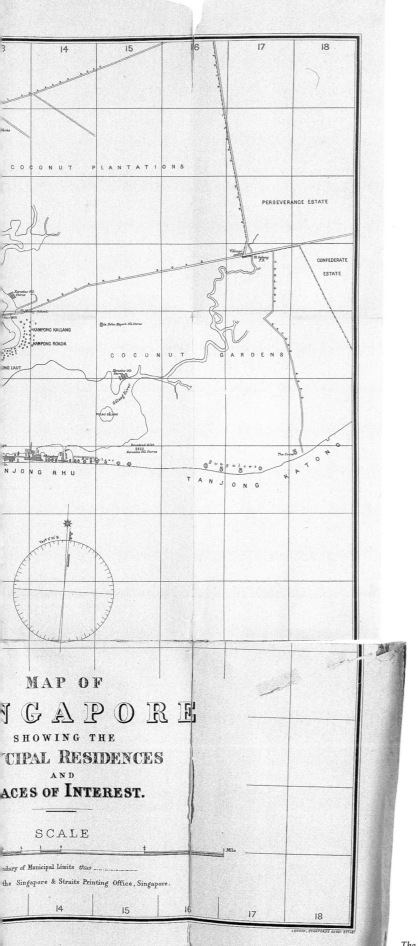

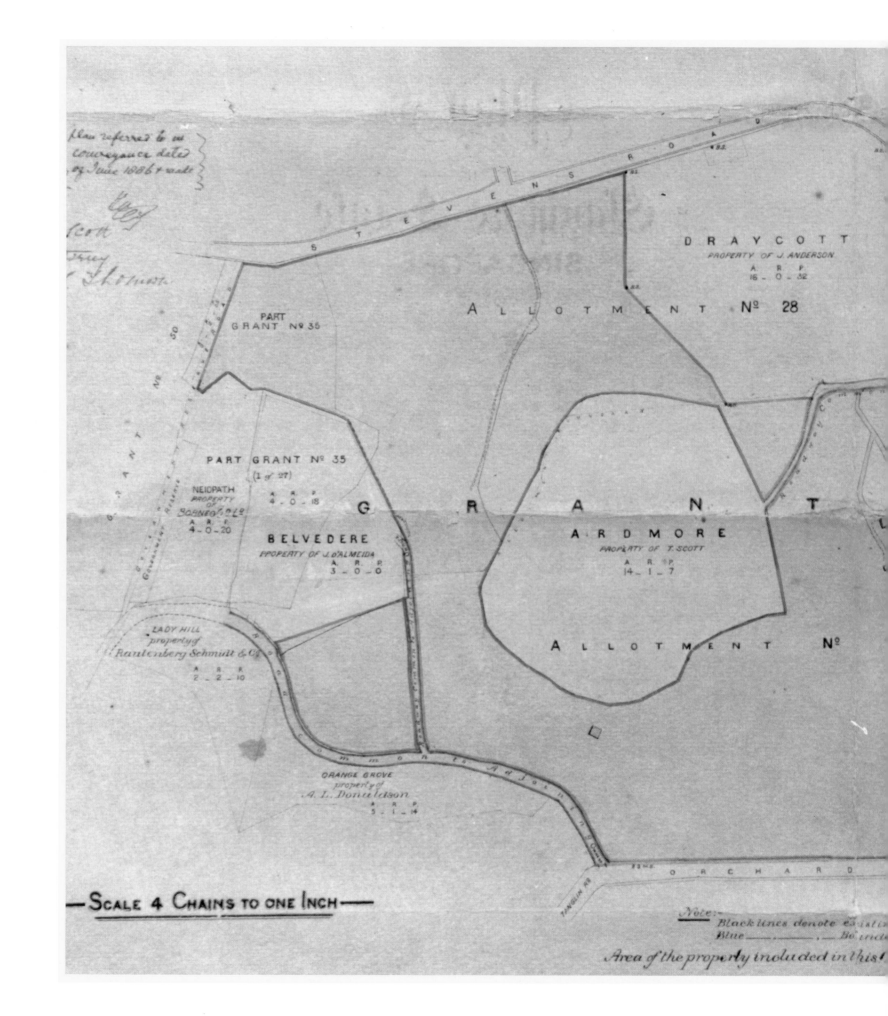

plan referred to in
conveyance dated
of June 1886 + made

PART
GRANT Nº 35

STEVENS ROAD

DRAYCOTT
PROPERTY OF J. ANDERSON
A. R. P.
16 _ 0 _ 32

ALLOTMENT Nº 28

PART GRANT Nº 35
(1 of 27)

NEIDPATH
PROPERTY
OF
BORNEO Cº Lᵈ
A. R. P.
4 _ 0 _ 20

A. R. P.
4 _ 0 _ 18

G R A N T

ARDMORE
PROPERTY OF T. SCOTT
A. R. P.
14 _ 1 _ 7

BELVEDERE
PROPERTY OF J. D'ALMEIDA
A. R. P.
3 _ 0 _ 0

LADY HILL
property of
Rautenberg Schmidt & Cº
A. R. P.
2 _ 2 _ 10

ALLOTMENT Nº

ORANGE GROVE
property of
A. L. Donaldson
A. R. P.
5 _ 1 _ 14

TANGLIN RD

ORCHARD

— SCALE 4 CHAINS TO ONE INCH —

Notes:-
Black lines denote existing
Blue _____ . __ Boundaries

Area of the property included in this

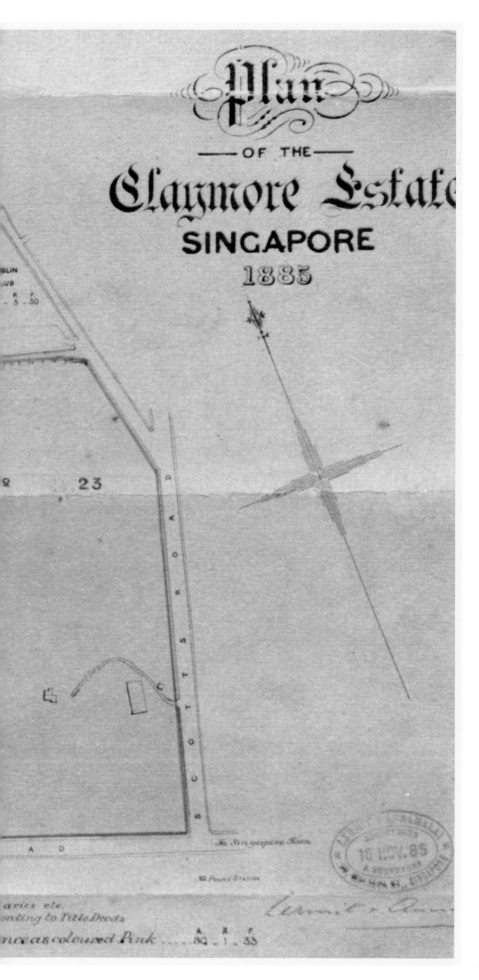

Allotments Nos. 28 & 29 with the property of the Tanglin Club, 1885 — T.C.

Contents

Water-colour of the Tanglin Club in the 1890's by Martin Gilmon, 1990 — T.C.

Preface

The Tanglin Club was founded as a social club that, over the years, has met the wants of a community and its members in a variety of ways. By 1990, one sees that its success has been and will be dependent on its relevance to such needs, a challenge as daunting today as it was in 1865. While there are still members who recall with wistful nostalgia the memorable New Year's Eve balls, the social occasions that accompanied tennis matches, the Sunday tiffins and the leisurely camaraderie of earlier times, the club today caters to a new generation of members whose lives are dictated by the stressful and competing demands of the last decade of the twentieth century. Few can imagine how the Tanglin Club will serve an exclusive membership in the next century; those who try to are certain that it will never be the same.... Kindly remember, fellow members, this sentiment was also aired one hundred years ago!

What Kind Of Men And Why

In 1977 writer Eric Jennings was commissioned to produce a short history of the Tanglin Club to coincide with the completion of the new clubhouse but the publication was never realised. Another proposal in 1989 was rejected as the cost exceeded expectations. In 1990 as the 125th anniversary loomed, the need to document the history of the club became an imperative. An editorial committee of members volunteered to produce a volume — with six months to research and write the text! — although some sourcing of materials had been initiated by Graham Bell, chairman of the Tanglin Club's 125th anniversary organising committee, over the previous year. Reseach tasks were allotted — Jan Bell to cover people, society and photographs, Graham Bell the gaps in the club's history, Andrew Jordan the club's properties — and all materials passed to me to be woven into an unfolding story of the Tanglin Club as a social institute defined by the environment of the times. In order to situate the chronological development of the Tanglin Club against the broad socio-economic and political trends that shaped the lives and interests of the élites who constituted its core membership, I divided the book into twenty-five-year periods, each organized around an evocative theme. With the spectre of constantly appearing and lapsing deadlines, the preoccupation with trying to do justice to a hundred and twenty-five-year evolution became a full-time daily routine. We all worked long hours to assess the available materials; if there are sections where our inexperience and omissions are obvious, our undaunted enthusiasm will call on members' forbearance.

There were many heated arguments over the gaps in our research on the early period of the club's existence, and various speculations could not be substantiated to everyone's satisfaction. Hearsay had it that after the Japanese occupation during World War II no records were to be found; yet, in 1965 Bill Kerr, then club manager, decided to clear out "a room under the ballroom chock full of papers and boxes some dating back to the turn of the century." Could the answers to many of our questions have been tossed out at this time? Why, for example, did Thomas Dunman, the first club president, make a point of distancing himself from the club so soon after its formation? What kind of 'good men and true' were those forty individuals who founded 'a suburban social institute to meet the wants of Britishers in the colony'? Why did these same men all share a passion for amateur dramatics? What role did affiliations with commercial, political or other institutions, for example, the Masonic Lodge, play in banding a select group of colonials together in a social club that upheld the privacy of its members? Readers can enjoy judging for themselves on what basis the club may have attained its historical exclusivity. Long-time members of the club familiar with the history of Singapore may recognise much of the background and source materials presented. More recent members perhaps will find in this review of the last century and a quarter of the club's existence some new and different insights into the contemporary life of the colonial island settlement of Singapore and its transformation into a global city-state, one of the brightest diamonds in the Pacific Rim tiara no less.

Barbara Ann Walsh

Foreword

Founded 1865

Tanglin Club Committee 1990
President:
George Sandosham (George Sandosham & Co.)
Vice-President:
Michael K.L. Khoo (Michael Khoo & B.B. Ong)
Honorary Treasurer:
Graham S. Bell (Crown Cork & Seal (Singapore) Pte. Ltd.)
Committee Members:
Dr. Colin Evans (consultant surgeon)
Robin G. Langdale (North Borneo Timbers Bhd.)
Ray F. Lynch (McDermott Equipment Inc.)
Roger H.W. Marshall (Chartwell Enterprises Ltd.)
Alexander C. McColl (Robbins & Meyers Canada Ltd.)
Noris Ong C.G. (Coopers & Lybrand)
Roger A. Prior (Roger Prior Associates)
Gilbert Whitesman (Ferranti Systems Singapore Pte. Ltd.)
[Back row left to right: Ray F. Lynch, Alexander C. McColl, Roger H.W. Marshall, Edward J. Grinsted, Norris Ong C.G. Front row left to right: Dr. Colin Evans, Michael K.L. Khoo, George Sandosham, Graham S. Bell, Roger A. Prior]

Justly Proud Of Its Premier Standing

The forty 'good men and true' who founded the Tanglin Club in 1865 would be justly proud of its premier standing with over five thousand members representing more than fifty different nationalities in the island of Singapore one hundred and twenty-five years later. Having survived the vicissitudes of debt and war, age and apathy, even a major transformation, the Tanglin Club still retains a certain exclusivity as one of the most prestigious social clubs in Singapore today. Many of the personalities who have graced the evolving scene of this social institution are those that have figured prominently in the greater drama of the history and development of Singapore; in 1990 the 125th anniversary of the Tanglin Club also had the added significance of being in the year when the Republic of Singapore celebrated its twenty-fifth year of independence.

The need to document the history of the club was acknowledged some years ago but despite the best intentions various efforts did not come to fruition. The impetus for this commemorative project came from Graham Bell, the chairman of the 125th anniversary committee, whose enthusiasm has inspired a publication which many members may see as coming almost too late. It has been an enormous task to present a review of one hundred and twenty-five years of the Tanglin Club. Facts and figures, writings and memories were compiled and sought from a variety of sources locally and abroad; the task of verifying and piecing these together was made no less easy by the unfortunate absence of club records — with the exception of a copy of the minutes of the 1922 AGM — for the years 1865 to 1946. Still, though much, regrettably, may have been lost with the passing of time, the dedication of Jan Bell as principal researcher, club members Graham Bell and Andrew Jordan (before his premature departure to Hong Kong) in providing supplementary research, and Barbara Walsh, wife of member Frank Walsh, in her work as author has at long last provided club members with a book to enjoy and treasure. The result is an historical account that provides not only an insight into the story of the Tanglin Club but also a perspective on life in Singapore as recorded in the diaries and letters of various personalities who have counted among the membership of the club.

My thanks go to all the members and individuals who have unselfishly contributed their time and effort towards the realisation of this book, one that stands as a fitting tribute to commemorate the 125th anniversary of the Tanglin Club in the island of Singapore.

George Sandosham
President 1990

A SUBURBAN

SOCIAL INSTITUTE

Tea on the lawn, c. 1890 — N.A.

The Singapore River from Fort Canning Hill, woodcut, artist unknown, 1866 — Travels in the East Indian Archipelago

When the Tanglin Club was founded in 1865, the island of Singapore was a thriving, boisterous place of diverse peoples. The town had developed on either side of the Singapore River which had been the heart of the island since Sir Stamford Raffles and seven ships of the British expedition arrived in 1819 to establish a new port within the East Indies. By 1865 business activities tightly packed the west bank; around Raffles Place (called Commercial Square until 1858) there were offices, warehouses, stores and native bazaars. On the east bank, site of the Law Courts and Padang, old houses of the principal merchants stretched from High Street to Beach Road. By the 1860's few of these were occupied as residences; the best had been taken up for hotels — like the Adelphi Hotel which opened in 1863 and the Hotel de l'Europe, which earlier had been functioning as the London Hotel — and one was used as a Masonic Lodge. St Andrew's Church, in the same vicinity, was consecrated in 1862. The 1860 census showed a population in excess of 80,000 and for the first time more than half were Chinese. Europeans were a small minority; of these there were less than 500 British, most of whom were employed in the colonial civil service. The remainder, along with Germans, Danes, Swiss, French, Dutch and Americans, were engaged in business. The greater number of Europeans lived about two miles out of town: River Valley Road and Cavenagh Road were the fashionable areas. Three miles out of town the houses thinned, and only a small number were sited beyond a four-mile radius.

...the finest nutmeg garden... The district of Tanglin was a beautiful place in the 1860's. Raffles had placed such faith in the soil and climate of Singapore that he had sent enthusiastic reports of the spices to be grown here. Convinced of the same, early settlers planted coffee, cotton, cinnamon, cloves and indigo; sugarcane was introduced and nutmeg-growing became 'a sort of mania'. By 1834 the town was surrounded by a belt of Chinese market gardens and, farther out, Chinese gambier and pepper plantations; coconut plantations thrived in the sandy coastal Katong area. By the 1840's great plantations had appeared in the Tanglin and Claymore districts of this 'veritable spice island'. The first of these in Tanglin, CARNIE'S HILL was established by Charles C. Carnie; W.W. Willans had a plantation at Mount Harriet, part being where Tanglin Barracks was later built; G.G. Nichol's SRI MENANTI was a 150-acre estate at Chatsworth; William Cuppage was established at Emerald Hill; C.R. Prinsep's plantation was on part of the land purchased in 1867 for Government House; Dr. T. Oxley's KILLINEY ESTATE, bounded by River Valley, Tank, Orchard and Grange

In 1846 the furthest plantation bungalow in Tanglin was that of Thomas Hewetson at Mount Elizabeth — then an area notorious for tigers — which, a few years later, was ransacked by a gang of thieves. Following the rise of unlawful secret societies and appeals from the householders in the relatively isolated bungalows in the area, the Orchard Road police station was established in the 1850's to deter such marauders; in 1863 the police went into uniform. [Orchard Road Police Station, c 1890's — The First 150 Years of Singapore]

roads, was described as 'the finest nutmeg garden'; and William R. Scott's CLAYMORE ESTATE included land on which the Tanglin Club now stands. Disease struck the plantations in 1855, and by 1862 European estate-type agriculture was defeated by soil deficiencies, plant diseases, pests and the absence of seasons. When the cultivation of nutmeg ceased, the land was subdivided into smaller estates as far out as TANG LENG, the property of William Napier, and symmetrical avenues of plants with their blossom and fruit took shape beyond the town limits. On the former CLAYMORE ESTATE, were such grand houses as John Anderson's DRAYCOTT, T. Scott's ARDMORE, William Scott's HURRICANE, A.L. Donaldson's ORANGE GROVE, The Borneo Company's property NEIDPATH (now the Shangri-la Hotel) where William M. Mulholland, a member of the first club committee, resided, the GOODWOOD between Scotts and Stevens roads, and BLANCHE HOUSE, an early home of the German club on Mount Elizabeth. As described by Lee Kip Lin in *The Singapore House,* "the houses were usually built on the highest ground of the estate, often in the middle of the vast domain, in quiet seclusion at the end of a long, winding carriageway. In the Tanglin district, where the land undulated, the houses were inevitably on top of a hillock. The estates were planted right up to the immediate grounds of the building. Viewed from a distance, the white stuccoed houses stood in splendid isolation against a somber backdrop of forest uncleared or only partially cleared."

Early coffee plantation — A.O.

The milieu in Singapore at the time the club was founded is described by Roland St. John Braddell in Walter Makepeace's *One Hundred Years of Singapore* as comprising "kind folk, hard at bargain, not very cultured perhaps...but — BRITISH — Oh, so British! ...Never mind the swarming masses in the streets, yellow, black and brown, or the chattering Babel of their many tongues — the place is British, stolid, prosperous, conservative, resentful of change, distrustful of enthusiasms, and commercial — above all, behind all, beyond all commercial." By other accounts, it was romantic and colourful: young military officers galloped their ponies round the Esplanade and bowed to the ladies on their evening stroll; military bands played twice a week on the Padang. However, old timers regretted the passing of the early informal days when wealth, race and colour were of little account. The everyday life of the British settlement in the 1860's "had become more sophisticated, snobbish and exclusively European... there were not 40 families who aimed at forming a part of society, and apparently there was a good deal of snobbery amongst them," relates John Cameron, who also comments, "when lovely woman sets out to adorn herself and invites the shopman to provide her with the wherewithal, the names by which she indicates

19

An Open-Air And Non-Commercial Exchange

In *Our Tropical Possessions in Malayan India* John Cameron, an early editor of *The Straits Times*, describes a day in Singapore in the 1860's: "By five o'clock a 68-pounder at Fort Canning ushered in the day. This was the accepted signal for all the old residents to start from bed. By six o'clock all were generally dressed and out of doors for a ride. This early morning walk for long remained an institution, friends were met, and gossip and news exchanged. During the training season for the races the horses did their practice in the early morning, as they do now, and the Stewards provided tea on the course, which made it the rendezvous for most of the residents, whether racing enthusiasts or not. Breakfast was at nine, 'fish, curry and rice, and perhaps a couple of eggs washed down with a tumbler or so of good claret.'

Arriving in town, a quarter of an hour or so was spent in going the rounds of the Square to learn the news of the morning.

"These Commercial Square gatherings were quite a characteristic of the place and of the community, and whatever channels they opened to the flow of local gossip, or even scandal, they were useful as serving the purpose of an open-air and non-commercial exchange. By half-past ten business proper commenced, and lasted without a break till the tiffin hour, one o'clock, when half an hour's relaxation and a very light meal were indulged in. About that time the daily newspaper came out, and there was a goodly flocking either to the Exchange or to the godowns in the Square for a perusal of it.

"Two o'clock was the Exchange hour, and though it was not much used as a

Straits Produce, Christmas, 1893

place of inter-communication on commercial subjects, yet as a rendezvous and place where the leading men of the mercantile community could have an interchange of ideas, even on irrelevant matters, it had the good effect of promoting and maintaining a more general intimacy than might otherwise prevail. Unlike the Chamber of Commerce, from which it was distinct, the Exchange as a body assumed no political influence; it was rather distinguished for its hearty and mixed co-operation in all that attended to ameliorate or enliven the conditions of life in the Settlement. Its place came to be taken by the Singapore Club.

"Business hours were not severe; by half-past four or five most offices closed, and the greater number then resorted to the fives court or cricket ground. The band nights twice a week on the Esplanade still remained a great institution. Except on such nights most people retired home before six o'clock, and dinner was at half-past six or seven, the former being the more usual hour. The dinner was as substantial as in the Thirties and the dishes remained of the same nature."

General Post Office and Exchange with a corner of Flint's Building on the left, c 1890 — A.O.

Raffles Square, Singapore.

Raffles Place, c 1895 — A.O.

her wants are apt to astonish the unfortunate male who accompanies her.... Heaven must have helped the husbands of the Sixties; fancy following your wife into Government House in the usual furtive and hang-dog manner, what time she was attired in a balzerine ditto or a tambourined muslin!" A certain Mrs. Beal was the presiding goddess of fashion in Singapore, "her temple being situate within the portals of Robinson & Co." an early advertisement of the firm informed in March 1861 in the *Singapore Review and Monthly Magazine.*

...a liberality
conducing to
good health and
long life...

Writing of the 1860's John Cameron also observes, "the good folks of Singapore are by no means inclined to place too narrow restrictions on their libations, and it has been found in the experience of the older residents that a liberality in this respect conduces to good health and long life." Beer was sold in kilderkins at John Little and Company; Emmersons soda was seventy-five cents a dozen, tonic one dollar and twenty-five cents, and lemonade one dollar (the esteemed firm of Fraser & Neave had yet to be established). The drink of the 1860's was 'brandy and Schweppes', the latter imported in casks. In the *Singapore Daily Times* of Friday, October 6, 1865, John Little advertised Jules Mumm & Co.'s champagne; Red & Brown Wax pints and quarts; Exshaw's brandy in barrels; beer — Inde Coope, Bass, Allsopps & Tennants and Guinness Dublin Stout in pints and quarts. Sydney beef was sold in tierces of 300 lb at twenty-two dollars per tierce; in barrels of 200 lb at sixteen dollars each; and in half barrels of 100 lb at nine dollars each. Robinsons advertised a new shipment of Nagasaki umbrellas (12- and 16-rib), sunshades, flannels and blankets, railway rugs, dinner sets ex NORFOLK, Guinness Stout, Bass Ale, Islay whiskey, dinner sherries, boots and shoes ex WEST. The Borneo Company advertised for "a small vessel to proceed to the wreck of the MARIBELLE in Acrimata Passage" and announced that they had been appointed agents for the Norwich Union Insurance Company. They also announced that Herbert Buchanan and William Mulholland (both members of the first club committee) were authorised to sign the firm "by procuration" at the Singapore branch. Boustead & Company (formerly Boustead Shwabe and Company) were agents for a good many ships in the harbour. Many press advertisements of the day quoted payments to be made in Spanish, Mexican or Peruvian dollars. There was no British standard coin available at the time due to the apathy of the Singapore authorities in not obtaining a sufficient supply of coins.

In April 1865 a disaster occurred in the harbour involving a 'schooner-rigged, paddle-wheel steamer of 150 tons burthen,' which belonged to His Highness the Temenggong of Johore, an independent Malay territory. The vessel, the JOHORE, was in Singapore on delivery from England with two of the Temenggong's brothers on board to pay a compliment to the British governor who, with a party of European residents, had been invited for an Easter Monday pleasure trip around the island. A trial run was planned for Saturday, April 15. Steam was got up at noon, intending that the vessel should leave at 2 P.M., but the steamer blew up, probably because cold water was pumped into an empty and red-hot boiler. About 30 people were killed, including one of the Temenggong's brothers, five Europeans, two Chinese and a number of Malays. Of those who survived were the Dato Bentara Dalam Ibrahim, who later played a leading role in the modernization of Johore; Jaafar bin Haji Mohamed, who became a distinguished mentri besar of Johore (his son Dato Onn Jaafar was the founder of UMNO and his grandson was Hussein Onn, Malaysia's third prime minister); Abdul Rahman bin Andak who was to play a pivotal role in the Johore sultanate's attempts to escape British tutelage. [Blowing up of the steamer JOHORE, 1865 — A.O.]

The Singapore Free Press, October 5, 1865; Singapore Daily Times, October 6, 1865

"High Street in the Sixties was composed of compound houses. On the left was the Studio of Schlacter the photographer and at the corner of North Bridge Road stood the famous Kugelman's bar, hotel and restaurant where the first Australian barmaids were employed. They all 'struck' and had to be sent back to Australia. Kugelman's was well patronised especially at night as it was the only place where a late supper — cold meats and grill could be got. Later on, much later it became the Egg Club. The Tanglin Club commenced in 1865 and until its bowling alleys were opened, and became an evening resort, the roisterer used to hie him to the Moses Pavilion where Hock Lam Street is now. Here bowls were played till all hours, losers paying for the game, and then three balls each for the winners to settle who should pay for the last drink. [Bowls is a dead game now since the Tanglin Club alleys were pulled down.]" John Cameron in Our Tropical Possessions in Malayan India. [Hotel de l'Europe, c 1890 — A.O.]

...new arrivals were immediately taken around to all the clubs ...

In the early months of 1865 the Singapore press was full of the American War of Independence and Lincoln's assassination after the Union Victory in April. Also covered was the arrival of the Confederate cruiser SHENANDOAH which visited Singapore on March 11 en route to Australia, the Philippines and the Far East. Early in April there was a report that the stock of American ice had run out (ice and fresh produce were imported from America); the efforts of a local company which had started to make ice in 1861 were unsuccessful, to the consternation of all the inhabitants. Real estate property in Singapore was a good investment and continued to maintain value. In 1865 four lots on a triangular block measuring 34,000 square feet between Princess Street and the sea wall were sold at auction for 47,000 dollars under a 999-year lease. Opium trading was also of great commercial interest to the colony and businessmen eagerly awaited the results of the regular opium auctions in Calcutta. A report in the Singapore Daily Times of September 11 that gold was discovered in a hill which was being levelled for site works behind the Tanjong Pagar Dock Company evidently led to a minor gold rush at the time — but nothing more was reported on it. After the opening of the Suez Canal in 1869, and with the advent of steamers a revolution occurred in travel. In 1867 the record passage for a ship between Singapore and London was 116 days; in 1870 'the SHANTUNG steamed from Glasgow to Singapore in 42 days, stops included.' There were many newcomers to Singapore in the years 1865 to 1890 and the small port founded by Raffles had developed into a thriving trading centre. New arrivals had much to learn not only about the conduct of the merchant houses and the boundless opportunities offered but also about the required code of conduct and dress; in those times they were immediately taken around to all the clubs and introduced to everyone.

In 1863 the Tanjong Pagar Dock Company was established. By 1865, 1,440 feet of wharves had been built at the New Harbour. Constructed from hardwood, and the godowns roofed either with tiles or corrugated iron, these fortunately survived the great fire of 1877, the greatest disaster then on record in the history of Singapore. Had they perished, it was said, Singapore would have been ruined for some years. In the days of sailing ships, the harbour was a magnificent sight — in 1865 there were 154 square-rigged vessels in the port at one time. Between 1861 and 1864 land to the seaward of Raffles Place was reclaimed and protected by a sea-wall. This formed Collyer Quay which consisted of a complete line of buildings joined by continuous verandahs on the upper floor where every merchant house had its telescope to scan the horizon for arriving ships, and which in 1866 was considered one of the great sights of the Far East. [*The Great Fire, 1877 — A.O.; Square-rigged vessels in harbour, section of lithograph, W. Gray, 1861 — N.M.; Collyer Quay in the 1880's — One Hundred Years of Singapore*]

The Policy Of Uniformity

From the early 1850's, the European merchants had become increasingly frustrated by the autocratic nature of the East India Company's governors and its inefficient bureaucracy. Despite its growing economic power, Singapore lacked a modern and sophisticated administration. In 1853 the East India Company's charter was renewed and the following year a new legislative council with enlarged powers set up in Calcutta. The governor-general of India, the Marquis of Dalhousie, with the engrossing duties entailed upon him by the government of India, could ill spare the time to consider the internal government of the Straits Settlements and matters of foreign policy connected with them. "Singapore was to suffer more than any other Indian-administered territory from the council's policy of enforcing uniformity, and its vigorous centralization campaign eventually goaded the Singapore merchants to demand a break with India," comments C.M. Turnbull in *A History of Singapore*.

By 1857 the crisis in the administration of Singapore, fuelled by the newspapers, strikes and riots, and public grievances, reached a peak. At a public meeting on September 15 support was promised for a petition to the British parliament from the European merchants of Calcutta demanding the abolition of the East India Company. Singapore requested that the Straits Settlements be separated from India and ruled directly from London in order to secure a local legislative council and participation in government. The matter was taken up as a practical issue by a young merchant, William Henry Macleod Read, which began a process that led eventually to the transfer of the Straits Settlements to the Colonial Office in 1867. In the meantime, the East India Company became extinct in 1858 and the transfer of India to the direct rule of the British Crown meant that the Straits Settlements continued to be administered by Calcutta — a change which had little impact in Singapore. The last governor of India, Colonel W. Orfeur Cavenagh, enjoyed unquestioning loyalty, support and respect, backed Thomas Dunman in strengthening the police force and promoted improvements in public works and administration. However, William Read and others kept the transfer issue alive.

On April 1, 1867, the Order in Council constituting the Straits Settlements a colony of the Crown was read, and after the gun salutes died away the first unofficial members of the legislative council met in the Town Hall with the first Queen's governor. The members included William Read who became Tanglin Club president in 1879.

The 1873 Legislative Council of the Straits Settlements. Standing: Thomas Scott, Dr. R. Little, Thomas Braddell (Attorney-General), W.R. Scott, H.F. Plow (clerk of the council), W. Willans (colonial treasurer), J.W.W. Birch (colonial secretary), Hoo Ah Kay Whampoa, Major J.F.A. McNair (colonial engineer). Seated: Mr. (later, Sir) Thomas Sidgreaves (chief justice), Major-General Sir Harry St. George Ord (governor) — N.A.

Worthy Representatives Of A Nation

The decision to start a suburban social club for the Britishers in the Tanglin and Claymore districts in 1865 — the German community had moved their club out of town to BLANCHE HOUSE which stood near the junction of Scotts Road and Stevens Road — can be viewed in relation to the article entitled 'A Young Men's Club' by Young Scotland which appeared in the correspondence column of the *Singapore Daily Times* on Friday, September 29, 1865: "Newly arrived in Singapore I claim the privileges of a stranger and if while letting you know what appears curious to a fresh arrival here I should ask some questions the answers to which are obvious to every old Singaporean — let this plead as my excuse. Wherever a colonising nation like England has sent out her sons, they will be found banded together working hard and persevering always, but nevertheless managing to enjoy themselves like worthy representatives of a nation where the truth of the maxim is recognised that 'all work and no play makes Jack a dull boy'. Even among the straggling colonies of gold diggers, theatres exist and are well patronised too — and when we read of a Cricket Club in France, a Gorse Club in Holland and a Highland Society in Denmark, we may be sure that even in the midst of foreigners, our countrymen are determined to enjoy themselves in their own way and be surrounded by as many national characteristics as possible. Knowing these things, it is no wonder that on arrival in Singapore — a British settlement with so few young Britons in it altogether, and with the character at home of being not all a slow place — a

Reputed to be the Tanglin Club, 1872 — Courtesy of Andrew Tan

newcomer is surprised that there is no place where he can meet and become acquainted with others, and enjoy himself quietly in the evenings. My first question is therefore, why have we not a Young Men's Club? A room of our own where we could meet and have a quiet game or a half-hour's reading. Considered along with the rather exclusive social habits of Singapore the object is a good one, and looked at from a moral point of view it is certainly not a bad one.

"More than one gentleman in the place, I understand, would be glad to give the grounds required for such a purpose and there is little doubt that some of our Towkays would be willing to help with the necessary funds. It is worth a trial at any rate, and even should the whole burden of the arrangements be thrown on the young men, there are surely heads clear enough and minds energetic enough among them to carry these through successfully.

"Perhaps the idea has been mooted before and been found impractical, but if not I hope as well for the sake of those newcomers occasionally arriving among us as for our own that the subject will soon be taken to hand by those able and willing to manage it. [I have just heard that the Germans have a Club of the kind for their young men and it seems a good model for such a place. They have a glee club in connection with it and this alone would be sufficient attraction for lovers of music.]"

New Year Regatta, c 1880 — A.O.

Singapore Cricket Club, c 1890 — Morgan/Betty Bassett collection, Singapore Methodist Archives

The forerunner of Singapore clubs was probably the Raffles Club, formed in 1825 to get up social entertainments on the occasion of the anniversary of the Settlement and other celebrations'; it lasted until 1835. The principal reason for the formation of clubs at this time was the pursuit of sport. The Billiard Club started after a meeting at the house of pioneer merchant Edward Boustead in 1829, but lasted only a year; the Yacht Club commenced in 1834 with the first sea regatta; a Fives Club was launched in 1836 in Empress Place; horse-racing at the Singapore Sporting Club began in 1842; and the Singapore Cricket Club (SCC) began in 1852. The Singapore Club, founded in 1862, was a business club for the tuans besar — the principals of the merchant houses, banks and law practices.

...forty 'good men and true'... Amid these stirrings, 'forty good men and true' convened a meeting in October 1865 for the purpose of forming a suburban social institute for Britishers. The exact foundation date of the Tanglin Club is uncertain; one suspects the date that had been determined by the Tanglin Club Centenary Celebrations Committee in 1965 was

the most convenient day on which to hold the celebrations. Two letters which respectively appeared in the *Singapore Daily Times* of November 11, and 13, 1865, allude to the formation of the club, and that in October 1865 legal documents show without doubt this club to be the Tanglin Club. The forty gentlemen elected a pro tem committee to carry out the stated objectives; they were: president — Thomas Dunman (commissioner of police); vice-president — Herbert Buchanan (The Borneo Company); honorary treasurer — Lancelot C. Masfen (Chartered

SATURDAY, NOVR. 11. 1865.

CORRESPONDENCE.

THE NEW CLUB,
To the Editor of the Daily Times.

DEAR SIR.—Nearly a month ago a meeting was convened for the purpose of forming an English Club, and forty 'good men and true' were enrolled on the spot. Office bearers and a committee were elected, and it was intimated that a general meeting should be called shortly to deliberate upon a code of Rules and Regulations, and to receive a report from the Executive. Well, so far as I can learn nothing whatever has been done since, and it is affirmed that the gentleman who was selected as Secretary has declined to act. Under these circumstances, I have ventured (in the hope that so desirable a movement should not be permitted to die of inanition —the more especially as the preliminary stages augured well for the vitality and success of the undertaking) to address these few lines to you calling attention to the desirableness of immediate action, or some explanation being given. It is important to all concerned to know how matters really stand, and to have an authorized Secretary, and it is due to the members that a meeting should be convened at an early date.

I am &c.
ONE OF THE FORTY.
Singapore, 8th November, 1865.

MONDAY, NOVR. 13. 1865.

CORRESPONDENCE.

THE NEW CLUB.
To the Editor of the Daily Times.

SIR,—I am sorry to see in your edition of to-day a letter signed by one of the forty members of the new club complaining of the dilatoriness of the committee.

It would probably have been a saving of time to himself and annoyance to others, if the writer of the letter I refer to had made enquiries on the subject before writing to a public paper on a matter which only concerns himself and thirty nine others, and is at present only a private undertaking. If he will take the trouble to ask the first member of the Committee he meets in the Square, he will find, as I have learnt myself, that they have been giving every attention to their duty, and so far from being inactive in the matter, they have taken measures which are likely, I believe, to result very soon in the permanent foundation of the club.

Perhaps the gentleman has a weakness for attending meeting and likes to spend his time in that way. If it is so no one can object, but there are no doubt a few others who do not wish to attend another meeting until the Committee have something definite to propose; and till that time I myself leave the matter in their hands with perfect confidence.

I am &c. &c.
ONE WHO VOTED FOR THE COMMITTEE.
Singapore, 11th November 1865.

Singapore Daily Times, November 11 & 13, 1865

There is no authority defining the origin or meaning of 'Tanglin'. There exists, however, an asok or asoka tree related to the saraca tree which is recorded in Malay, although, the Malays generally refer to this native species as gapis, talan, tengalan or tanglin. Sacred among the Hindus, and particularly sacred to the Buddhists as being the tree under which the Buddha was born this beautiful flowering tree with golden-orange flowers and deep purple pods up to twelve inches long is not common in present-day Singapore.

Another derivative for Tanglin may be a corruption of the Chinese tang leng — tang being eastern side, and leng (or ling) a small hill. In the 1860's there were plenty of hills in the districts of Tanglin and Claymore: Nassim Hill, Mount Alma, Mount Victoria, Mount Elizabeth, Cairn Hill, Claymore Hill and Goodwood Hill — coming from town, Orchard Road followed the course of a valley between these. In 1854 William Napier, Singapore's first lawyer, built a large house which he named TANG LENG on his 67-acre estate. (It was subsequently bought by the Sultan of Johore and renamed TYERSALL.)

It may never be known how the name Tanglin originated, but as there are many places in Malaysia named after trees it is possible that the club was named after the tree of the same name — perhaps one growing on the very spot where the clubhouse stood. To mark the occasion of the 125th anniversary of the Tanglin Club, a commemorative tanglin tree was planted in the grounds of the present clubhouse.

Bank of India, Australia and China); honorary secretary — Jos. M. Webster (The Borneo Company); committee members — William Mulholland (The Borneo Company), Walter Oldham (Boustead & Co.), Edwin A.G.C. Cooke (Cumming, Beaver & Co.) and John R. Forrester (Cumming, Beaver & Co.).

...a clubhouse with bowling alleys, billiard rooms and stables...

On June 26, 1866, a property was purchased in the District of Claymore from Arthur Hughes de Wind for 600 dollars. The title deeds for this, the club's first acquisition, and the numerous indentures executed in connection with it contain a wealth of invaluable and previously unknown information about the club's formation, in particular the considerable financial difficulties encountered by the forty men who founded this 'suburban social institute to meet the wants of Britishers' living in the settlement. In December 1866 the trustees of the Tanglin Club borrowed 5,000 Spanish dollars to build a clubhouse with bowling alleys, billiard rooms (in which smoking was not allowed) and stables. The 1865 committee held office in 1866, but for some reason none served in 1867; Thomas Dunman is on record as refusing to continue to act 'in the trusts of the Club'. Of the original trustees only Charles Dunlop remained. Robert Barclay Read of A.L. Johnston & Co. was elected president in 1867 (his tenure continued until 1870), supported by a strong committee drawn from the leading merchants and bankers of Singapore, four of whom served for another year. By the end of March 1867 the clubhouse was completed and the Tanglin Club opened its doors for members. At this early stage it seems that some financial difficulties had been encountered, and the appointment of James W.W. Birch as president in 1871, a mere six months after his arrival from Ceylon to assume the post of colonial secretary, invites speculation that he was sought out by the committee to add a degree of prestige to an institution on the wane; that he was appointed only as a caretaker president for the impecunious and ailing club. It is proved, however, that James Birch was club president from 1871 to 1873 only, not, as previously believed, 1874, when he was appointed the British resident of Perak, or 1875, when he was murdered and when, it appears, the club had no president. During his term there were only three trustees: Lewis Fraser, Charles Dunlop and Jonas Daniel Vaughan; Dunlop held concurrently the positions of secretary and treasurer. In 1874 there were only two instead of five committee members: James L. Ogilvy of the Oriental Bank Corporation and Andrew Currie of The Borneo Company, a member of the legislative council; Dunlop continued to act as both secretary and

The structure of the clubhouse itself was basically of load-bearing brick wall construction. Walls were usually of one-and-a-half or two-brick thickness (the bricks measured 10 inches in length, 4 inches in width, and usually two and a half inches thick, slightly smaller than imported English or Indian bricks). Local bricks were produced to British standards by Indian convict labourers and may have been supplied by the brickfield started in the Serangoon area around the 1850's by the Public Works Department. Mouldings to capitals of pilasters, columns and piers were pre-cast in timber moulds and applied to the building, then lime-washed either in pale yellow or white as the design required. Walls, both external and internal, were rendered in lime plaster and later cement plaster, and either washed or distempered.

The Tanglin Club from a portfolio of photogravures entitled 'Malay Peninsula' by Charles J. Kleingrothe, c 1907 — T.C.

The upper floor of the clubhouse comprised of floor boards of *changai* timber one and a half inches thick, supported on timber joists resting on bilian timber beams spanning the brick columns or piers. In some cases, particularly under the dance floor, additional intermediate supports of cast iron — made from columns imported from Calcutta or Glasgow — were also constructed. The main activities of the club were held on the upper floor which opened onto verandahs on all four sides. The ground floor housed the kitchens, the changing rooms and toilets. The floors were slabbed over either in brick or large, red Malacca tiles, fifteen inches square and one and a half inches thick. The ceilings of the ground floor rooms were usually exposed floor boards of the rooms above — suspended or false ceilings were not yet common. The roof, of half-round Chinese red, clay tiles, was supported on a mansard truss. On the underside of the rafters the ceiling was often of sailcloth or latterly in asbestos sheeting held up to the rafters by timber strips. The eaves extended beyond the face of the building to give protection from the sun and rain. The long overhang of the roof structure was a feature of those early days when most buildings were open to give through ventilation; punkahs were constantly in use before the days of electric fans. Until the introduction of glazing between 1870 and 1880, window openings were of slatted wood louvres, hinged right back or top hung, kept open by a wooden strut.

The best remembered feature of that original clubhouse was the main entrance staircase which rose from street level up to the dance floor and the attractive use of bottle-green, vase-shaped, glazed balustrades which lined the sides of the staircase and the vestibule above. After the 1930's, a stout, brass handrail, donated by 'Frosty' Dyne, ran up the middle of this staircase, and many stories were told of the support this gave members at the close of an evening's entertainment.

An affiliation shared by many early members of the Tanglin Club was the Singapore Volunteer Rifle Corps founded in 1854. William Read was Captain Commandant from 1856 to 1864; Herbert Buchanan, the club's first vice-president, and committee members William Mulholland and Walter Oldham were on the corps list. Given the security concerns of the resident Europeans and that the first club president Thomas Dunman was the commissioner of police, it is logical to assume that many of the original club members, as well as other Britishers and Europeans residing in the colony, would have been Volunteers.

The Singapore Chamber of Commerce was another organisation supported by prominent businessmen. The chamber formally came into being on February 8, 1837, which Alex Josey chooses to describe in From Early Days as "the fourth day of the first moon of the seventeenth reign of Emperor Tao Kuang in the Year of the Cock," and which was also the year Queen Victoria of Great Britain ascended the throne. Names of presidents and members of the Tanglin Club can be traced from the inception of the chamber whose activities have been closely related with the development of Singapore itself. Between 1865 and 1890 chamber presidents included William Read, Samuel Gilfillan, Louis R. Glass and John Finlayson. It is also recorded that many of the early members were prominent Freemasons, an affiliation that may have been as pertinent then as in recent times. [SVA Officers. Standing left to right — G. Bruce-Webster; E.M. Merewether; J. Fabris; W.G. St. Clair; R. Dunman. Sitting — F.W. Barker; H.E. McCallum; W. Jennings. Sitting Front — T.C. Mugliston; C.J. Davis, c 1893 — A History of the Singapore Volunteer Corps.]

treasurer in the absence of a club president. The future of the club in 1874 must have seemed bleak indeed and it is a wonder that it survived. In April 1876 the mortgagees for the club gave notice demanding payment plus interest in arrears of all outstanding monies: on failure to repay, they intended to sell the clubhouse at auction: to all intents and purposes the club was insolvent. On July 29, 1876, the Tanglin Club was auctioned and sold for 4,000 dollars to the merchant William Henry Macleod Read. The 1877 president of the Tanglin Club is listed as Julius Brussel, supported by M. Trasher as vice-president and C.B. Dalman as secretary; in the 1878 Singapore Directory for the Straits Settlements these gentlemen, stalwart members of the German community, were also listed against the same honorary positions for the Teutonia Club. Despite the close relationship which the two clubs enjoyed, it may be assumed that this double entry is a misprint. It is more likely that when William Read became the trustee for the club in February 1877 he also took up the position of president. In the 1879 Directory — which only lists the Singapore club secretaries for 1878 — Charles Stringer, a prominent sportsman of the day, is listed as being secretary of both the SCC and the Tanglin Club. In 1879 William Read was elected president of the club. Having been actively and financially committed to the affairs of the club since 1876, his efforts attracted a new and dedicated committee who then laid the foundation for the future success of the Tanglin Club.

The Lots Marked Nos. 28 & 29 In The Government Map In The District Of Claymore

The sole surviving records of the earliest days of the Tanglin Club are the deeds which recorded the club's real estate acquisitions and borrowings. Complicated as they are to follow and interpret for those unfamiliar with legal language, the vital fact of their existence, given the dearth of other available historical material pertaining to the club's precise origins, makes a closer examination of these documents crucial to any attempt to understand or reconstruct the club's early fortunes. [Even so, no information could have been extricated without major restoration work being first undertaken in London to several of the crumbling and somewhat pulverized title deeds and indentures of a hundred and twenty-five years ago.]

The present clubhouse premises extend over numerous plots of land which were acquired piece-meal over a period of nearly a century. The first acquisition in 1866, barely seven months after the exchange of letters between two of the forty promoters of the English club, is the most intriguing. Several trustees of the club had been appointed and were subsequently authorised by the committee of management to acquire a plot of land to erect a clubhouse in the District of Claymore. This can be deduced from the fact that seven months after the publication of the letter to the editor of the *Singapore Daily Times* dated November 8, 1865, an indenture was made on June 26, 1866, between Arthur Hughes de Wind of the one part, and Thomas Dunman, James Davidson, David Rodger, Charles Dunlop and Jonas Daniel Vaughan, described in the indenture as "Trustees of

a certain Club or Association in Singapore called the Tanglin Club" of the other part, by which the said Arthur Hughes de Wind sold a plot of land "being part of the lots marked Nos 28 and 29 in the Government map in the District of Claymore," and said to comprise "an area of one acre, three roods and thirty eight poles," to the trustees of the Tanglin Club for the price of 600 dollars. This indenture appears to be the earliest written record alluding to the existence of the Tanglin Club by that name.

According to the recital in the Indenture of Conveyance, the land bought from de Wind in 1866 had originally formed part of a much larger parcel of land, "estimated to contain eighteen acres and twenty five poles," owned by William Scott and described in the indenture as being "bounded on the North by Steven's Road, on the South by Orchard Road, on the East by Scott's Road, and on the West by William Scott's Plantation." Scott was a well-known nutmeg plantation owner who, like the other planters including Carnie, Oxley, Cuppage and Prinsep, was probably compelled to sell much of his plantation for development purposes after the nutmeg disease swept through the island in the years 1855-56. The land had first been sold by Scott on November 1, 1859, to the Reverend Jean

Marie Beurel (the Pro-Vicar Apostolic who had built the Cathedral of the Good Shepherd in 1832 and who is best remembered for his contribution to the field of education, notably the founding of St. Joseph's Institution in 1852). This parcel of land was subsequently vested in de Wind before its purchase by the club.

A restrictive covenant was included in the indenture which declared that the purchasers "shall not use the houses and building to be erected on the said premises or any of them as a Hotel or Tavern nor shall nor will permit or suffer any person or persons whomsoever to use or follow in or upon the said premises or any part thereof the trade or business of a Hotel-keeper, victualler, retailer of spirituous liquors or any noisy or offensive trade or business whatsoever." It had been agreed between the parties that a breach of this covenant would entitle the vendor to damages agreed at 500 Spanish dollars.

Apparently the committee of management, as it was then called, decided to borrow the princely sum of 5,000 Spanish dollars for development purposes and John Crum, a clerk with W. Mulholland in The Borneo Company, agreed to lend that sum to the club. This loan was secured by a mortgage of the property to Crum, evidenced by an Indenture of Mortgage dated December 4, 1866, executed by John Crum and the Tanglin Club's trustees, the recital of which declares that the club's land was mortgaged to Crum in consideration of a sum of 5,000 Spanish dollars borrowed from him. The recital further states that the trustees of the club had been authorised by the committee of manage-

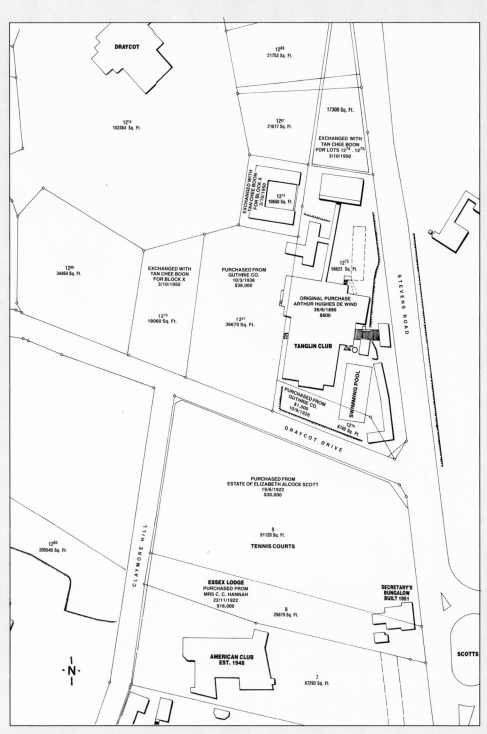

DRAYCOT

12⁸⁶
21753 Sq. Ft.

17300 Sq. Ft.

12⁷⁶
152384 Sq. Ft.

12⁸⁷
21617 Sq. Ft.

EXCHANGED WITH
TAN CHEE BOON
FOR LOTS 12⁷⁴, 12⁷⁵
3/10/1950

EXCHANGED WITH
TAN CHEE BOON
FOR BLOCK X
3/10/1950

12⁷⁴
10650 Sq. Ft.

12⁸⁸
34464 Sq. Ft.

EXCHANGED WITH
TAN CHEE BOON
FOR BLOCK X
3/10/1950

PURCHASED FROM
GUTHRIE CO.
10/3/1938
$38,000

12⁷³
56623 Sq. Ft.

STEVENS ROAD

ORIGINAL PURCHASE
ARTHUR HUGHES DE WIND
26/6/1886
$600

12⁷⁵
18060 Sq. Ft.

12⁵⁷
36670 Sq. Ft.

TANGLIN CLUB

PURCHASED FROM
GUTHRIE CO.
$1,000
10/8/1926

SWIMMING POOL

12¹⁶
8740 Sq. Ft.

DRAYCOT DRIVE

PURCHASED FROM
ESTATE OF ELIZABETH ALCOCK SCOTT
19/6/1922
$30,000

9
91120 Sq. Ft.

TENNIS COURTS

12⁸²
205540 Sq. Ft.

CLAYMORE HILL

ESSEX LODGE
PURCHASED FROM
MRS C. C. HANNAH
22/11/1922
$18,000

8
25679 Sq. Ft.

SECRETARY'S
BUNGALOW
BUILT 1951

SCOTTS

-N-

AMERICAN CLUB
EST. 1948

7
67293 Sq. Ft.

Property acquisitions of the Tanglin Club since 1865

ment "in accordance with the rules thereof to raise and borrow for the construction of a club house and other buildings connected therewith and furnishing the same."

The money advanced on the property was to be repayable in instalments, as to 2,000 dollars on November 30, 1868, and 3,000 dollars on November 30, 1871, and it was agreed that the trustees "should in the meantime and until the whole of the said principal sum was repaid pay interest on the sum or part thereof as should remain unpaid half yearly on the Thirty-first of May and Thirtieth of November in each year after at the rate of nine per centum per annum."

At the time of the borrowing, it was stipulated and agreed that as an additional security for the repayment of the loan and of the interest thereon in the manner designated, the trustees should execute in favour of Crum a bill of sale of the furniture and other effects then belonging, or that might thereafter during the subsistence of the loan, belong to the club. Pursuant to this, Crum apparently made the request to the trustees since a bill of sale was duly executed on March 25, 1867, between the trustees and Crum whereby in consideration of the sum of one dollar paid to the trustees they, "assigned unto the said John Crum his executors and assigns, all and singular the household furniture, billiard tables, and other goods, chattels and effects belonging to the said Club, and wherever situated or being: And also all the house-hold furniture, billiard tables, goods, chattels and effects, which shall or may at any time or times during the continuance of this security belong to the said Club or be appropriated to the use thereof, whether in addition to or in substitution for the said furniture, billiard-tables, goods, chattels and effects now belonging to the said Club or the members thereof in, to or upon the same or every part thereof: to have and to hold the said chattels and ... premises hereby assigned or expressed so to be unto the said John Crum, his executors, administrators and assigns, subject to the proviso for redemption hereinafter contained." This indicates that a new clubhouse with the usual amenities of an exclusive British social club was built and furnished by March 25, 1867.

This loan of 5,000 Spanish dollars appeared to be the forerunner of the club's financial problems, resulting in a series of other loans being obtained in substitution for the original, which formed part of an intriguing web of refinancing intended to re-schedule payment of the original loan.

The costs of construction of the clubhouse and the provision of amenities together with the expenses involved in running the club must have placed a tremendous burden on its financial resources, because the committee of management was unable to repay the first instalment of 2,000 dollars due on November 30, 1868. The committee, however, obtained the consent of a trustee Lewis James Fraser to advance that sum to Crum, in consideration of which an indenture was executed that day between Crum and Fraser whereby the former covenanted that he held his interest in the land by virtue of the mortgage in trust for Fraser as to 2,000 dollars.

When the second instalment of the principal mortgage sum fell due on November 30, 1871, the club was also unable to pay both that and the sum of 2,000 dollars previously advanced by Fraser, who then advanced and paid to Crum the further sum of 3,000 Spanish dollars, taking no security for the same, and thus assumed the whole debt. When the debt of 5,000 Spanish dollars was not repaid to Fraser by the due date of November 24, 1873, one of the trustees of the club, Charles Dunlop, a partner of Maclaine, Fraser and Company, Merchants, together with two others, the lawyer Bernard Rodyk (a Dutchman acting either for himself or as a trustee on behalf of a client), and John Gottlieb Brinkmann, partner of Brinkmann & Co. and a prominent member of the German community, agreed to make repayment of the 5,000 Spanish dollars to Fraser to assume the mortgage.

An indenture was accordingly executed between Crum and Fraser (who by then were living in Manchester and London respectively) and the new mortgagees, by which Fraser assigned his interest in the principal sum and interest to the new mortgagees "and all the right title and interest of the said John Crum therein or thereto," and Crum thereby assigned "all that piece of land with its appurtenances ...and the Club house, Bowling Alley, outoffice and premises thereon erected" to the new mortgagees to hold the same, subject to the equity of redemption then subsisting in the premises under the Indenture of Mortgage.

Of the sum of 5,000 dollars paid to Fraser, 2,000 had been contributed by Rodyk, which was repaid to him on March 24, 1875, by Dunlop and Brinkmann upon which Rodyk assigned his share and interest in the club's property to them by a tripartite indenture executed between Rodyk, Crum, Dunlop and Brinkmann. Crum's interest in the Bill of Sale of 1867 was also assigned to Dunlop and Brinkmann, who by this time were the principal creditors of the club. Brinkmann in turn assigned his share to one Willie Krohn, another prominent German, on April 6, 1875. [The German community had rented BLANCHE HOUSE at 28, Scotts Road from Mrs Hewetson in 1856, and around 1862 built a new Teutonia Club on this land. We may surmise that the proximity of the two clubs resulted in not only the documented social interaction but also some financial involvement to the benefit of the almost defunct Tanglin Club at this time.]

It is apparent that by this time the club was in dire financial straits. Ten years after the loan of 5,000 dollars had been taken from Crum, the club could not afford to repay any of the principal sum borrowed; even the club's servants could not be paid their wages. On April 4, 1876, the mortgagees Krohn and Dunlop, who appeared to have lost all hope in the club ever being able to repay them the mortgage sum and outstanding interest, gave to the committee "notice demanding payment of the mortgage debt of Dollars Five thousand together with all arrears of interest thereon then owing to them ...and of their intention to sell the premises" in the exercise of their paramount right of sale as such mortgagees. A extraordinary general meeting of the club was then called on June 20, 1876, by the trustee Dunlop, to resolve the problem of the club's indebtedness.

The minutes of that meeting mention a report put up on proposals to rescue the club from closure. One of these was an offer by Dunlop that if 500 dollars was raised by the subscription of the members and on the consumable stores to cover all servants' wages and outgoings up to that time, then if all moneys in hand were to be handed over to him, he would liquidate and discharge all the debts of the club "so that the Club be freed from all liabilities whatever excepting the mortgage debt to which the Club Buildings, and fittings and furniture are subject." His offer however was further conditional upon the mortgage to the trustees of Mrs. Mitchell for 5,000 dollars with interest from March 31, 1876, being paid off by the members and that he be authorised to receive the debts due to the club up to the March 31, 1876. It appears from this that there had been another mortgage of 5,000 dollars, though it is unclear whether this loan was secured on a second charge on the land.

The general meeting passed four resolutions, namely: To appoint a committee to enquire and report to an adjournment of this meeting whether any person will advance 5,000 dollars on a mortgage of the club; That if a person be found to take a mortgage of the club the present mortgagee be requested to sell under his power of sale, and that a member of the club be appointed to purchase the property and re-mortgage the whole property to the new mortgagee; That if

the committee find a person willing to advance 5,000 dollars on a mortgage of the club then the offer of Dunlop be accepted and the assets mentioned in his offer be handed to him and a call of 13 dollars on the members be made and thereout 500 dollars be paid as suggested; and That Messrs Burkinshaw, Miller and Henderson form the committee to enquire and report as to the mortgage, and that they appoint the members referred to in the above resolutions to purchase from the present mortgagee and to re-mortgage. From the call made on members it can be deduced that there were now less than forty 'good men' remaining.

Singapore Daily Times, July 27, 1876

No records of subsequent meetings of the club are available but it is evident that the Tanglin Club literally went under the hammer. An Indenture of Conveyance dated September 20, 1876, entered into between the mortgagees Dunlop and Krohn of the one part, and a merchant

named William Henry Macleod Read of the other records the fact of the demand for the repayment dated April 4, 1876, having been made, together with the notice of the mortgagees' intention to sell given to the committee, and consequent to default having been made on the demand, with the result that "all the said lands and tenements and all the said household furniture, billiard tables, chattels and effects" of the Tanglin Club were put up for sale by public auction by the mortgagees Krohn and Dunlop on July 29, 1876.

The Indenture of Conveyance to Read contains further recital that "the said William Henry Macleod Read was the highest bidder for and was declared the purchaser of the said lands, tenements, household furniture, billiard tables, chattels and effects at the price of dollars Four Thousand Now this Indenture witnesseth that for effectuating the said sale and in consideration of the sum of Dollars Four Thousand by the said William Henry Macleod Read paid to the said Willie Krohn and Charles Dunlop upon the execution of these presents ... they, the said Willie Krohn and Charles Dunlop do hereby grant, convey and assign unto the said William Henry Macleod Read, his executors, administrators and assigns All that piece of land containing an area of One Acre Three Roods and Thirty Eight Poles situate adjoining Stevens Road in Claymore District in the Island of Singapore Together with the Clubhouse, Bowling Alley Shed, Bowling Alleys, Carriage house and other erections standing thereon...."

But that was not to be the death-knell of the Tanglin Club. By an Indenture of Mortgage dated September 21, 1876,

Read mortgaged the Tanglin Club, its chattels, furniture and fittings to another merchant named Matthew Little, a partner in John Little & Co., for a loan of 3,500 dollars for a period of one year, with the proviso that if the mortgagor Read repaid the loan with interest at the rate of eight percentum per annum on September 21, 1877, Little was obliged to reconvey "the herediments and premises" to Read at his cost.

The proviso contains a very important further stipulation that "in the meantime and until the twenty first day of September next, the said mortgagor, his heirs, executors, administrators or assigns shall remain in the enjoyment and possession of all the said lands and premises," strongly suggestive of the fact that the Tanglin Club was to continue with its use of the premises. This inference is reinforced by a further recital which mentions that the committee of management shall, during the currency of the mortgage, "keep the buildings furniture and effects …insured against loss or damage by fire in the sum of Dollars Three Thousand Five Hundred."

The actual position regarding the properties vis-a-vis the Tanglin Club can be unravelled only by investigating yet another indenture, this time dated February 22, 1877, whereby Read conveyed unto himself and one John Burkinshaw, a partner of the law firm of Aitken, Donaldson and Burkinshaw, the equity of redemption of the September 21, 1876, mortgage to Little. It is expressly declared that "the said William Henry Macleod Read and John Burkinshaw … shall stand and be possessed of the said piece of land Club House, Bowling Alleys Shed, Bowling Alleys, Carriage House and other erections standing thereon and all the said Household furniture, billiard tables, fixtures, fittings, furniture and chattels … (which are hereinafter referred to as the Trust Premises) upon the Trusts hereinafter declared or expressed concerning the same respectively, that is to say: (1) Upon Trust for the persons who now are or hereafter when any such directions of Members in general meeting may be given as hereinafter mentioned, shall be active members for the time being of the association of persons known as or constituting the Tanglin Club in the Island of Singapore (2) And upon trust at the absolute will and discretion of the said William Henry Macleod Read and John Burkinshaw or the survivor of them or the heirs, executors or administrators of such survivor or his assigns to convey and assign the said Trust premises to the persons who for the time being shall be and constitute the General Committee in whom is vested for the time being the management of the affairs of the said Association to hold the same for the use of and benefit of the persons who are active members for the time being of the said Association (3) And subject to the trust last hereinbefore declared and with regard to the said Trust premises so far as they may not have been conveyed assigned or dealt with pursuant to the trust hereinbefore declared concerning the same upon trust that the said William Henry Macleod Read and John Burkinshaw or the survivor of them or the heirs executors or administrators of such survivor or of his assigns shall convey charge mortgage dispose of or deal with the said trust premises hereinbefore expressed to be hereby granted conveyed and assigned in such manner as the members of the said Association shall by a resolution or resolutions in general meeting convened and held according to the rules thereof for the time being direct or sanction."

From the foregoing it is evident that the club had continued to function notwithstanding the charge and conveyance of its property, but probably only so because of the somewhat complex financial arrangement that had been devised to permit the continued use of the club and its facilities by its members. The saga of the original loan of 5,000 dollars was to continue until almost the turn of the last century, when the club's membership numbered around two hundred. By a supplemental indenture executed on June 21, 1899, between Little and Read and Burkinshaw it was stated that in consideration of all monies under the principal indenture having been paid to Little as mortgagee, Little conveyed the club's lands and premises vested in him, subject to redemption, to the latter in their capacities as trustees of the club, whereupon the loan of 5,000 Spanish dollars first obtained in 1866 was repaid and the club's indebtedness arising from that loan was totally discharged.

Many founder members of the Tanglin Club were involved in the production of amateur theatricals in the settlement, and this shared interest may have contributed to the genesis of the club. In 1844 William Read assisted Captain Calbeck of the Madras army in reviving theatricals, with performances held at the Theatre Royal, a room in Dutronquoy's London Hotel in Coleman Street. In those days actors took stage names and female roles were always played by men — the ladies did not consider such activities respectable and hesitated even to attend such functions. Some of the early performances of this Amateur Club featured many personalities associated with the social history of the Singapore colony and especially the Tanglin Club: William Read (Miss Petowker), Thomas Dunman (Mr. Johnson), Jonas Daniel Vaughan (Mr. Jingle), Archie Spottiswoode (Miss Ledbrook), the low comedian Farleigh Armstrong (Bono) and the light comedians William Adamson and Robert Barclay Read.

The first production at the Theatre Royal in 1844 featured two plays, *Charles II*, also called *The Merry Monarch* (the lead played by lawyer William Napier who later became the lieutenant governor of Labuan), and a satirical farce, *The Spectre Bridegroom*. In the second piece Miss Petowker (Read) made her debut as Lavinia and Mr. Johnson (Dunman) appeared as Dickory. C.B. Buckley provides the full account: "Miss Petowker for several years played ladies' parts. She had the smallest waist, and smallest foot, of any lady in Singapore, and was the envy of all the sex, for it was acknowledged

she was the prettiest little chambermaid on the stage and a clever little actress, and played everything she attempted most successfully. One night, after a performance, she was taken to the house of a lady friend, where there was a lady visitor who talked to the actress for some time and seemed much impressed with her lady-like bearing, &c., when the pert little woman came out with a rather strong expression which aroused the old lady's suspicions; so she walked up to Miss Petowker and said in tragic tones, opening her eyes as wide as she could, 'Why you naughty creature; you are a man,' and so it was — Mr. W.H. Read! Since then he has played important parts in his own character on another stage quite as successfully, but he probably often looks back with pleasure to the days

Jonas Daniel Vaughan, self-portrait

when he tripped the boards in petticoats. But when speaking of the 'Soubrette' the Prima Donna should not be forgotten. Pretty, graceful, always well-dressed and careful in his acting, Miss Ledbrook for several years took the leading female parts, and was a decided public favourite. Some still alive remember the then well-known voice of Archie Spottiswoode. Lieutenant Dunlop also took to the petticoat, but it took so much chalk and care to tone down his 'black muzzle' to 'maiden's blush' that he had to return to male attire." The diary of George Mildmay Dare in *One Hundred Years of Singapore* provides another anecdote: "*December* 1857. — Since last writing I have joined the Corps Dramatique, which consists of gentlemen amateurs: young men like myself in business. I came out as Lucy in the farce *John Dobbs* under the name of 'Miss Flora Macfungus,' which has since been changed at my request to 'Miss Brani,' the Malay for Dare. It was a difficult part, but they say I performed it to everyone's satisfaction, and made what they called 'a stunning girl'! I went in a crinoline made out of rattan, and even after the theatre was not known till I commenced kicking the syce's back on account of his not opening the door wide enough, which elicited a roar of laughter from the men in the portico of the theatre, who were all seeing four young ladies into their carriage."

The Tanglin Club's first president Thomas Dunman made his debut in *Charles II* and was considered 'the greatest low comedian Singapore had ever seen.' He was married to the second daughter of Thomas Crane, a pioneer merchant. There were nine children in the Dunman family, and with the other Crane families they organised and produced most of the concerts, musical entertainment and plays for society at the time. Dunman continued performing until his appointment as commissioner of police, when his sons, Robert and William, carried on the family tradition.

In 1861 a second amateur society was formed, the Savage Club, which performed at Barganny House. Jonas Vaughan, the president and stage manager, was yet another talented amateur actor, musician and singer. (From 1861 to 1869 he was an assistant magistrate and resident councillor; he was a trustee of the Tanglin Club in 1866, 1870 and 1871, and a committee member in 1870.) As an officer of the East India Company based in Singapore, Vaughan had appeared as Whisk in *Damp Beds* and was praised for his "excellent acting, complete self-possession and modulation of voice." When he made his second appearance on the Singapore stage as Whisk in the *Chimney Corner*, the *Singapore Daily Times* of October 9, 1861, assigned "to Mr Whisk the place of honour in last night's performance." The low comedian of the Savage Club was Charles Emmerson of Emmerson's Tiffin Rooms (now located with a different cast at 51 Neil Road) and their leading lady was William Mullholland, a Tanglin Club committee member 1865, 1866, 1871, of whom C.B. Buckley writes: "as a delineator of female characters he was never surpassed. His Portia was excellent and as Maritana in 'Don Caesar' he was exquisite, and no stranger visiting the performance would have supposed that the character was represented by a man." The Savage Club enjoyed a brief career of only two years but the Amateur Corps Dramatique continued performing at the Town Hall where it had moved in 1861. After the 1867 Transfer there was little interest in theatre although enthusiasm was revived after the first professional dramatic company visited Singapore in 1876. J.C.D. *'Panjang'* Jones of the Telegraph Company and Tanglin Club committee member Jules M. Fabris of the fire department gained the reputation as the best actors in Singapore. Playbills featured names such as Maxwell, McCallum, Stringer, Swettenham, Cadell, Braddell, Salzmann, Dare and Owen, all of whom were no strangers to the Tanglin Club.

In 1885 the Amateur Club expanded into the Singapore Amateur Dramatic and Musical Society. Concerts and musical evenings were then the popular entertainment among Europeans. Popularised by King Edward VII when he was Prince of Wales, Black and White Minstrel Shows were all the rage in the 1880's; the first of these to be presented at the Tanglin Club was in November 1888 by a party who called themselves the "Bulbuls."

HMS BACCHANTE, c 1880 — The Cruise of HMS 'Bacchante'

Unveiling of the statue of Raffles on the Esplanade, June 27, 1887 — N.A.

In the social calendar of 1880, the event of the decade was the visit of the 'Sailor Princes.' The Prince of Wales' two young sons — Prince Albert Victor and Prince George (later King George V) — who had set out to see the world as teenage midshipmen on board HMS BACCHANTE, reached the island of Singapore the day after Prince Albert's eighteenth birthday. The town was reportedly *en fête* and band concerts were a highlight of the festivities. In the account of their voyage, *The Cruise of HMS 'Bacchante'*, compiled from their journals, letters and notebooks, is an entry dated January 10: "At 4 P.M. we landed at Johnston's Pier.... where Mr. W.H. Read, the oldest inhabitant of the Colony read an address.... One address only was presented by all the various races to typify the unity which pervaded the whole community...."

Another major event was the Golden Jubilee of Queen Victoria, celebrated by all in June 1887. The statue of Sir Stamford Raffles was unveiled on the Padang. Otto Ziegele, a diarist of the time, noted: "June 27: First Jubilee day, holiday. Military parade and salutes from the fort and the men-of-war in the harbour at 6 A.M. June 28: Second day of Jubilee, most awful rain all the morning till 3 P.M. Went to the races and lost ten dollars. Ker won the Queen's Jubilee Cup. Large Chinese processions and Governor's ball in the evening." From a social point of view dinner and tennis parties provided the usual form of entertainment, "there were no cinemas and no Happy Valleys; ...no Rings and boxing, and if we wished to let off our animal spirits we went to the Tingle Tangle in South Bridge Road where after a little friendly argument with a German as regards the ladies of the orchestra, there was always a good chance of a marble top table coming into contact with one, or of getting more beer than one had paid for," according to J.S.M. Rennie in his *Musings of JSMR, Mostly Malayan*. "The Swimming Club was little more than an attap shed, ... the Cricket Club was, comparatively, a tin pot building and 90 per cent bar where pukkah Tuans Besar used to congregate... The Gap was not known, though Lover's Lane in the Gardens, on a band night, had its devotees."

1865 1866 DUNMAN, Thomas,

(born 1815) came to Singapore in 1840 as an assistant in the merchant firm of Martin Dyce & Co. Entered the police force in 1843; from 1844 sat as police magistrate; made superintendent of police, 1851, and commissioner of police, 1856. Recognised for raising and training an efficient police force. After retirement in 1871 spent the next few years on his coconut plantation, GROVE ESTATE, at Tanjong Katong. Still remembered by Dunman Road and Dunman Lane. Returned to England where he died in 1887 aged 73. C.B. Buckley relates: "he was known and liked in the place by all classes of the community, European and native, who were willing to give him information and assistance. They looked upon him as a friend and not as a military martinet. They never saw him in uniform and spurs.... He did not spend all day in the office and all night in bed, and it was not an unusual thing, especially if there was any feeling of insecurity about to meet him the same night in widely different directions."

1867 1868 1869 READ, Robert Barclay, (born 1828)

arrived in May 1848 to join A.L. Johnston & Co., became a partner in 1862 and resided in Singapore for 36 years. Died in Yokohama in October 1884 aged 56. According to C.B. Buckley: "he was very popular in the place, a leader in all its affairs, like his cousin W.H.M. Read, both commercial and social. He was Consul for Sweden and Norway.... The Swedish Government made him a Knight of the Order of Wasa and the Dutch Government conferred on him the Knighthood of the Netherlands Lion for his valuable assistance in discovering and following up the threads of a conspiracy at Palembang.... Socially Mr. Read was for years the life and soul of the place. He had a good appreciation of the enjoyments of life, and, especially in his younger days, the capacity for inspiring and diffusing them. He was an enthusiastic yachtsman, and took great delight in his cruises.... In the amateur theatricals of those days he was always considered an indispensable associate.... He was president of the Singapore Club, and a handsome centre-piece was subscribed for by the members to be kept in the Club in memory of him."

1870 PADDAY, Reginald Henry, a member of a well-known Straits family, was a partner in one of the colony's oldest firms, Hamilton, Gray & Co., founded in 1832 (other partners of that time included Walter Buchanan, W. Hamilton, G.G. Nichol, John Jarvie and George Henderson). Founder member of the Singapore branch of the Straits Settlements Association an organised political forum established in London a year after the 1867 Transfer and served under W.H.M. Read on the committee.

1871 1872 1873 BIRCH, The Hon. James Wheeler

Woodford, (born 1826) son of a clergyman, was a midshipman in the Royal Navy. Worked in Ceylon from 1852 as a government servant; in May 1870 appointed colonial secretary, Straits Settlements; nomination as British resident in Perak was delayed until the end of 1874 when certain charges of financial impropriety were cleared. Murdered in a floating bath-house in Perak in 1875. His life was complicated by the death of his wife in England, leaving four children there, soon after arriving in Singapore. Tired of the trivialities of the colony's restricted social life; described by Winstedt and Wilkinson as "having no insight — he had about as much sense of humour as the average Victorian was allowed to display. He had reached an age where from habitude the East no longer held any illusion and glamour. Years in the tropics had tinged his Nordic energy with nervous irritability." His life and work are extensively documented in his own *Journals* and *A History of Perak*. His son Sir Ernest Birch, British resident in Perak, 1904-1911 married Margaret Niven, the daughter of the director of the Botanical Gardens and a member of both the Singapore Cricket Club and Tanglin Club.

1879 READ, William Henry Macleod,

(born 1819, Scotland) arrived in Singapore in 1841 to take the place of his father Christopher Rideout Read in A.L. Johnston & Co., a pioneer European mercantile firm. Wrote in his memoirs, *Play & Politics*, that he found the place dull, so set about putting some life in it. Was instrumental in building the first race course in 1843 and won the first race on a horse named Colonel; also a Steward of the Course, Organiser of The Race Ball. After the first Masonic Lodge was opened in 1845, the second to be initiated, following William Napier; later became the first Provincial Grand Master of the Lodge in Singapore. Commodore of the Singapore Yacht Club for many years. First on the roll of the Volunteer Corps in 1859. Consul for Holland in 1857 at a time when relations between England and Holland were strained over Java and Rhio and made a Knight of the Netherlands Lion; retired from the position and returned to England in 1885. The first unofficial member of the legislative council after the 1867 Transfer and played a noteworthy part in bringing the Native States under British protection. With his cousin R.B. Read, recorded as a resident of SPRING GROVE from 1868 to 1885 (the writer John Cameron lived with them in 1875), and was the first to install a six-lamp chandelier in his drawing rooms, fuelled by oil imported from Batavia. Active in community work involving the Library, the Sailors' Home, the Paupers' Hospital, and the on-going campaign against piracy at sea. President of the Chamber of Commerce in 1867 and the first president of the Singapore Club In 1886 Queen Victoria made him a C.M.G. Died in 1908 aged 89. Described as an energetic man of many remarkable and varied talents. Read Bridge on the Singapore River and Read Street honour his memory.

1880 GILFILLAN, Samuel, arrived in Asia in 1842 and worked with McEwen & Co. (which later became part of The Borneo Company). In 1867 Gilfillan Wood & Co. was formed.

Shared the credit for instituting a weekly half-holiday, taken either on Saturdays or Wednesdays whichever suited the mail. Visited Australia in 1879, encountered western smelting methods for the first time and returned to Singapore with the belief that if a smelter were built here it could attract most of Malaya's tin-smelting business. Retired to London in 1881 but continued as a director with Sir William Adamson of Adamson Gilfillan & Company until 1914.

1881 BISHOP, Frederick Clark was manager of The Mercantile Bank and served on the legislative council and committee of the Chamber of Commerce.

1882 CUTHBERTSON, Thomas, (born 1843) became a partner of Boustead & Co. in 1874. Was a office bearer of the Presbyterian Church and donated the church organ. Served on the legislative council, 1885-1887; was deputy chairman of the Chamber of Commerce, 1885-86. Retired 1911. Was greatly involved in the commercial, public and social life of Singapore. Had a special interest in agriculture in Penang, Malacca and Singapore, particularly in tapioca and sugar estates in Province Wellesley and Perak. Under Cuthbertson, Bousteads was one of the first business houses to understand and grasp the great possibilities of

the plantation rubber industry in the Peninsula.

1883 FRASER, John, came to Singapore for the Chartered Mercantile Bank in 1865, left and went to Shanghai for two years but returned and joined Alexander Gentle in business as brokers and accountants. Became involved in the bill broking business, and in partnership with David Neave founded the Mission Press (which used to print the race-books) and established the soda-water factory subsequently known as Fraser & Neave. Renowned for his Highland costume worn as auctioneer at the race lotteries. Joined by J.B. Cumming in the business of brickmakers, housebuilding and whatever else would make money — some of his houses in the Dalvey Road area still stand including CREE HALL and GLENCAIRD. Was president of the Singapore Club, a prominent Freemason and Secretary of Lodge Zetland, one of the original members of the Singapore Cricket Club, a municipal commissioner, a Justice of the Peace and on the committee of the SPCA. Nicknamed Our Jolly Old Octupus, his picture in the *Straits Produce* was captioned: A man so various that he seems to be not one but all mankind's epitome.

1884 1887 CUTHBERTSON,
1890 1891 John Reid, brother
1892 1893 of Thomas, joined
1894 the Boustead partnership in 1882, served on the legislative council, was chairman of the Tanjong Pagar Dock Company and involved in the business

and social life of the island. Supported British intervention in the Peninsula. A strong supporter of the Presbyterian Church and reported to have been musically talented. Had a keen interest in racing; was trustee of the Singapore Sporting Club and on the first committee of the Golf Club. Assisted in the revival of *The Singapore Free Press* in 1887.

1885 1886 ANDERSON, Sir John, (born 1852, England) came to Singapore aged seven and was educated at Raffles Institution. (His mother, a grand-daughter of the English astronomer Edmund Halley, taught at Raffles

Girls' School.) Spent twelve years in government service, joined Boustead & Company in 1871, then in 1876 Guthrie & Co. which, under his direction, became one of the great trading and plantation houses of South-East Asia; was a founding director of the Boustead Institute and chairman of the board of Guthries until his death in 1924 aged 72. Member of the legislative council at various times from 1886; presided over the opium commission in 1907 together with Dr. W.R.C. Middleton. Was president of the Singapore Cricket Club in 1880 and patron of the Singapore Recreation Club in 1883 with W.H.M. Read. For many years the consul-general for Siam in Singapore; knighted in 1912. Resided at ARDMORE in the Claymore district.

1888 FINLAYSON, The Hon. John, was a partner in Boustead & Co. with John and Thomas Cuthbertson. Assisted in

the foundation of Boustead Institute for Seamen; was involved in many commercial, public and social aspects of life in Singapore. Served on the legislative council; was chairman of the Chamber of Commerce in 1889 and chairman of the Tanjong Pagar Dock Company. Supported British intervention in the Peninsula; vice-consul for Sweden and Norway. Was a founding member of the Golf Club. Remembered by Finlayson Green at Collyer Quay.

1889 MURRAY, Sir George Sheppard, was manager of the Mercantile Bank of India (which later became part of the Hongkong Bank Group). Recognised the opportunities offered by rubber plantations and supported the development in the Peninsula. Served as unofficial member of the Legislative Council. With John Finlayson and John Cuthbertson was a founding member of the Golf Club. Reported to be a tower of strength to the government in financial and trade matters in *One Hundred Years Of Singapore*, in particular he gave invaluable assistance to the government in its difficult task of the note issue and establishment of a gold standard. His wife, Miss Dennys, well-known for her participation on the amateur stage and a member of the Ladies Lawn Tennis Club, was the daughter of Dr W.B. Dennys, assistant protector of Chinese under William Pickering (who established the Chinese Protectorate in 1877) and honorary secretary of the Raffles Museum.

IN SINGAPORE

COUNTY

Opening of the Ladies Lawn Tennis Club at Dhoby Ghaut, November 10, 1884 — A.O.

Finlayson Green and The Borneo Company, c 1910 — A.O.

By 1901 Singapore was a cosmopolitan place with a population of 206,000, of which 2,800 were European. A heterogeneous society existed "in order and sanitation, living and thriving and trading, simply because of the presence of English law and under the protection of the British flag. Remove the pieces of bunting from Government House, and all that it signifies, and the whole community would go to pieces like a child's sand castle when the tide rises. Its three supports are free trade, fair taxation and even-handed justice," contends H. Norman in *The Peoples and Politics of the Far East*. At the turn of the century the Raffles statue still stood on the Esplanade; the old Hotel de l'Europe — to be rebuilt in 1903 — comprised a range of buildings as far as Coleman Street occupied as bachelor or family quarters; the Singapore Recreation Club for Eurasians had been established at the northern end of the Padang; Raffles Hotel was renowned as the premier hotel (the Adelphi Hotel was considered second-rate); the celebrated Tingle Tangle was the local edition of a continental dance floor on North Bridge Road just past Bras Basah Road; Orchard Road was the principal traffic outlet from the town, with local shops on either side from Dhoby Ghaut to Cavenagh Road.

...everything was green, a wonderful vivid green...

"Everything was green, green grass, green trees, green undergrowth, green hedges, a wonderful vivid green," observes Edwin Brown in his *Indiscreet Memories*. The Esplanade was bordered by "magnificent, old, sturdy trees that had grown to a big height. They were of so luxuriant a foliage that there was a definite 'roof' of greenery the whole way along the road." In the evenings both sides of the drive were full of stationary carriages, "the lady occupants of which would walk about, or sit in each other's carriages and chat, while their husbands played their games on the Padang, or discussed business in the Singapore Club or the Cricket Club." An entry dated June 17, 1895, in the diary of Rowland Allen, club president, 1910, 1911, reads: "on Saturday, I went 4 miles into the country and stayed until Monday with one [Brompton] Matthews, a leading barrister to whom I had introductions. His house is beautiful, being one of the palaces of one of the Sultans of Johore, and the grounds are very fine, full of curious plants of which I do not know the names. M's wife was away so we lived in bachelor-freedom spending Sunday in pyjamas until afternoon when we put on whites and went and played golf on the Sepoy Lines. The round is most sporting — all sorts of bunkers from Chinese gravestones to deep ditches; it seemed most curious playing over a graveyard."

The Esplanade and Padang, water-colour by A. Watson, c 1905 — N.M.

Singapore Ice Works and bullock cart at Rochor Road, 1910 — A.O.

...to hear something spicy about your forbears...

Heavy jungle still covered much of the island and 'general dampness was the rule,' causing mildew on clothes and footwear. There were few motorcars, the most popular conveyances being bicycles, rickshaws imported from Japan via Shanghai, or carriages drawn by horses or small Java ponies. The tuans besar also employed a syce. The rickshaw, introduced in 1890, was a popular mode of transport, "but to experience a puller who had become completely 'broken-winded' was enough to put one off a rickshaw forever," Violet Marks recalls. In 1900 some rickshaw pullers installed carbide lamps in place of wick and oil lamps and charged three times the usual rate of six cents a mile; " a journey to Serangoon for croc shooting or to Johore for a flutter at the gambling farm was done by rickshas in relay, the fare being 3 cents a half-mile. If you wanted to hear something spicy about your forbears, give a rickshaw coolie 3 cents for a half-mile now, and he will astonish you with details of your ancestry if you understand the Chinese language," recounts J.S.M. Rennie. Riding was popular on the soft laterite roads and since 'Holland Road, Ayer Rajah Road and Buona Vista Road were not even metalled (they) were splendid places for a good gallop.' Gallop Road was so named, "because it was there that we let the nag have its head for a decent gallop

on turf," Rennie elucidates. John Little and Robinsons made Tanglin deliveries by horse and van but the usual commercial transport was the bullock cart and hand cart. "We had no electric light and the use of gas was mainly confined to street lighting; in bungalow and office, kerosene lamps were used; no electric fans but something far more comforting by way of the punkah. Bananas were cheap and well ripened and the table always sported a dish of these, largely used to keep the punkah wallah awake on the verandah. We had no Cold Storage and no Sunkist Oranges but did quite well on ayam and Calcutta kambing, and local fruits (like) Mangosteens, Chekoes, Dukoes, Pisang Mas, and Nanas," reveals Rennie. Until the turn of the century, Europeans lived on local produce, adding curry and spices to local meat and chicken. For some, "tiffin was 'cold' from the previous evening's dinner and was taken to the office in a tiffin-box and consumed behind a screen in the office, no forty winks in a long chair afterwards then, but back to work until five o'clock," reminisces J.S.M. Rennie. When cold storage was introduced in 1903 food habits and many familiar dishes disappeared from their tables: 'dry curries of eggs or prawns, the different fish kedgerees and the soused and spiced *ikan tenggiri*, all of which made such delicious breakfast.'

Still life of local fruit, c 1910 — A. O.

Creaking Carts With Iron-Bound Wheels

The years 1890 to 1895 were lean years for Singapore. With the slump in trade and finance, some small business firms collapsed. Despite a scarcity of money, the legislative council demanded a military contribution of £100,000. In protest against this levy, in 1895 the unofficial members of the council, Justices of the Peace and the members of the Chinese Advisory Board all resigned, a gesture that did not serve to set Singapore on the road to recovery.

By contrast, the economy of Malaya was buoyant with large increases in tin production and the export of padi (unhusked rice) and sugar. From the mid-1890's Henry Ridley's rubber plant seeds were much in demand and by the early 1900's individual planting gave way to company speculation as plantations were bought up, merged and enlarged. Situated at the crossroads of major trade routes, the port of Singapore had yet to expand to reap the benefits of the huge trade potential of Malaya. On July 1, 1896, the Protected States of Perak, Selangor, Negri Sembilan and Pahang were drawn under one administration as the Federated Malay States and Singapore was forced to reconsider its position as the entrepôt warehouse of the peninsula. Facilities in the New Harbour were grossly inadequate: ships were lined up for repair, cargoes had to wait their turn at the wharves, godowns were overcrowded and, compounding all this, the roads leading to

Straits Produce, July, 1894

town were also congested. While the world was turning to steam trains, electric trams and petrol-driven vehicles, cargoes in Singapore were still transported in creaking carts with iron-bound wheels pulled by oxen.

In 1903 the governor, Sir Frank Swettenham, departed with the observation, "you have in Singapore a city of 200,000 inhabitants, which will one day be a million, and a port reckoned by the tonnage of its shipping as the seventh largest in the world. That is something to begin with. Then you have a magnificent natural harbour (Telok Ayer Bay) on which nothing has yet been spent, but which, if it were protected by works, could afford 1,300 acres of sheltered anchorages. You have wharves and docks which have already fame beyond these shores, and are capable of vast improvement...." The improvement began with

Boat Quay, 1890's — A.O.

Telok Ayer, 1890's — A.O.

Sir John Anderson, who arrived in 1904 and was one of the colony's most notable governors. In 1908, the Telok Ayer Basin, with a breakwater and sheltered wharves, was built.

The *cause célèbre* of the early 1900's was the Tanjong Pagar Dock Company arbitration in 1905, in which the government sought to expropriate the company when its London board, in an effort to maintain receipt of dividends, rejected a $12 million proposal for modernization put up by the Singapore management. Former Tanglin Club members by then residing in London, and current members in Singapore were involved on both sides of the arbitration, especially Adamson, Gilfillan and Anderson; W.P. Waddell, club president 1898-1899, was the chairman of the dock company in 1905. On July 1, 1905, the docks and wharves of Keppel Harbour came under government control and entered a period of expansion more extensive than any dreamed of by the old company.

Having been refused permission to store kerosene or petroleum in the vicinity of the port, Syme & Co. began a tank depot on Pulau Bukum. The first bulk stocks of kerosene were imported from Russia for lighting and cooking. Later, Dutch supplies from new oilfields in Borneo and Sumatra arrived and from 1902, when Dutch and British interests were merged under the Asiatic Petroleum Company, Pulau Bukum became a centre of supply for the region.

The 1900's saw the appearance of electric trams and motor lorries in town. C.B. Buckley, a writer and authority on the early history of Singapore, was the owner, in 1896, of the first 'auto-car', a Benz motor velocipede, more popularly known as the coffee-machine. By 1913 there were 500 passenger cars on the roads, by 1918 the number had grown to 1,300. Currency of the new Straits dollar was established in 1903 and of dollar notes in 1906. International banking facilities were established; insurance companies agreed to cover the transport of rubber from plantation to factory; almost unlimited credit facilities were made available to the merchants. Public health and welfare became a matter of concern. Dr. W.R.C. Middleton, the club president of 1902, was the municipal health officer for 25 years during which he also served on the opium commission and was remembered by the isolation hospital which bore his name (subsequently the communicable disease centre within Tan Tock Seng Hospital). In 1911 Roland Braddell, club president 1914, 1917, 1918, began a successful campaign in *The Straits Times* with the editor Alexander William Still for the introduction of anti-malaria measures. That, too, was something to begin with.

HEALTH LECTURES

Singapore is not too well provided with intellectual entertainment, a fact that is much more due to the want of initiative on some one's part than to distaste among the many. The spell is about to be broken; individual energy has secured the needed co-operation and seems to secure us a somewhat novel and exceedingly useful course of address during the next few months. Health lectures by our leading medical men are to be given on alternate Monday evenings, with a break at the New Year, beginning on November 7th. Seven well-varied subjects are announced for popular treatment, illustrated (when practicable) by magic lantern demonstrations and by experiments. The lectures are to be given at the Tanglin Club, the sympathies of the Committee with the promoters of these lectures being, we hope, an indication of the general support that will be forthcoming from the community . . . The price of the tickets is only just sufficient to cover unavoidable expenses—two dollars for the whole course, a very cheap education, or fifty cents a lecture (obtainable from Messrs. Little & Co.). The following is the full syllabus:—

November   7—"Contagion and its Prevention"—Dr. Simon

November 21—"The Roentgen Rays"—Dr. Middleton

December   5—"Water"—Dr. Ellis

December 19—"Diet and Exercise in the Tropics"—Dr. Fowlie

January   9—"Digestion"—Dr. Lim Boon Keng

January   23—"The Care of Children in Tropics"—Dr. Galloway

February   6—"The Influence of Dress on Health"—Dr. Glennie

TANGLIN HEALTH LECTURE

The second of the series of health lectures at the Tanglin Club will be given on Monday evening nine o'clock when Dr. Middleton will speak upon "The Roentgen Rays". Mr. W. Grigor Taylor will occupy the chair. The tickets for the remaining six lectures of the course are to be had from Messrs. John Little & Co. for $2, or a ticket for a single lecture can be obtained for 50 cents. It is proposed to divide any surplus funds from the sale of tickets, after necessary expenses in connection with the lecture have been paid, towards the purchase of new batteries for the Roentgen Rays apparatus.

The Straits Times, October 24, 1898

IN THE TROPICS.

DIET AND EXERCISE.
HOW TO LIVE HEALTHFULLY.

"Diet and Exercise in the Tropics" was the subject chosen by Dr. Fowlie for the health lecture delivered by him last night, at the Tanglin Club. The Chairman was the Hon. W. R. Collyer, who, in introducing the lecturer, alluded to the eminently practical nature of Dr. Fowlie's subject that evening, and expressed the hope that his listeners might profit much by what they heard.

Dr. Fowlie remarked that it was not too much to say that almost all the ailments of the European in Singapore arose from indiscretion in eating and drinking, and the taking of too little exercise. One great danger people in the tropics did not realize was that of always attributing feelings of general seediness to the climate. That was a mistake. Singapore climate was a good one, and an appreciation of the general laws of health should enable us to live as well here as at home. What he wished to do more particularly was to give young and healthy men in Singapore a little advice as to the best method of keeping their health so that life here might be a pleasure rather than the reverse. The young man in the tropics could generally eat an enormous meal and digest it, but, as a matter of fact, that meal was too much for the maintenance of health. The result of this over-eating might not be apparent for many years, but when the period of youth was passed and the young man was young no longer, the result would be felt in those excruciating twinges of pain in the small of the back or elsewhere, and complaints of the liver. Then, as Rudyard Kipling had said, the stomach and other organs must not be called names; they were as human as their possessors and deserved a fair chance. It was a fact that less food was required in a hot climate than in a cold one. The three square meals to which the average Britisher in Singapore subjected himself every day were too much for him. What people in the tropics, as a rule, want is a more rapid removal of the waste products of the body; on the proper regulation of the income and expenditure of our bodies in this climate depended our good health. It would be madness for the European in the tropics to live as

the native; a proper diet was that which lay midway between what we were used to at home, and the quantities of food devoured by the Kling or the Malay. There was much to indicate, Dr. Fowlie continued, that the generality of men were best fitted for work mentally and bodily on a mixed dietary of animal and vegetable food. He was not a supporter of the starvation diet advocated by some physicians. The fact was that no two men were alike in regard to the diet they could usefully take. There must be a difference in the diet given to the brain-worker, and to the man who is engaged in manual labour. To bring the case nearer home, the Singapore merchant stewing in his office must have different food to the planter. The planters were, he thought, the most healthy set of men in the tropics. They were continually in the open air, and their meals were so arranged that the stomach was enabled to digest one quantity of food and take a rest before being called upon to deal with more food. Take the ordinary day of the sedentary person in Singapore. He generally had early breakfast at six or a little later; there might perhaps be some form of exercise before breakfast, but only in a few cases. After breakfast came the drive to the office and a morning's work, followed by an attempt to get outside a Singapore Club tiffin. By five o'clock or so, there comes on a feeling of sleepiness and inactivity, and a stimulant is needed before dinner. This was asking the poor liver to do too much; not only was the liver useful in forming bile, but it had also to stand sentinel over the circulation and keep away impurities from it. It stood to reason, therefore, that if the liver were overworked, the circulation was affected and consequently the general health. People should remember that they eat to live and that they live not to eat but to work. They should have only a light tiffin, and if that course were followed he would guarantee that many men in Singapore would be saved a great deal of misery. To ladies he would say, make your tiffin parties earlier, go to your tiffin at 11.30 without any breakfast, take nothing more until 4.30, and dine at 7.30. Alluding to drink, Dr. Fowlie said it was unquestionable that people imbibed far too much alcoholic liquor in the tropics; for those whom it suited, teetotalism was far the best course to pur-

sue. The best drink with tiffin was a light wine or light beer. The favourite "stengah" was not rational or to be defended; as a matter of fact the beer-drinker was, as a rule, in better health than the drinker of ardent spirits. Turning to the question of exercise, the lecturer remarked that if the merchant did nothing but stick to his office, and the clerk to his desk, the result would be physical ruin for that man's family, and consequently it would affect the whole nation. The body required to be kept up to pitch in the tropics even more than in a temperate climate; the enervating effect of heat told very much on the organs and especially on the heart, and one should be careful, therefore, that exercise threw no excessively heavy strain on the heart. Moderation in exercise was the thing in the tropics as elsewhere. Cycling was excellent for ladies and men; cricket, as an exercise, was inferior to a great many other forms of amusement; lawn tennis was a pleasant method of exercising the muscles; horse-riding, with an occasional canter or gallop, was the best exercise in this climate; the constitutional walk he had not much faith in; while, as to the value of Indian clubs and dumb-bells, there could be no doubt. He considered that the afternoon was the best time to go in for physical recreation. In conclusion, Dr. Fowlie gave a piece of advice to those whose children were at school at home. It was, of course, important that the school should be a good one as regards its masters, but a more important matter for the child was the character of the food and the amount of exercise he got. Depend upon it, concluded the lecturer, the youth's career is as much in the hands of the cook and the school doctor as in the hands of the head-master. (Applause).

The Chairman, in moving a vote of thanks to Dr. Fowlie, said he was convinced that the advice they had heard that evening was the right advice to follow, and he related his personal experiences on the Gold Coast, where those men who went in for the most exercise were, as a rule, those who best withstood the deadly climate.

The vote of thanks having been unanimously accorded, the Chairman announced that the next lecture would be given on January 9th by Dr. Lim Boon Keng, who would speak on the subject of "Digestion."

The Straits Times, December 20, 1898

By Their Chota Pegs Or Stengahs Did Ye Know Them

Rowland Allen, a founding partner of the law firm of Allen and Gledhill, arrived in Singapore in June 1895. In his diary recording his voyage and first days in Singapore, he relates: "I have during the last few days been introduced to so many people that I feel sure I'll not know one quarter of them when I see them again. They all seemed very nice and are exceedingly hospitable to a newcomer though I believe there are many 'sets' and all that sort of nonsense.... The Bar here consists of some 40 members and most of them exceedingly nice people and there are several very able men. The élite of Singapore meet every evening if fine on the Club ground (generally called Gymkhana Ground) round which there is a public road and you see some very nice turn-outs; the rich Chinamen have the

finest carriages and horses. The Chinese boys are very quaint little men, the two who look after my rooms at Raffles Hotel have the usual full moon faces and pigtails coming down lower than their knees with bright silk thread plaited in with the hair and front part of head shaved—the Servants here are dressed in blue trousers with white gaiters, jackets and shoes. I shall have to provide myself with a boy, who generally valets you and accompanies you out to dinner-parties and waits upon you; this is a necessity here.... You never pay ready money here for anything, you sign 'chits' which are presented to you at the end of each month so you have to be careful and keep account or you have not at the end of a week the least idea how much you have spent." Since it was common practice for Europeans not to

Raffles Hotel, c 1900 — A.O.

carry money, there was a significant concession to local custom for church goers: it was even possible to sign a chit for collection.

In his *Lights of Singapore* Roland Braddell declares: "To distinguish between the *burra sahibs* (India) and the tuan besar (Malaya) and the tai pan (China), there was only one shibboleth. By their *chota* pegs, or stengahs or half pegs did ye know them. Otherwise they were peas in a pod. Go into any of their clubs and save for the different way in which you had to order your whiskey and soda, you were always in the same place, supremely satisfied and blissfully ignorant of everything outside."

Salubrious Singapore, 1920

The presence and influence of the Grif-fith-Jones family in Singapore certainly left its mark on the Tanglin Club. Oswald Phillips 'O.P.' Griffith-Jones, was president of the Tanglin Club six times between 1923 and 1938. O.P. and his wife Edith had three children, Gwen, Eric and Lionel. Gwen, who is still a member of the Tanglin Club, married John Pickering, the 1959 president of the club, and served on the ladies subcommittee for fifteen years. Eric returned to Singapore in 1935, and was an honorary secretary of the Tanglin Club in 1937. In his memoirs *That's My Lot* Lionel, who was a Tanglin Club committee member in 1960 and 1961, depicts the living conditions of the 1920's, also typical of the earlier decades.

"We lived in a bungalow on short stilts — monsoon rains in due season tended to slop about somewhat — at Mount Rosie, a few miles out of town. A flight of steps up the front of the bungalow led into a spacious front verandah which was our sitting room. A wide corridor with two bedrooms and a bathroom on either side led off that, straight to the back of the bungalow, where the dining room was located. From there, there were steps down to the kitchen and to the servants' quarters. Lighting was by oil lamps. We all slept under mosquito nets suspended on wooden frames from the ceiling over our beds.

"In a pantry alcove adjoining the dining room was a large icebox standing shoulder-high which was replenished with a huge block of ice delivered early every morning before the heat of the day from the Cold Storage Company. Next to the icebox was a big, bulbous stone filter, like a huge udder, with a Shanghai jar, so-called because of its Chinese origin, underneath it. The legs of the wooden frames holding both icebox and filter stood in earthenware saucers filled with neat Jeyes fluid. This precaution applied to all wooden, floor-standing furniture or impedimenta which would normally not be moved about, such as tables, wardrobes, beds, to guard against marauding creepy-crawlies, and particularly against white ants which could devour wood from the inside, and most other material of those days, apart from steel. They could even burrow up through cement. They had not yet been confronted by plastic but would probably have thrived on it. Well-water was tipped into the filter to drip steadily into the large earthenware jar, which was of a size to match the cooking pot in popular illustrations of cannibals, stewing wide-eyed, bemused, and for some reason, invariably behatted missionaries. After being filtered, the water was boiled for drinking and kept in stoneware bottles. Other Shanghai jars filled with unfiltered cold water stood in

Europeans outside bungalow, c 1915 — A.O.

each bathroom, with soap and a dunker (known as a *tong*) handy with which the water was scooped up from the jar to douse head and torso. The water then drained away beneath wooden slats laid on an angled cement floor. It was primitive but effective.

"The only other furniture in the bathrooms was a row of three or four thunder boxes, each with a lid and free-standing, known also more prosaically as *jampans*. Both terms could be said to be aptly descriptive. These were the lavatories of the pre-watercloset days. For piddling purposes one simply used the one which had obviously had fewest previous visitations. After big jobs however, the required procedure was to pour in a generous dollop of Jeyes fluid, always kept ready to hand in a corner, and then close the lid on it all. A closed lid meant give it a miss. A very junior Chinese member of the household staff, known as a *tukang ayer* (literally water worker), had the unenviable job of daily clearing all used *jampans*, usually after breakfast. As a disinterested small boy I do not recall ever enquiring about what happened to the contents: presumably they went into some pit at the back of the compound and were earthed over. Household servants, whether *amahs* (children's nurses), cooks or house-boys, were Chinese, gardeners *(kebuns)* were Tamil Indians, and car drivers *(syces)* were Malays. They were all my friends. Now and then I used to pull rank but they did not take it very seriously. We conversed together in an ungrammatical, bazaar Malay, with which I grew up and which I learnt to speak as I learnt to speak English."

In his <u>Indiscreet Memories</u> Edwin Brown informs: "in 1901 we had no fans, only punkahs; oil lamps were our lighting mainstay. No electricity whatsoever (except the telephone) was available, and we all had to wear blue suits to go to church in! The ladies wore high-necked blouses, flowing skirts with lots of petticoats, and long, kid or suede gloves. But in the offices men from the Tuan Besar downwards—wore the white suit—the <u>Baju Tutup</u>; collars were never seen except at parties, the races, or in Church!" The <u>tutup</u>, a jacket, featured a one and a half-inch stiff collar held together by two small gold or EPNS studs. The five large buttons down the front were usually of mother-of-pearl, or EPNS; sometimes twenty-cent coins from Queen Victoria's reign were used. With changing fashion trends the coat was lengthened and a six to nine-inch vertical slit at the back was introduced which enabled "the nuts of the day to strut the town with one hand in trouser pocket, white topee, or a boater worn slightly on a slant; well-polished brogue shoes, and a cigarette in a holder being puffed at vigorously."

[European wearing <u>baju tutup</u>, 1910 — N.M.]

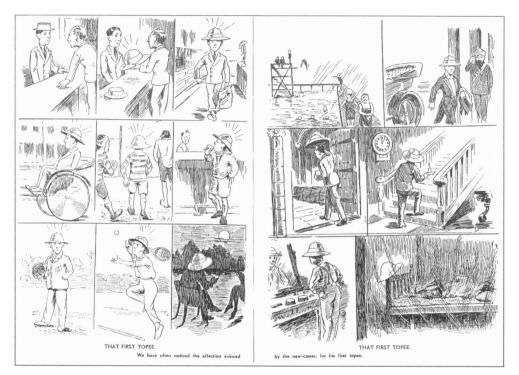

THAT FIRST TOPEE.
We have often noticed the affection evinced

THAT FIRST TOPEE.
by the new-comer, for his first topee.

Straits Produce, December, 1926

The Claymore district at the turn of the century was no longer isolated. Residential districts contained large estates and Grange, Scotts, Stevens, Balmoral and River Valley roads were prestigious areas where well-known Europeans lived. The residents occupied spacious two-storey bungalows with wide verandahs shaded by chick blinds, standing in two or three acres with tennis courts or lawns surrounded by flowering trees and bushes. Everyone "kept out of it (the sun) as much as possible from eight in the morning to five in the afternoon," notes Rowland Allen, who ventured "to give a warning to all those under a tropical sun in the words of the 'Barrack Room Ballad': But the worst of your foes is the sun overhead/You must wear your helmet for all that is said/If he finds you uncovered he'll strike you down dead/An' you'll die like a fool of a soldier!"

...members were entitled to privacy...

After a struggle to survive its first quarter century, the Tanglin Club in 1890 was finally an established institution.

It may be supposed that the influence of such past presidents as William Read, Samuel Gilfillan, John Fraser, John Anderson and George Murray, all senior partners in major firms, and the force of their renowned personalities would have added prestige to the standing of the club. There are no records for the 1880's and 1890's; it is known that members of that time regarded the club's

ADVICE TO A "GRIFFIN."

1. As soon as possible after your arrival in Singapore, call on your "boss"'s wife. If she is at home (which is improbable) tell her you think Singapore a very one-horse sort of a place. Repeat this to any other ladies you may meet later on. They like it.

2. Never wear a white coat, but put on a stiffly-starched shirt every day and wear it in office with your coat off. It will be evidence that you are hard at work.

3. Invest in a $500 turn-out as soon as you have found one to suit you. What were the Chetties made for?

4. Then take the Directory and call on every third person from A to Z. They won't be at home, so it doesn't matter; and by the time they return your call (which won't be for a year or so), you will have found out whether they are the sort of people you want to know or not.

5. When you do go out in Society, show by your manner that you think it very inferior to what you were used to at home.

6. Never get into a jinrikisha till after dark. When you do, it is useless to attempt to tell the coolie where to drive to. He will probably guess; and if he happens to go wrong, you can always hit him across the back with your stick. On arriving at your destination keep him waiting for an hour or so, and then give him a chit or say, "Mari besok." This also applies to gharry-syces.

7. When you have sufficiently mastered the vernacular, make a point of saying "lu" to every person you address in it; especially Arab merchants and the Sultan of Johor. They are used to this mode of address and it puts them at their ease.

8. Cut your cook 20 per cent. every time you take his account. It won't make any difference to him, or to you, in the long run, but will be a source of periodical satisfaction to yourself.

9. If you have occasion to go on business into a Government office, do not remove your hat or cigar, but just sit down in the most convenient chair. Government officials are the servants of the public, and should be treated accordingly. Remember you are part owner of the Building and Staff.

10. Let it be generally known that your principal motive for coming to the East was a desire to see the world or to benefit your health; and that your present pecuniary position is not nearly so good as the one which you held at home.

Straits Produce, July, 1894

WANTED, A CLUB.

To the Editor of the "Straits Times."

DEAR MR. EDITOR,—Is it not time that some effort was made to add to the natural beauties of Singapore some attractions in way of social recreations?

For the size of the place we possess undoubtedly many clubs, but all must admit that general comfort has not been studied in connection with those institutions, whereas so much might be done if only a good scheme for a Country Club in a central position could be placed before the community. Everyone in Singapore appears to be so deeply engrossed in the advancement of his own affairs that it is difficult to find the person with leisure and inclination to promote what is really wanted to make this increasing town more attractive to visitors as well as to residents. Such a club has been mooted on more than one occasion, but lack of support has disheartened those who have made the attempt.

The difficulties of securing an eligible site and of raising funds are always brought forward, but, I believe, these could be overcome by *esprit de corps* if only a good scheme could be laid before the community, and be shown to be acceptable to old and young alike.

I emphasize my contention :—

(1) What is there in Singapore for anyone to do on a wet afternoon after business?

(2) Many young men are in the place with nowhere to spend their evenings nor anywhere to congregate, and spend a convivial few hours after work.

(a) The Singapore Club is deserted after dark, and is practically nothing more or less than a tiffin club.

(b) The S.C.C. is closed at 7 p.m., and on wet afternoons has only one attraction, "The Bar."

(c) The Ladies' L.T.C. has such an abbreviated apology for a pavilion that it hardly affords shelter in case of rain, and, except in fine weather, is deserted.

(d) The Tanglin Club was lately condemned as dangerous, and even if repaired temporarily, will serve only for an occasional dance or concert and is shut up except on those rare occasions. The Bowling alleys are better patronized, but are only used after dinner, being situated too far from town for play on wet afternoons.

(e) The numerous golf, boating, chess, and other clubs, are all limited in accommodation and have practically no comfort.

Any attempt to remedy the above state of things, deserves the support of everyone in the community.

The Teutonia Club is an example which should put the British community to shame, seeing the wigwams they possess as Club buildings.

This letter is written with a view that abler pens will come forward, but I offer a few suggestions :—

The Raffles Reclamation would be preferable to the Fort Canning or Old Jail sites, if the Government would entertain any proposals. I believe a covenant exists that no building may be erected on the reclamation in front of Raffles School, but would objection be raised if the ground was laid out with tennis and croquet lawns, and with a nicely kept garden? The Club house could be placed to the eastward, and in no way interfere with the above mentioned covenant.

The Club house itself depends so much on whether it is decided to build a residential club, or only a recreation club. The former, of course, requires a large sum of money, and such a sum could only be raised by making it a limited company concern, so that men located here for a limited period, or liable to be moved, would have something tangible to hold and easy to realize if leaving the Colony when their shares or debentures could be either taken over by their successors or otherwise disposed of.

The terms of payment should be made easy, and spread over a period, so that those with limited incomes could all join.

For instance say young men who could not afford a subscription of $100, out of hand, would possibly give even more if the amounts were made payable by monthly instalments of $10.

If a recreation club only is decided upon, the expense would be less, but it should include a ladies' drawing room, or a ladies' club should be attached, and then they might abandon the Tanglin Club and the Ladies' Lawn Tennis Club.

I am, etc.,
Nil Desperandum.
Singapore, 14th March

The Straits Times, Tuesday, March 15, 1904

On Sunday, April 21, 1901, the Duke and Duchess of Cornwall and York (later King George IV and Queen Mary) arrived on the SS OPHIR on their way to Australia. Elaborate preparations were made to give the royal visitors a splendid welcome: troops were positioned in the area of the Town Hall where a choir of over 100 performed; the royal carriage was headed by a mounted detachment of Sikhs in scarlet uniforms who were known as the Perak Lancers, a private bodyguard of about twenty men and an officer maintained by the Sultan of Perak and lent to Singapore for the occasion. The atmosphere of the town was frequently charged by a visit from members of British royalty so it was not surprising that the death of Queen Victoria in 1901 stunned Singapore: 'it seemed like a city struck with the plague; it was a perfectly silent town as far as business went.' This occasion marked the end of the century, indeed of an era, though life rolled on very much the same as before. [The Perak Lancers, 1908 — Twentieth Century Impressions of British Malaya]

affairs as no matter for public record and newspaper editors conceded that members were entitled to privacy. Nevertheless accounts of the club exist in the published works and personal writings of several prominent members and writers. *Twentieth Century Impressions of British Malaya* carries the record: "the Tanglin Club was founded shortly after the German Club in 1868 as a suburban social institute to meet the wants of Britishers living in the Tanglin district. Formerly it contained reading, smoking and billiard rooms but these have now been discontinued in consequence of the growing popularity of rival institutions in town. The club bungalow in Stevens Road is used principally for monthly dances and occasional concerts. The ballroom has for years had the reputation of having the best dancing floor in Singapore. In the grounds are four bowling alleys which are freely used by members. The membership numbers about two hundred and the club which owns the bungalow and grounds forming its headquarters is carried on by members' subscription alone. Some years ago a scheme was projected for rebuilding the club premises as a residential club but nothing came of it."

...the building was old and rather dismal looking...

The Tanglin Club was regarded by some as a white elephant. The building was old and rather dismal looking and in 1900 had been condemned as unsafe; various schemes were proposed by 'authoritative committees' and private individuals to modernise the club, including suggestions for complete alterations. One committee in 1904 even proposed the removal of the club to the corner of Orchard Road and Orange Grove Road, to land believed to be owned by John Anderson. This scheme was to cost Straits Dollars 300,000 for the land, a new building with residential quarters for men, tennis courts, stables, bowling alleys and 'all the other necessities of an up-to-date social club of that day.' The proposal was not taken up and the club remained on its original site, consisting as it did until 1980 of the original condemned building and later extensions. Another proposal in 1904 to establish a 'country club' was, like the former efforts, 'an agitation ...started, taken a certain distance and then dropped.' Several years later, assisted by a few liberal-minded seniors, a group of younger men revolted; according to Roland Braddell, who played a role in the instigation, "this happened after we had made a gallant attempt to convert the old Tyersall Palace, now pulled down, into a Country Club. Despite official support the scheme was killed by the old boys at the Singapore Club, largely out of pique." The Tanglin Club did not, it seems, offer sufficient attraction to Britishers in the colony.

During the rebuilding of their clubhouse between 1899 and 1900, members of the Teutonia Club enjoyed the hospitality of the Tanglin Club. The German community was the life and soul of European social life in the colony and the Teutonia Club was the scene of some of the finest entertainments and the centre of musical life. The bar was stocked with German beer and wine; as bowling was a popular sport, the alleys of the Teutonia Club and the Tanglin Club saw many highly contested matches followed by evenings of beer and sausages. The new Teutonia Club was opened on September 21, 1900, by Sir James Alexander Swettenham, then acting-governor of the colony. More than 500 guests attended the function, including all members of the German community and, among other distinguished guests, the chief justice Sir Lionel Cox and the Honourable W.R. Collyer; the president of the Teutonia Club was Theodore Sohst, a municipal commissioner in 1890.

...great times
at the
Teutonia...

The handsome new building, erected by Swan and Maclaren, put in the shade any similar social institution in Singapore at that time — it was even rumoured that the tower of the new Teutonia Club was built to look down on the Tanglin Club. Of a general feeling at the time, C.M. Turnbull writes: "British merchants had viewed with some distaste and resentment the invasion in the early

The Teutonia Club from a portfolio of photogravures entitled 'Malay Peninsula' by Charles J. Kleingrothe, c 1907 — N.A.

years of the century of a new breed of aggressive young German businessmen, very different from the suave German merchants of earlier days. German goods flooded the Singapore market, the German community expanded rapidly, and the opulent Teutonia Club overshadowed the nearby British Tanglin Club, which was almost deserted and its buildings in a dangerous state of disrepair." In 1901 the German community numbered 236, by 1911 their numbers had dropped to 181; in 1914, with the outbreak of World War 1, the Teutonia Club was seized by the custodian of enemy property. Until then, however, the activities of the Tanglin Club continued to benefit from its proximity to the German club and the sharing of common interests between the members of both clubs. On March 15, 1906, the AGM of the Tanglin Club was held at the Teutonia Club during which approval was sought to borrow $25,000 from Commercial Union Assurance for renovations to the clubhouse. In July 1907 the musical farce, *The Rajah of Stengahpour*, produced by Roland Braddell and J.N. Briggs was staged at the Teutonia Club which had much better facilities than the Tanglin Club. Recalling a bygone era in his *Musings*, J.S.M. Rennie writes: "The Germans gave us great times at the Teutonia Club, now Goodwood Hall, with Dances, Smoking Concerts, and Bowls, and once a year a delightful evening with a real Fair, very well got up, and 'all the fun of the Fair', even to the biergartens."

Volunteers Flocking To The Colours

Echoing the fortunes of the British Empire, the number of members of the Singapore Volunteer Artillery (embodied by proclamation on February 22, 1888) ebbed and flowed: during crises Volunteers flocked to the Colours, in between only the stalwarts remained. Meetings of the general committee of the SVA were held at the Singapore Cricket Club. As the social aspect as well as the social responsibility became predominant, dancing, smoking concerts, and other entertainments were arranged to popularise the Volunteers. Sporting cups and trophies were competed for annually and included the Finlayson and the Murray trophies. The standard of shooting in the colony was high; in 1905 Captain F.M. Elliot, SVI, one of the best shots in the Straits, was tenth in the King's Hundred at Bisley, England.

On August 4, 1914, Britain declared war on Germany. Although the European conflict seemed far away to residents of Singapore, on August 5, two hundred men of the Singapore Volunteer Corps which included a number of Tanglin Club

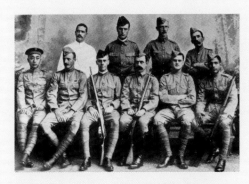

Rifle Club prize winners, (left to right) Otto Jaeger, Peter Fowlie, Pullar, 'Old' Flanagan, Tan Soon Bin, 'Ginger' Thompson, Charlie Phillips, F.M. Elliot, A.E. Murray and De Silva, c 1903 — Indiscreet Memories

members and the Chinese and Malay contingents, marched to Military Headquarters at Fort Canning. The government issued notice of a state of war: local forces were placed under the army act and mobilised; German ships were seized and their crews brought ashore; German inhabitants signed internment papers; the movement of foodstuffs was regulated; export business was brought to a halt; the tin market was suspended; immigration of Chinese and Indian labour was prohibited.

By August 10, 1914, local shipping began to move and Keppel Harbour was busy again. On August 23, the Japanese, an unknown quantity in the East, declared their allegiance to Britain. On September 21 the German cruiser EMDEN appeared in the Bay of Bengal and attacked British shipping; after a raid on Penang in October 1914, she was de-

During one SVA route march through the exclusive Tanglin district on April 13, 1891, forty-five Volunteers, headed by the drum and fife band of the 41st Battery Southern Division, made various stops before arriving at the Tanglin Club, "where there was a brief halt for refreshment." In A History of the Singapore Volunteer Corps Capt. T.M. Winsley writes: "owing to the halts which took place so conveniently, this march was known as 'The Battle of Tanglin' and the following verse was written regarding it:

> ..And now their Captain issues bold
>   command:
>   'High Tanglin must be stormed and
>   sacked to-night.'
>   Undaunted e'en by this the gallant
>   band
>   In serried ranks marched forward to
>   the fight.
> ...Thus press they onward to the
>   towering height
>   Where Tanglin Club their way doth
>   seem to bar.
>   With loosened ranks they rush in to
>   the fight
>   On every side arise loud sounds of
>   war.
> ..Zeal so unquenchable what can
>   withstand?
>   Within brief space their victory's
>   complete,
>   The ranks reform, on marches this
>   brave band
>   Though some perchance can scarcely
>   keep their feet."

[The Singapore Volunteer Rifle Corps 1865 depicted on the cover of the SVR March reprinted after 1888 — A History of the Singapore Volunteer Corps]

At the S. V. A. Smoking Concert at the Tanglin Club on Tuesday, there is to be some good orchestral music. We understand also that some new amateur vocal talent will appear.

— ◆ —

— ◆ —

The Straits Times, October, 1893

CORRESPONDENCE.

V. D.

The Editor,
   Straits Produce.

Dear Sir,

As a woman—and a mother—it grieves me to see such charming men as the Dear Bishop and MR. STILL quarrelling and writing harsh things about each other over the above subject and their statistics and figures are very wrong indeed. There are only about six gentlemen in Singapore who have the V.D. and they only got it through being in the Volunteers for 20 years

Yours etc.,
"Dear Old Lady."

❖   ❖   ❖   ❖

Dear Sir,

I am very sorry to see the letter signed "Dear Old Lady" because now my father won't let me join the Volunteers and this is a great disappointment to me and Colonel Spencer because my two weeks practising and four lessons on the bugle are wasted now or do you know someone who wants a bugler or someone who wants to buy a bugle nickel plated or I would exchange for a hand camera or thoroughbred Pomeranian dog, male, must be all black.

Yours
"Straits Born Chinese Schoolboy."

❖   ❖   ❖   ❖

Straits Produce, April, 1924

stroyed at the Cocos Islands by HM Australian Ship SYDNEY. When the German fleet was destroyed at the Falklands on December 9, any menace to Singapore disappeared.

The period of calm was shattered in February 1915. After the British Regiment had departed for the front in November, the only regular troops left were the Indian Regiment, the 5th Light Infantry, who were preparing to sail to Hong Kong and a few Royal Garrison Artillery and Royal Engineers. The Singapore Volunteers, augmented by the Volunteer Rifles and the Veterans Company, numbering 450, manned the forts and undertook garrison duties. On February 15 the 5th Light Infantry who were guarding German military prisoners mutinied. After murdering some of their officers, the Indian soldiers seized Alexandra Barracks, released the prisoners-of-war in Tanglin Barracks and set about murdering any Europeans they encountered. By February 22, with the assistance of British, French, Russian and Japanese naval landing parties and Japanese civilian special constables, the mutiny was suppressed. Roland Braddell prosecuted at the special court martial held on February 23 where the sentence of death was passed on 37 mutineers and carried out at Outram Road Gaol; 89 mutineers were transported for life and the remainder sentenced to lesser terms of transportation and imprisonment.

THINGS THAT NEVER COULD HAPPEN IN SINGAPORE
The Master Attendant Performs on the High "C."

Hampered by the letting of the Town Hall for the Tanjong Pagar Dock Company arbitration in 1905 and the demolition of the hall in 1907 to make way for the Victoria Theatre, the Singapore Philharmonic Society stored their music at the Teutonia Club, practised at the Tanglin Club and until 1911, 'some excellent concerts were given.' In One Hundred Years of Singapore *Edwin Brown remarks that no mention of music during the earlier part of the 1900's would be complete without some acknowledgement of the military bands in Singapore. Straight from the South African War, the first white regiment to arrive was the Manchesters followed by the Sherwood Foresters, both with no bands to speak of although individual members played regularly in the Singapore Philharmonic Society, established in 1891. Later on, the settlement was lucky to be the abode of a battalion of the West Kent Regiment stationed at the Tanglin Barracks from 1907 to 1908, with a band reputed to be one of the finest in the marching regiments of the British army. Edwin Brown recounted in 1919, "there are people here who will still remember the shock they got when, at a concert at the Tanglin Club, the band laid down its instruments and sang an unaccompanied glee." [Straits Produce, October, 1925]*

Putting The Sing Into Singapore

In 1894 Jerome K. Jerome's *Sunset* and William Brough's *Trying It On* were staged at the Tanglin Club. Though performances were not open to critics, the press reported them to be a success. Among the stars were Mr. and Mrs. Brompton Matthews, Mrs. W.E. Hooper (wife of a later club president), Mr. Haigh, Mr. Harwood, the Solicitor-General, and Mr. E. Ormiston. In 1901 a Russian operatic singer of good repute performed at the Tanglin Club, but even she could not equal Kate Salzmann's rendering of a simple little English song, a great favourite of hers, 'The Old Grey Mare'. Kate Salzmann was a popular and highly acclaimed performer who used her beautiful voice to perfection in the amateur theatricals, especially the Gilbert and Sullivan productions. Her début in *The Wonderful Woman* in 1884 was described in the press as "...irresistible. Her pretty face, engaging manners and natural acting took the house by storm!" Her final stage performance was in *His Excellency the Governor* which was also the first performance in the new Victoria Memorial Hall in 1906. Her husband Edward Salzmann, the organist at St. Andrew's Church, was a professional pianist whose name was associated with every English musical and dramatic production in Singapore for more than a quarter of a century. In 1887 the stage production of *Charley's Aunt* starred Miss Dennys (Mrs. G.S. Murray) and Miss Wishart (Mrs. J.D. Saunders); C.I. Carver, president 1909, is reported to have given his best performance as Brassett the butler in the 1901 production of this play.

E. Lehrenkrauss of Behn, Meyer & Co.,

a vice-president of the Teutonia Club, is described by Edwin Brown as a fine vocalist, "about the only foreigner whose name will be found figuring as a soloist." Edwin Brown arrived in Singapore in 1901 to join Brinkmann & Company, the Singapore house of Hiltermann Brothers of Manchester. In addition to being a later commentator — his *Indiscreet Memories* was described as 'straightforwardly anecdotal and opinionative pages' — Edwin Brown was also said to be the man who "put the sing into Singapore." In a 1925 issue of the *Straits Produce*, a columnist quips: "We learn that the Singapore Amateur Dramatic Committee is reviving that well-known Gilbert and Sullivan Opera *Edwin A. Brown*." Brown's stage début was at a private concert for the

TO SINGAPORE'S SONGSTRESS.

I've come from a Smoker
I'm wearied with noise,

Last night I played poker
With some of the Boys,

And I think as I lie back,—I'm not sleepy yet,-

And I drowsily puff out a last cigarette.

What is the use of it when it's all done,
  Blatant tom foolery, where is the fun ?
And I know, that's the worst, that none of the throng
  Can move me as you, with one simple sweet song—

'Queen of the Fairies,' ' Ruth,' proud 'Gypsy Queen,'
  ' Katisha,'—each in their turn you have been,—
As each you've excelled ;—yet I do you nò wrong
  In preferring to each—one simple sweet song.

Full of soft dignity, graciously sweet,
  Rings out round melody, ever replete
With womanly sympathy. May you e'er long
  Entrance me again with a simple sweet song.

Straits Produce, April, 1895

Salzmanns at the Tanglin Club, and his first public appearance was in April 1901 at a farewell concert for Walter Makepeace who was going on leave. He is 'remembered with gratitude' as an actor, singer, stage manager and voice trainer in musical productions. In 1901 he appeared in *The Grass Widow* and *Charley's Aunt*; as Lieut. Reginald Fairfax in *The Geisha* he was 'magnificent...see E. Brown at his best'; he was the pirate king and stage manager for the triumphant success *The Pirates of Penzance* which opened the new Victoria Theatre in 1909. Valois, an instrumentalist, is described as 'that prince of good fellows and most versatile performer on the cello... an excellent soloist,' and E.E. Sykes reportedly gave a very memorable performance in June 1904 when amateurs performed *The Duchess of Bayswater & Co* and Offenbach's *The Rose of Auvergne*.

Another leading light in the social life of Singapore, F.W. Barker, a one-time committee member of the Singapore Club and a keen cricketer who for many years served on the committee of the Tanglin Club, also rendered valuable service in connection with the amateur theatricals. His wife was always a popular performer and starred as the leading lady in the 1903 production of *Liberty Hall*, which also marked the final appearance of J.C.D. Jones and A.Y. Gahagan. The daughters of Howard Newton, Maud (Mrs. W.J. Mayson) and Edith (Mrs. O.P. Griffith-Jones) delighted audiences for many years. Maud, a choreographer and singer, made her début in *Liberty Hall*; Edith made her début in *Dream Faces* in

Tanglin Club.

Cigarette Smoking Concert.

Friday, 22nd January, 1904.

❄ PROGRAMME. ❄

1.	March	"Carmen"		Bizet.
2.	German Song	"Spirito Santo"		C. Loewe.
		Mr. Lehrenkrauss.		
3.	Solos (Violin)	{ (a) "À la Valse"		Coleridge-Taylor.
		{ (b) "Moto Perpetuo"		Carl Bohm.
		Miss A. M. Stringer.		
4.	Song	"Love the Pedlar"		Ed. German.
		Mrs. Salzmann.		
5.	Romance	"Salut d'Amour"		E. Elgar.
		Orchestral Arrangement.		
6.	Plantation Song	"De Low Cut Shoe"		Ivan Caryll.
		Solo:—Mr. Sykes (With Chorus).		
7.	Quartett	(Robin Hood)		G. Macfarren.
		Mrs. Wilson Barker, Messrs. E. A. Brown, Cunradi & A. Westerhout.		
8.	Solo (Violoncello)	"Arioso"		H. Rabaud.
		Mr. Valois.		
9.	Song	"Japanese Love Song"		Clayton Thomas.
		Mrs. Wilson Barker.		
10.	Plantation Song	"Piccaninny Mine, Good Night"		Trotere.
		Miss Maud Newton.		
11.	Orchestral Morceau	"Loin du Bal."		E. Gillet.

Programme courtesy of the Dyne Family

1906 — the last performance in the old Town Hall. After Billy Dunman (son of Thomas Dunman) and Howard Newton left the colony, there was no tenor to match their talents. The Braddell family had played a large part on the changing Singapore scene since 1862, a tradition continued by Roland Braddell and Dulcie Winslow, whom he married in 1906 and who became a significant figure in amateur theatricals and Singapore society. Roland Braddell wrote and managed many shows in which Dulcie successfully appeared, including the skit *The Pirates of Pulau Brani*. Gilbert and Sullivan operas were popular in Singapore; *Iolanthe* was first performed in 1889 and *The Geisha* and *The Mikado* were reviewed as 'the two greatest successes and most perfect performances our amateurs have ever given.'

The residents of Singapore also enjoyed visiting entertainments which were always popular, including the circus. Two such companies frequented Singapore, Harmstons and Warrens. Harmstons, "a monument of progress, prosperity and business integrity, unequalled, unapproachable, the 'mastodon' of modern amusement enterprise," was considered the better. Warrens advertised as "a stupendous Federation of the World's Wonders; a sterling, diverting, electric success, successful beyond the most extravagant praise." Everyone, from the governor downwards, 'could be found sitting round the sawdust ring.'

On July 6, 1901, the 'new wonder of the world, the Biograph' appeared and, for the first time, moving pictures were shown at the Singapore Town Hall: the first shows depicted Queen Victoria's funeral and scenes from the Boer War.

ocial customs in Singapore at the beginning of the century reflected what was sometimes called 'Old Singapore', also dubbed 'Singapore County'. Each of the leading mems held a regular at-home reception at which the social lights were expected to appear and "at which the Towkays attended in real Chinese handsome costume, and the Arabs in all their glory," describes J.S.M. Rennie. At well-known bachelor messes, Christmas dinners were a special feature. Throughout its history, the sartorial elegance of members of the Tanglin Club has provided a subject of comment: in earlier days the code of dress was never questioned and before the Great War social life at the club was very formal.

Kerengga Dance at Tanglin Club, 1908 — <u>British Malaya</u>, October, 1934

...the annual fancy dress ball given by the Kerenggas...

In May 1911 Roland Braddell wrote to his mother of plans to celebrate the Coronation of George V: "we are having a fancy dress at the Tanglin Club, there's a public ball at the Town Hall, a Chinese procession, and all the rest of it. I am going to the fancy dress as Coronation Billy, in a costume made up of flags, crowns and red, white and blue ribbons. Dulcie is going as a Yankee Doodle Girl. They were a troupe of dancers and singers we saw and the costume is made on the lines of the American flag and very smart." The social highlight of the year was undoubtedly the occasion when "the County came out in all its glory at the annual fancy dress ball that used to be given at the Tanglin Club by the Kerenggas, a self-chosen band of some 15 or so of the leading bachelors in the town," according to Roland Braddell. (The *kerengga* is a large, red, biting ant.) The Tanglin Club hosts sported red tail-coats with white silk facings and wore a silver *Kerengga* on each lapel. An invitation to the Kerengga Ball was the supreme social accolade, "more prized even than invitations to private dinners at Government House, which in those days meant the Grande Entrée." At the club's monthly ball the band of the British regiment in the garrison played in attendance, and 'festoons of greenery were hung up and huge blocks of ice put in different places to cool the building more than the long hand-pulled punkahs could,' as quoted by Eric Jennings. The programmes of the ladies would be booked, with the supper dance being the most prized of the evening and the bar profits were inflated by the large number of unattached gentlemen. Looking back, J.S.M. Rennie testifies: "girls of the genus white were few and far between and for about a week prior to the monthly dance at the Tanglin Club the telephone was busy in endeavours to secure lady partners. We knew them all and all knew each other. A new arrival was something to write home about... [we] greatly enjoyed the rush for the few eligible partners, and the 'sing-song' afterwards, and then 'Home John' in a rikisha, and woe betide the wallah who dared to wake you up at your destination. Some of us have slept in the rick until 6 A.M., haven't we."

1895 1896 CADELL, William A., was manager of The Borneo Company in Sarawak, Singapore and Bangkok. Interested in horse racing and amateur theatricals; in 1884 was honorary secretary and clerk of the course of the Sporting Club. Assisted in the 1876 revival of the Amateur Dramatic Corps "rescued from decay by the energy and public spirit of the young men of the Colony (which) if its records had been diligently chronicled, would have now presented an interesting story of the social life of the Colony," declared the *Daily Times*.

1897 JONES, John C. D., better known as 'Panjang' Jones, was chief electrician for the Telegraph Company for 25 years. Considered for years to be one of the 'leading spirits in amateur theatricals as an actor and stage manager.'

1898 1899 WADDELL, William P., affectionately known as 'Pa' Waddell, was a partner in Boustead & Company. An unofficial member of the legislative council, chairman of Tanjong Pagar Dock Company in 1905 and involved in the arbitration of 1905, and chairman of the Singapore Chamber of Commerce in 1901 and 1908. Married the daughter of Colonel Samuel Dunlop who succeeded Thomas Dunman as the inspector general of police. Resided at DRAYCOT, in Tanglin.

1900 MACLAREN, James Waddell Boyd, (born 1863), trained in Edinburgh as a civil engineer, came to Singapore in 1887 and joined A.A. Swan to form Swan and Maclaren, an architectural firm which designed some of the finest ornamental buildings in Singapore and the Federated Malay States — in Singapore these included the Hongkong and Shanghai Bank Building, the Chartered Bank Building, Raffles Hotel, the Adelphi Hotel, the Hotel de l'Europe, the Sultan Mosque, the new Teutonia Club building, the pavilion of the Singapore Cricket Club, Syme & Co., Fraser and Neave Ltd. and various other business premises. Resided at HARTFELL in Tanglin. Was a Justice of the Peace, for some years a municipal commissioner and a committee member of the Singapore Club and the Golf Club.

1901 MACTAGGART, Francis W. David, was employed by Boustead & Company. Committee member of the Singapore Club, 1901 and of the Cricket Club.

1902 MIDDLETON, Dr. W. R. C. came to Singapore in 1890, already qualified as a Master of Arts, Doctor of Medicine and Master of Surgery, with a Diploma of Public Health. Was vice-president of the Malaya branch of the British Medical Association; in 1894 appointed municipal health officer and

for 25 years implemented progressive improvements in sanitary conditions of the city. Served on the opium commission; was chairman of the municipal commission. Took a keen interest in the Volunteer Corps of which he was Surgeon-Major; was a committee member of the Singapore Club. Lived at CLARE GROVE in Orchard Road.

1903 SAUNDERS, J. Dashwood, (born 1862, Surrey, England) went to Hong Kong in 1886 after the Old Oriental Bank failed, then Shanghai, before entering the service of the New Oriental Bank in Singapore. When this failed in 1891, returned to England and came back to Singapore in 1892 to found Saunders & Co., exchange and share brokers (in 1901 his partner was F.W. Barker; in 1903 the firm included A.E. Mulholland, son of William Mulholland). Committee member of the Singapore Club and member of the Sporting Club. His wife was a committee member of the Ladies Lawn Tennis Association; they resided at GOODWOOD in Scotts Road.

1904 COLLYER, The Hon. William Robert (born 1842, England) arrived in Singapore as a puisne judge in 1892. (Not to be confused with Colonel G.C. Collyer of Collyer Quay.) As Attorney-General supported the passage of 37 ordinances through the legislature — a number only previously

equalled by Sir Walter Napier — particularly the Municipal Ordinance of 1896 and the Women and Girls' Protection Ordinance of the same year. Conducted the principal Crown prosecutions at the assizes and advised government departments. In 1903, first president of the YMCA; president of the Philosophical Society 1894-1901 and 1902-1906; member of the committee of Raffles Library and Museum and president of the Art Club, the Rowing Club and the Children's Aid Society. 'His true value as a public servant was never realised until he retired.'

1905 1908 HOOPER, William Edwards, (born 1858, Surrey, England) grandson of the Rt. Hon. John Kinnereley Hooper, Lord Mayor of London 1847-48. Came to Singapore in 1881 to join A.L. Johnston & Co. In 1884 appointed acting-consul for Norway and Sweden and the following year made a Visiting Justice and Justice of the Peace. In 1890 appointed by Sir Cecil Clementi Smith to the labour commission; elected representative of Tanglin ward on the municipal commission; registrar of the hackney carriage and jinricksha department, 1892; in 1901 the census officer for Singapore. Was on a commission of inquiry into the detective branch of the police force, superintendent of the prevention of cruelty to animals department, deputy acting-coroner, member of the Straits Settlements Association, chairman of Visiting Justices for 16 years, committee member of the Golf Club, secretary of a 1919 Singapore centenary celebrations sub-committee (with D.Y. Perkins and R. St. J. Braddell), a prominent

Freemason, and a keen tennis player—with G.P. Owen won the professional pairs in 1892 against John Anderson and G. Muir; brother-in-law of Lady Birch. Lived at Paterson Road; remembered by Hooper Road.

1906 1907 ELLIOT, Frederick Mitchell, nephew of writer C.B. Buckley, was senior partner in the law firm of Rodyk and Davidson from 1877. A Volunteer officer, golfer, prominent

Freemason, amateur actor, founder member of Singapore's first photographic society in 1889 (formation meeting held at the Tanglin Club in 1887) and in 1894 exhibited his own work, president of Singapore Swimming Club, committee member of the Singapore Bar and the Singapore Rowing Club, president of the Straits Settlements Association, a champion tennis player and champion shot. Remembered by Elliot Road in Siglap.

1909 CARVER, Cedric Ingram, (born Gibraltar) was educated at Sherborne, England and entered the chambers of Sir Rufus Isaacs (later Lord Redding) before joining the law firm of Donaldson & Burkinshaw in Singapore in 1899; retired in 1919. Married the widow of Frederick Cumming of McAlister and Company in 1907 and built TILTON on land given to him as a wedding present by Burkinshaw his partner; his wife died during the 1918 influenza epidemic. Served on legislative council, 1911. A founding member of the Singapore Automobile Club,

1907; president of Singapore Cricket Club 1912-1914, and 1916-1918; committee member, Singapore Golf Club; honorary secretary of the Singapore Bar for a number of years. As an amateur actor appeared in *Charley's Aunt*, 1901 and as Colonel Fairfax in *The Yeomen of the Guard*, 1903. Died in Sussex in 1941.

1910 1911 ALLEN, Rowland, (born 1868, Staffordshire, England), obtained a B.A. and LL.B. from London University in 1889 and came to Singapore in 1895 to join Messrs. Joaquim

Bros.; took over the practice after the death of Mr. P. Joaquim and continued it under the name of Allen and Gledhill. Was a notary public; member of the municipal commission elected for Tanglin ward, 1906; joint-editor of the Straits Settlements Law Reports; honorary secretary and treasurer of the Straits Settlements Association; committee member of the Singapore Bar; Past Master of the Masonic Lodge St. George; a Lieutenant of the Singapore Volunteer Infantry. Married Maud Bacon in 1900 and built WOODSIDE in Grange Road. Retired in 1912; died in 1928 aged 60.

1912* PERKINS, Donald Yarbury, was a partner in the law firm of Drew and Napier. Served on the legislative council, 1918; on the 1919 centenary celebrations committee with F.M. Elliot and Roland St. John Braddell.

Treasurer of the Straits Settlements Association, committee member of the Singapore Sporting Club and president of the Singapore Cricket Club, 1919, where he was known as a "solid enough citizen but less noteworthy character than Presidents of the past." Married the younger daughter of Sir John Anderson, a governor of the Straits Settlements.

1912* FOWLIE, Dr. Peter, (born 1867, Scotland), was educated at Aberdeen University and came to Singapore as a physician and surgeon. Was a captain and

surgeon in the SVC, a Rifle Club prizewinner with F.M. Elliot, and a Golf Club champion seven times from 1891 to 1914 also winning the Straits Championship in Penang. In 1908 represented Tanjong Pagar (No. 1) Ward of the Municipal Commission. His wife is remembered by the Mary Fowlie Scholarships established in 1918 for commercial classes at the YWCA. Remembered by Fowlie Road in Katong. Resided at ROCHALIE in Grange Road.

1913 1914* HEWAN, The Hon.
1915 Elliot Dunville, worked for Boustead & Company for 55 years, becoming a partner in 1909. He earned the esteem of governors and British residents for his commitment to pub-

lic duties in the FMS and Singapore where he was regarded as an outstanding authority on all shipping matters;

assisted the War Relief Fund; honorary treasurer for 24 years of Straits and FMS Benevolent Society; member of British Association of Straits Merchants; committee member of The Association of British Malaya.

1914* 1917 BRADDELL, Sir Ro-
1918 land St. John, (born 1880, Singapore) was the eldest son of Sir Thomas de Multon Lee Braddell, after whom Braddell Road is named; and a member of one of the most distin-

guished families in the colony. Completed law studies at Oxford and returned to Singapore in 1905 as an advocate and solicitor in Braddell Brothers. In 1908 married Dulcie Winslow, grand-daughter of the celebrated mental specialist McNaughten; they lived at Orange Grove Road. As a municipal commissioner worked with Dr. Middleton on health reform; highly regarded for his public service on the housing commission. Legal advisor to United Malays National Organisation during Constitutional negotiations 1946-1947 resulting in the establishment of Federation of Malaya in 1948. Was Commander (*Dato Paduka*) of the Most Honourable Order of the Crown of Johore; member of the executive council and the council of state, Johore; fellow of the Royal Geographical Society and the Royal Society of Arts; president of the Malayan branch of the Royal Asiatic Society. Founding chairman of the Rotary Club, Singapore; also authored legal, historical and local books and essays. Retired to England in 1956.

GO EAST,
YOUNG MAN

Up-country planters, c. 1910 — A.O.

Unveiling the memorial tablet on the Raffles Statue at Empress Place, 1919 — Singapore Centenary, A Souvenir Volume

News of the armistice reached Singapore at 8 P.M. on November 11, 1918. The following day, amid festivities and rejoicing, a public proclamation of the allied victory was made on the Esplanade. The Straits Settlements had reportedly raised more than $5 million for war causes; led by the Straits Chinese, sufficient funds were collected for Britain to purchase 53 war planes, the first tank and, with funds from the Federated Malay States (FMS), a battleship for the Royal Navy. Also in support of the war effort, the amateur dramatic committee in Singapore had staged a series of revues, some written by Tanglin Club members Roland Braddell and Francis Graham in which Dulcie Braddell starred, and from 1915 to 1919 a total of $26,500 was collected for war charities. Preparations had already begun for the centennial celebration of the founding of the colony on February 6, 1819, by Sir Stamford Raffles. As a tribute to Raffles' interest in education it was decided, following an appeal in 1917 by the Straits Chinese British Association for tertiary and technical education, to establish a college of arts and sciences which would lay 'securely the foundations upon which a university may in course of time be established'; Raffles College was subsequently opened in 1928. The centenary day celebrations committee, which included Tanglin Club members Braddell, Elliot and Perkins, also decided to move the statue of Raffles from the Padang to Empress Place. The occasion of centenary day, held on the old racecourse (later named Farrer Park), was also a celebration of peace and 'unexampled commercial prosperity': the earliest postwar figures place the value of imports and exports at more than $1000 million, with over six million tons of shipping entering the port annually; the population was estimated at 305,000.

...equal to any port in the Mediterranean Apart from resulting in a greater demand for tin, rubber and oil, World War I had hastened the revolution in locomotives and motor vehicles. In *A Tour in Southern Asia* Horace Bleackley describes the most famous drive of all which "takes one across the island from south to north — a distance of fourteen miles — to the Johore Causeway. This is the artificial isthmus — a fine engineering feat completed recently — that joins Singapore to the mainland of Malaya. It spans the narrow strait, which is only half a mile in width, over which it conveys both a motor road and a railway. It is possible now to travel by train from Singapore to Bangkok in Siam through the whole length of the Malay Peninsula." Visitors in the 1920's could drive through the coconut groves of Tanjong Katong and Pasir Panjang; a good road led to the top of Mount Faber from where Keppel Harbour

A Busy Night for Misses Woods.

The Cabaret entertainment given by the Misses Aileen and Doris Woods at the Tanglin Club last night was well attended by the members of the Club and their friends, and the performance of these talented ladies was greatly appreciated, not only for their vivacious and smart rendering of the heavy programme they presented of the latest inspiriting patriotic songs and the most popular themes sung by them during their recent successful tour in Malaya; but also for the quaint originality they imparted to their various items.

Each song was thorough and responsive in character, and the audience did not hesitate to join the singers in their choruses. Part of the proceeds of the entertainment was generously devoted to the Red Cross Fund. At the end of the entertainment a supper and dance followed. The full programme, every item of which was enthusiastically encored, is too extensive to give in detail, for no fewer than twenty-four songs were rendered.

Tanglin Club Concert.

At the Cigarette concert to be held at the Tanglin Club this evening, in addition to string trios and vocal quartettes the audience will have the pleasure of listening to Miss Carry Pool and Mr. Onderwyzer, who were so successful at the Dutch Club last night. It is hoped members—both of the Tanglin and Dutch Clubs—and their friends will avail themselves of this opportunity of a musical treat, and so help forward the Red Cross work for the wounded undertaken by the ladies of Singapore.

Malaya Tribune, October 9 & 13 and September 22, 1915

ANOTHER SHOCK FOR POOR OLD NEPTUNE!

Opening of the Johore-Singapore Causeway, September 1923 — Straits Produce, October, 1923

and the distant islands could be seen spread out across the horizon, with the town and docks to the east. Describing his arrival in Singapore in 1925 Bleackley relates, "there is an air of grandeur about Singapore and everything appears to be on a large scale. The size and populousness, the wealth and importance of the great seaport are manifest at first sight. It has natural surroundings of much beauty; it is a handsome and stately city in itself....All around the shores of the harbour there are docks and store sheds, workshops and factories, indicating the extent and volume of its commerce. Its numerous wharfs always seem to be occupied by great liners and cargo ships from every country in the world. The Roads within the breakwater are crowded with coasting vessels of all descriptions. When driving from the quay through the business part of the town its opulence is still more conspicuous. The offices and warehouses, the shops and stores suggest that its trade must be equal to that of any port in the Mediterranean." The huge houses around River Valley Road were by now mostly boarding houses and rubber and coconut plantations fringed the innermost suburbs; in 1919 the island had 24,000 acres of rubber, 10,000 acres of coconut palm, as well as Asian holdings under minor crops such as pepper and market vegetables.

On the morning of Friday March 31, 1922, HMS RE-
NOWN steamed into Singapore with her royal passenger
HRH Prince of Wales, later Edward VIII. The visit was
timed to coincide with the Malaya-Borneo Exhibition,
an important event planned to stimulate trade and
bring the products of the two territories to world
attention. Prince Edward struck a golden padlock
and, declaring the exhibition open, toured it briefly.
The itinerary then took the royal party, which also
included Lord Louis Mountbatten, to the Stadium, the
Yacht Club, the Polo Club and, as dusk fell, to Government House for a banquet and ball — said to have
been the largest ever held in the colony. Apart from
the serious business of the exhibition, other diversions
included military bands, Malay music and dance,
fencing displays and top-spinning demonstrations.
Evening entertainment ranged from Malay shadow
puppetry to European plays at the Victoria Theatre
and Italian grand opera. After the torchlight tattoo
organised by the Chinese Community, films were
screened, including Charlie Chaplin's The Kid which
attracted special interest when it was found to be a
pirated version (an irate cable was received from
Chaplin authorising the immediate seizure of the
film). When the gates closed on April 17 more than
300,000 people of many nationalities had passed
through them and Singapore was no longer regarded
as merely an exchange port but as among the greatest
in the world with resources and capabilities that
inspired confidence in the future. [Prince of Wales chatting to
the Hon. Lo Chong (Chinese Consul-General) at the Malaya-Borneo
Exhibition, 1922 — 'The Sphere']

During the early 1920's, the Tanglin Club purchased additional blocks of land. The first, in 1922, opposite the clubhouse in Draycott Drive, was intended to house at least 12 tennis courts and a bowling lawn. Subsequently Essex Lodge was purchased as the site for 3 squash courts. By this time several necessary additions and alterations had been made to the club buildings; the minutes of the AGM of April 11, 1922, read: "I do not think your Committee could have pleased Members better even if they had built the most spacious supper and billiard rooms than by building our new dressing rooms and lavatories. Changing over to the Municipal Electric Supply has been expensive but again I think satisfactory. You will remember that our last General Meeting was held by candle light." In 1926 a further 8,740 square feet fronting Draycott Drive was acquired for $1,000. Four years later when John Chippindale, who worked for Asiatic Petroleum Company (later Shell), became a member of the club his expertise was frequently called upon as a sort of resident engineer. He helped to design the original squash courts, spent months attempting to iron out a condensation problem that left the walls dripping with moisture and, when there were difficulties with the roof of the club, he and another member, D.R. Howgil, an engineer with Ritchie & Bisset, were asked to inspect it: "We had to climb up into the roof, and it was full of cobwebs, dust, funny things like bats, and it had started in on woodworm. So we had to advise the committee to get someone in to squirt goo into the timber."

...men of more than
five years standing...
Towards the end of the 1920's, the finances of the club were severely strained. Membership was still restricted to those of managerial rank or professional men of more than five years standing and it had become the sort of place where 'one old boffin had his own chair and if anyone sat in it there was hell to pay.' The men congregated almost entirely in the (men only) back bar and billiard room while ladies were restricted to the ballroom — where Wednesday afternoon at-homes were held, the library and the pool area. Gwen Pickering, who joined as a junior member in 1928, remembers leafing through English magazines with her mother on the verandah while her father freed himself from the bar: "In those days the club was very much a gentleman's club and was not used much before 4 P.M. Meals were not available in the early days and anyway the club was too far out from the central business area to be used as a lunchtime watering hole. Ladies were able to use the facilities for activities such as tennis, bridge and lawn bowls."

In An Interesting State Of Transition

Charles Wurtzburg, a shipping manager who became chairman of Mansfields and of the Straits Steamship Company Limited, was a commentator on the Singapore social scene who arrived in 1920 when the postwar period of reconstruction was just commencing and found the colony "in an interesting state of transition — physically and spiritually.... In general, there was a Victorian atmosphere in Singapore, probably due to its isolation from the Western world during the war. England had advanced a long way between 1914 and 1918, but Singapore was only beginning to wake up. It also had its own particular problems, quite apart from those common to the world at large. The return

John Chippindale first visited the Tanglin Club in 1927 as the guest of A.C. Potts of the Cold Storage Company after dinner at the Hotel de l'Europe, apparently the traditional end to an evening out in fashionable circles because "everything closed down at twelve o'clock except the Tanglin Club." Then members paid $5 for the privilege of introducing guests for after-dinner drinks, so it was quite an honour for the young engineer to be invited. [Hotel de l'Europe, 1905 — N.A.]

of ex-servicemen was one of those problems. Feelings ran rather high between those who had been to the Front and those who had stayed in Singapore and had improved their financial position not a little thereby. They were called 'stokers' on the grounds that they had kept the home fires burning. There was in fact, a good deal to be said on both sides, but it was a pity that this cleavage should have existed — the healing hand of time, however, gradually obliterated it.

"Clubs were far more exclusive and the business of being introduced to the Committee was taken very seriously. At the same time, social life was extremely vigorous and entertainment on a generous scale — that is to say, on an extravagant scale, so far as the senior members of the Community were concerned. Juniors were not expected to entertain lavishly, and anyone who gave parties at the Europe (the Hotel de l'Europe on the later site of the Supreme Court) was suspected, and generally with reason, of living far beyond his means. No junior was ashamed to entertain inexpensively, and that was one good feature which later tended to disappear.

"My first Mess — the old Dutch Club, in Grange Road — was lit by most indifferent gas, which gave at the best of times very little light and flickered continuously (electric light was still a rarity, mostly supplied from private plants at great expense). Refrigerators had never been heard of, and we had dubious ice boxes with their attendant hoards of cockroaches. Modern sanitation was a distant dream and mosquitoes a very present reality. Food was quite good, but of a very

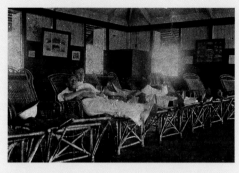

At the Swimming Club, c 1910 — E.W. Newell collection, N.A.

limited variety. Cars were limited to the rich and most of us had our own rickshaws. To get to the Swimming Club, a very modest and ramshackle establishment, you left by launch from Johnston's Pier, as the modern East Coast Road (like the other fine roads which now distinguish Singapore), was still only on the drawing board." [Charles Wurtzburg writing in the December 1940 journal of the Association of British Malaya, of which he was president, 1946 -1948.]

THE MORNING AFTER.

"What'll you have?"

"O, anything to make me feel more like a man and less like a bottle!"

Straits Produce, April, 1927

The Great Depression which began in 1929 caused a particular problem for Singapore as the economy was dependent on international trade. The price of rubber fell from £284 a ton in 1926 to £100 a ton in 1932, and an unwanted 600,000 tons was on the market. Tin prices dropped to $60 per picul in 1931. Retrenchment was a normal consequence of those difficult years for everyone including Europeans; the 1931 census showed there were 567,433 persons on the island, of whom 8,147 were Europeans. In *A Beachcomber in the Orient*, Harry Foster portrays a Singapore overflowing with human derelicts: professional

PROCEEDINGS OF THE COMMISSION TO ENQUIRE INTO CLUB LIFE IN SINGAPORE.

(BY OUR SPECIAL MISREPORTER.)

As our readers will be aware, the recent agitation against the licentiousness of Club Life in Singapore caused H. E. the Governor to take most drastic steps. He appointed a Commission of Enquiry under the Chairmanship of Adolphus Etheldred Odell, Esquire, F.R.S.P.C.* As one of the leaders of the agitation Mr. Odell was marked out for the position of Chairman. Who indeed will forget that dreadful night when the Middlesex took farewell of Singapore and the youthful crews of the Royal and Ancient Yacht Club behaved in such an outrageous way that the Great Man went to bed with tears in his eyes and r signation on his lips?

The proceedings at the first meeting of the Commissioners were frequently lively and always interesting. Right and left of the Chairman sat the other members, Messrs. Soon Goh Futt, Arokiosamy Pillay and Ebenezer Benisrael, with Mr. Augustus Daffy-Dilly of the Civil Service, as Secretary.

The first witness was the Right Rev. the Bishop of Tanjong Katong who made a lasting impression upon the Commissioners. His Lordship was attired in a crimson coat, purple apron and red velvet gaiters, it being the Eve of St. Herbaceus.

The witness said he had received trustworthy information that on the occasion of the Patronal Festival of St. Andrew, couples not joined together in the bonds of matrimony had been seen with their arms round each other's waists in full electric light at the Town Hall. He regretted to say that his informant told him that this had been done even in the presence of H. E. the Governor. (Here the Commissioners rose to their feet and stood for a full minute in solemn silence.) Moreover, not only had this occurred at the Town Hall but the same informant had assured him that it had been seen at the Tanglin Club on the Third Friday after Michaelmas. Witness believed that it frequently happened there on Fridays. The Chairman asked the witness if he had heard of anything similar occurring at the Hotel Europe (Managing Director, A. E. Odell, Esquire, F.R.S.P.C.). The witness said that he did not know there was such a place but he would make enquiries.

Mr. Soon Goh Futt asked the witness whether his informant was prepared to come forward and substantiate this extraordinary and disgusting story.

Witness said his informant was one of the lay-workers at the Banana Mission and of a very retiring disposition with a slight impediment in her speech. He was sure that she would shrink from the—ah—if he might coin a phrase the fierce light of publicity—ah—ahem!

Mr. Arokiosamy said informant never coming and all things, how Commission making findings, much botheration?

His Lordship was thanked for his evidence and withdrew.

*Fellow of the Royal Society for the Prevention of Chimes.

Straits Produce, April, 1924

In a letter of May 1990 G.McCallum 'Tiger' Coltart recalls: "In 1930-31 the financial strains of the slump in rubber and tin prices affected most clubs and Tanglin was no exception. One of the social features was the Saturday night dances, very popular as a follower to the dinner parties of the social 'leaders' (mems besar). These suffered when a paid orchestra could not be afforded — gramophone records were a poor substitute. Several of the younger set who were budding jazz musicians suggested they might get a dance band together and the committee of the day were delighted and offered club membership without payment of the entrance fee: that's when I joined the club! After some weeks of intensive practice the band gave its opening night and was hailed as a great success; we were called the Wig-Wogs, Archie Wigginton of Borneo Motors being the leader. We played on alternate Saturday nights for some 18 months, after which the idea gave up owing to members going on leave. Not long after, the slump lifted and professional bands became available." In another interim attempt to provide a variation of musical entertainment, a group of members formed a ukulele band called The Tangy Ukes, with John Chippindale as the drummer. [The 'Wig Wogs' at the Tanglin Club, including (left to right), Jack Barker of Barker & Ong Siang on piano, 'Tiger' Coltart of Rodyk & Davidson on banjo, J. Barclay of National City Bank, New York, on trumpet, Archie Wigginton of Borneo Motors on drums, and Peter Cork of Dupire Morrell Limited, on piano, 1931 — Courtesy of 'Tiger' Coltart]

beachcombers, well-meaning but weak-willed sailors who had missed their ships, and others who "were discharged employees from the rubber estates or the tin mines, for with the slump in rubber and tin — the principal industries of the Malay States — many better-class Europeans were finding themselves stranded. Nowhere in my travels have I ever found a city so full of the down-and-out as was Singapore at that particular moment...." Adding to this general downturn, Chinatown and the rural districts were at the mercy of street gangs, gunmen and members of secret societies (in 1927 Singapore was reputed to be the 'Chicago of the East').

...I'm going to lose $5,000 this month... As the slump lifted and commodity prices improved, moves to rejuvenate the club gained momentum. There were, of course, many members who were perfectly satisfied with the conservative and rarefied atmosphere of the club, who continued to sit on the verandah drinking their stengahs and discussing rubber prices, little realising that plans were afoot to haul the Tanglin Club into the modern era. In the mid-thirties a 'young and vigorous new committee' with bold ideas for modernization and an ingenious scheme to boost club finances was

CLUB FEVER.

(With apologies to JOHN MASEFIELD'S
" Sea Fever ")

I must go down to the Club again for the
    Mah Jongg call is strong,
I want to throw the dice again, I want to
    Pung and Kong;
And all I ask is a flowery hand with
    Dragons showing,
And the luck to draw just what I want,
    and an " East Wind " blowing.

I must go down to Club again, the Club
    that I can't pass by,
And all I ask is a gin sling to quench my
    thirst when I'm dry,
And the balls kiss on the green cloth of
    the billiard table,
And a long break, and a long drink from
    the right coloured label.

I must go down to the Club again, though
    it is but half a life,
For a lonely man 'tis the only way, for a
    man without a wife;
And all I ask is a game of bridge, and
    a hand full of aces,
And a merry yarn in the crowded bar
    and cheerie fellow faces.

Dorothy Tobutt, Straits Produce, July, 1924

The first is Patricia, oh what a sad sight!
For the doctor has said that she must not, pay-hit.
But she risks it on Saturdays : yes, that's the rub
She can't keep away from the Tanglin Club.

Straits Produce, April, 1927

Straits Produce, December, 1929

elected. "Gentlemen," announced the newly-elected treasurer at his first meeting, "I'm going to give you a shock; I'm going to lose you $5,000 this month"; despite cries of horror he proceeded to suggest that "we invite one hundred new members to join the Tanglin Club at no entrance fee," [at the time $50]. As a close investigation of the club's accounts had shown that bar takings constituted the greatest source of revenue, there was no intention of allowing free entrance to teetotallers: 'they got four or five hundred applications and they went through them and picked out the ones that would be free spenders at the bar.' This new crop of members — who included Arnold Thorne, Eric Henton, 'Tiny' Mason, Donald Stewart, Charles Auchmuty, Ken Hatchard, Harold Smyth, Peter Frend and other SCC rugby and cricket players — became known as the Hungry Hundred and 'from then on, the Club never looked back.'

Go East, Young Man

In the twenties and thirties many young men, sharing a British middle-class background and an English public school education, took up careers in the Far East or South-East Asia. A career in the East, whether in government or business, 'offered a standard of living that could not always be guaranteed at home,' and also offered an outlet for some who had survived years in the trenches in the Great War. Applicants, whether for government services or the business firms, faced interviews designed to ascertain whether they could play games, mix with people, display some degree of leadership and were accustomed to open-air life; a reasonable academic record and athletic ability almost guaranteed a position. In the years before 1929, two of the biggest trading concerns, Dunlop and Guthries, took on as employees players of international standard to play in their respective rugby teams. Some of the larger Eastern trading houses, as well as the two major banks — the Hongkong and Shanghai and the Chartered — were more selective; 'the chaps you found in Bousteads and A.P.C. (the Asiatic Petroleum Company) were the best of all.' Looking back, Edward Tokeley recounts in a recent letter, "the European community throughout Malaya (as the entire area was then called) was relatively small and one's knowledge of people, and what was going on in those pre-war days was much greater than became the case postwar. The atmosphere overall was more relaxed. They were lovely days. Malaya was a career, so one had years during which to know a great many people extremely well. From the beginning of 1946 onwards the pace

Four gentlemen of Pahang, 1893, including Sir Hugh Clifford, (right) governor of the Straits Settlements 1927, 1929 — British Malaya, *November, 1929*

quickened ever increasingly, the European community grew and grew to a point when one hardly knew the juniors in your own company leave along those in others." 'Teddy' Tokeley, a Tanglin Club committee member in 1962, came east to Penang in 1935 with Boustead & Company, moved to Singapore the next year and returned again after the war (he was a prisoner of war in Siam) and was chairman of Bousteads from 1966 to 1970.

Young men reared on the romance of Kipling knew little about conditions overseas — some had learnt a little from reading Somerset Maugham — however, their youthful enthusiasm was more important. Their contracts or letters of appointment allowed for a starting salary of about thirty pounds a month; after five years they could expect their first home leave — "there was nothing in the letter of appointment about marriage but it was made clear to you that in order to get the partners' approval to get married you had to earn a certain sum of money a month, which took about ten years' service to achieve,'' informs Tokeley in Charles Allen's *Tales From the South China Seas*. In her memoirs, compiled by Isabella Lau, Cynthia Koek, whose husband came from an old Singapore family (they once owned a nutmeg plantation inherited from William Cuppage which was taken over by the government at the turn of the century and became the well-known Orchard Road market), affirmed that the social scene was greatly enhanced in those days, from the female point of view, by the young bachelors who came out from Britain to join the old established trading firms. In their first few years they were not permitted to marry and were limited by their meagre salaries, but they were much sought after for such social functions as the competition dancing at Raffles Hotel, which had an excellent ballroom floor.

After contracts were signed, the tropical kit was purchased with practical tips from experienced colonials: 'Buy only the more formal articles of clothing in Britain and have the rest made up at half the cost by Chinese tailors and shoe-makers in Singapore where a white suit costs three dollars, a pair of shorts one dollar fifty cents and socks about a dollar for half-a-dozen.' Shoes were made to measure with English leather for three dollars; other essential prerequisites to good health in the tropics were a green-lined

OUR ROADS.
Portrait of a Singapore Merchant, fully equipped for the journey from his residence (Pasir Panjang) to his office (Robinson Road).

Straits Produce, October, 1927

umbrella, a Straits Settlements solar topee, and the ubiquitous *tutup*, a special jacket with a spine pad: 'a thick felt pad that you had sewn into the back of your uniform with red cloth inside and khaki exterior.' For dinner in the tropics 'the short white jacket, worn with black trousers, known as the bum-freezer' was *de rigueur*. In the daytime, the men wore a white cotton jacket buttoned up to the neck, white cotton trousers, black socks and black shoes. If the company were mixed, men were expected to wear a dinner jacket and a stiff collar, which, Tokeley insists was "a bit of a bore — but not so much of a bore as it was on a dance night, because the collar that one wears with tails gets pretty limp if you're dancing in a temperature of eighty degrees, and so one had to change one's collar two or three times during the evening." Horace Bleackley considers the ballroom costume of the men to be "the

Whiteaway Laidlaw & Co at Hill St. and Stamford Rd. Junction, c 1908 — Twentieth Century Impressions of British Malaya

In the chummery for employees of E.E.A. & C. Telegraph Co. Ltd., River Valley Road, 1910 — E.W. Newell collection, N.A.

most unsuitable attire for dancing in the tropics that could be imagined. But some are wise enough to wear a drill mess-jacket, and soft shirts are not uncommon. At Government House, however, a tail-coat is compulsory, with white tie and waistcoat in addition, terrific instruments of torture when the temperature is eighty-five degrees in the shade. Its wearer feels just like an ancient Crusader must have felt in his suit of mail armour on a midsummer's day in the Holy Land. Yet, in spite of the heat the men of Singapore are the keenest of dancing men, which is not strange since they have pretty and pleasant dancing partners. There is a dance on six nights of the week either at the Europe Hotel or at the Raffles."

As far as creature comforts were concerned, newcomers were assured that Singapore would do them proud; acquaints Roland Braddell in *The Lights of*

Singapore: "all kinds of sport all the year round, a good table, owing to cold storage, and a magnificent fish supply, comfortable houses, lovely green gardens, superb roads on which to motor, and plenty of places to go by road, rail, or sea." In *Tales from the South China Sea* the memories of many young men graphically depict their lifestyles. Mervyn Sheppard joined the Malayan Civil Service in 1928, was interned in Singapore during World War II, and was a director of the Public Records Museum between 1957 and 1960 (he subsequently became Tan Sri Dato Mubin Sheppard). Sheppard describes how in the bedrooms "we had no means of keeping cool and they were rather hot and mosquito-ridden, but over the dining-room there was a series of pleated fans called punkahs — not a Malay word but an Indian word which had been introduced from India. These

hung from a wooden frame which was connected to the roof by struts. It had pleated blanks of cloth and a long rope which was pulled when required by a small boy, who was probably the son or grandson of one of the staff." Accommodation provided by a company was usually the mess, a bungalow consisting of about a dozen single rooms opening onto a very large central dining room. Not all companies provided a mess, in which case, explains Gerald Scott, who joined A.P.C. in 1939, "you hunted round the various chummeries — maybe four engineers or sales people or accountants or whatever there were of that particular company — and you went and had dinner with them and if you liked the sort of life they lived you became one of them. ...all expenses including food, drink and servants were divided at the end of the month and one share was no more than about $120 in all."

Newcomers, sometimes referred to as griffins, were taken to sign the book for the chief secretary, the resident and the chief justice, which were kept in little boxes in the bottom of their gardens. As soon as they were established, relates Cecil Lee who arrived in Malaya in 1934

Returning from the hunt, c 1905 — A.O.

to join Harrison and Crosfield, there were certain formalities to be observed. The first was the business of calling and card-dropping: newcomers in the mess were advised that they would not be invited to the house of a certain senior member of the firm unless they dropped cards. "This was a very important part of life in Malaya and Singapore in those days because the British community went out of its way to look after the new arrivals and see that everything was done to make them welcome and to bring them into that community. And in order to do that, you had to have some name cards printed. Then the mentor who met you gave you a list of senior people — married people of course — upon whom you had to drop these cards. We were supposed to do it in

the evening time, and not be seen. All houses in those days had a little card box at the entrance to the drive, so you waffled around with your list with your mentor, who'd be driving you to show you where everybody lived, and you dropped a card in the proper boxes, and then it became obligatory upon those people on whom you dropped a card to invite you to their houses for a meal or a drink, so that within a very short space of time a newcomer became known and knew other people as well," details Tokeley. At the Singapore Club facing Battery Road, relates Bleackley, apart from the exceptional cuisine offered "the visitor is cordially received and made a temporary member for the duration of his stay; and here he can learn all about the country

Picnic, c 1915 — The British in the Far East

from the lips of Mr. J.D. Saunders, the genial president of the race-course, one of the celebrities of the colony." Recalling earlier colonial life, "set in a pleasant background of evergreen gardens and comfortable domestic architecture," Sir Richard Winstedt writes a *British Malaya*, "for the days work done, Europeans and Chinese turn to golf, or tennis, or football, or swimming or sailing; the Malay to football, the Japanese to tennis...there are common meeting places like the race course, the football field, the golf-course, a wedding feast, a Chinese birthday party, a Government House At Home on the King's Birthday."

The names of many young men and families who came to Singapore, stayed for years and enjoyed successful careers in the East can be found in the annals of some prominent organisations and clubs in the island. Sir Eric Griffith-Jones who joined the Law firm of Donaldson and Burkinshaw in the thirties before working in the colonial legal service was an officer with the Singapore Volunteers before World War II and among the prisoners of war who worked on the 'death railway' in Siam and Burma. He was later appointed

At the races, c 1912 — A.O.

ON LEAVE.
Do look, Mummy, at the Mata Mata with the Pussy-cat **topi**!

Straits Produce, July, 1927

acting-governor of Kenya before joining the Guthrie Group, eventually becoming chairman of Guthrie Corporation. His brother Lionel joined the Singapore Harbour Board in 1938; during World War II he escaped to Bombay and joined the Royal Indian Naval Voluntary Reserves. Some, such as Andrew Gilmour, later controller of shipping for Singapore and secretary for economic affairs after World War II, joined the Malayan Civil Service; others served with the business houses, like Sir John Bagnall who first visited in 1911 as a purser on a Blue Funnel Line ship, returned in 1912 to join the Straits Trading Company, and from 1923 to 1965 was chairman and managing director of what became the first public

company in Singapore. In 1929 his sister, Bobbie, came to Singapore to entertain as his hostess and met Ewen Fergusson, who had travelled to Singapore in 1920, aged 23, after leaving the army (he read accountancy in the trenches) and being advised that his future was not in Scotland, but in the East. Fergusson joined Straits Trading Company and married Bobbie, and their story of coming East can be paralleled with others of their time. Usually on contract for five or six years, local leave allowed them to explore the region as they were moved around in different parts of Malaya. For those who joined the Tanglin Club, a special category of 'up-country member' allowed them to maintain an interest and enjoy the facilities on

their return to Singapore. These men also served on government bodies, including the legislative council and business councils such as the Singapore Chamber of Commerce (Sir John Bagnall was chairman in 1928, 1929, 1931, 1932 and part of 1936, and Sir Ewen Fergusson was chairman from 1946 to 1952); their contemporaries included John Pickering, Jimmy Paterson, Bobby Craik, and others whose names are remembered by club members of the present generation. Dr. M.C. 'Cammie' Bain, who came to Singapore from Scotland in 1924, practised medicine in Singapore for 56 years and founded the practice of Bain and Partners. He was a one-time president of the Singapore Amateur Swimming Association and a golf champion — interned at Changi and Sime Road prison camps during World War II, one of his duties was to plough up his beloved Bukit golf course to plant cassava. Dr. Bain joined the Tanglin Club in the twenties and in 1986 was among the longest-standing members of the club (where a third generation membership is now enjoyed).

George Peet, who arrived in Singapore in 1923 and joined *The Straits Times*, observes in his *Rickshaw Reporter* that throughout the interwar period the senior men in the British business and professional community followed in their predecessors' footsteps, taking an active part in public life, particularly in the municipal commission and the local branch of the Straits Settlements Association. These expatriates believed that an Eastern career was not incompatible with being a good citizen of the colony in the civic and moral sense. In the changing circumstances of their time, with wider horizons and a more varied and

"THIS IS A NICE TIME TO COME HOME, JOHN HENRY! BEEN WITH YOUR LOOSE FRIENDS AT THE SPOTTED DOG AGAIN, I SUPPOSE."
"YOU'RE WRONG, MY DEAR, THEY WERE ALL TIGHT!"

Straits Produce, April, 1924

interesting life, Singapore no longer meant to this later generation what the early settlement had to the old-timers. In 1937 the Friends of Singapore Society was inaugurated with Sir Song Ong Siang as president and Dato Sir Roland Braddell as vice-president. The governor, Sir Shenton Thomas, speaking for this later generation declared: "We regard Singapore as our home away from home....It seems to me that all of us who live here have a duty to our city as well as to ourselves."

In the thirties, complaints were aired by old-timers about the decline in the quality of the British colonial civil servant, who had come to be regarded as spineless, disinterested in the colony, and lacking the presence and dignity of his predecessors. The colonial service no

longer attracted the best type of young man in Britain: the rewards were less attractive, the sense of security and the glamour of adventure had diminished and the chances of individual advancement limited by the practice of promotion by seniority. In 1934 R.H. Bruce Lockhart, who returned to spend a month among local British residents after an absence of 25 years, felt that "the pioneer days are ended, and to many, including myself, the loss in attractiveness of life in Malaya is immeasurable."

Lockhart's impressions in his *Return to Malaya* are tinged with the poignant vividness of earlier memories of Singapore as a garrison town; in the early 1900's officers were welcomed by the local British for the colour and distinction which they lent to the social life of the colony, for the added zest of rivalry they infused into the local games and the valuable support they gave to the Singapore rugger and cricket teams in their matches against Hong Kong and the FMS. Lockhart remembered men who showed a public spirit in advance of their times and signed up for volunteer soldiering, but whose example "attracted few recruits from among the vast majority of selfish and easy-going residents who, like myself, saw little use or no amusement in devoting part of their spare time to drills and shooting practice in the heat of the tropical sun." By 1935, every young Englishman, "be he planter, miner, or merchant, is urged to join the local Volunteer forces which now include tanks and also local flying units attached to the Royal Air Force." The new defence scheme placed a new and heavy responsibility on the shoulders of local British administrators, whose work was infinitely harder and more complicated than

that of the colonial servants of the previous generation. During his visit Lockhart renewed his friendship with Sir Andrew Caldecott (who is listed in the Tanglin Club records against the post of president for 1935, although the *Straits Directory* for that year lists H.W. Hawkeswood) and found him "tired and overworked.... During the last four years he had had nine different jobs, including those of Resident or Acting Resident in several states, Acting Chief Secretary of the FMS Government, and Acting Governor in Singapore. His present official post was that of colonial secretary of the Straits Settlements, the official on whose shoulders falls the detailed work of administration. In his case it had been complicated by the additional burden of piloting a new Governor through those difficult initial months of a new term of office." Lockhart recalls the days when Caldecott, as assistant district officer in Jelebu, had been his nearest European neighbour, and the football matches when they transported their teams of Malays by bullock-cart and bicycle. In his esteem Caldecott was "a good Malay scholar with literary tastes and a genuine interest in the poetry and folklore of the language. He had a piano and played it well. More wonderful still, his bungalow was decorated with attractive water-colours of his own painting.... He was a very exceptional figure in a community which in those days, and even now, is chiefly remarkable for its healthy low-browism."

Social amusements could be found in the three so-called Worlds, all Chinese owned — the Great World, the Happy World and the New World — "where you will see how the Asiatic, and particularly the Chinese, amuses himself. Here you will find all sorts of entertaining side-shows, best of which are the Malay opera and the Chinese theatrical performances which so fascinated Charlie Chaplin when he was here.... The amusement park called the Great World, off the River Valley Road, is well worth a visit, but it is not so boisterously alive as in the New World, since it caters to a much smugger class." Roland Braddell in Lights of Singapore. *[(Left to right) Mrs. Alta Goddard and Mr. Julius S. Fisher of Amalgamated Theatres, Ltd., Charlie Chaplin and leading lady Miss Paulette Goddard in Singapore —* British Malaya, *September, 1936]*

In 1931 'Esperantist in Embryo' wrote in to the Straits Produce *"to suggest the conspicuous posting in first-class Railway Carriages of a notice in the words:* Jangan Hoick Ptoo.*" [Buffet parlour car on Singapore-Kuala Lumpur Express —* Handbook to British Malaya, *1935]*

In the late 1930's Singapore was in every way the Exotic East. The realities of everyday life may have been noise, dirt and humidity, but those who wrote about Singapore before the war described a languid and elegant life of tiffins and stengahs, tea dances, tennis and bridge. "In those happy days, Singapore was the last resort of yesterday in the world of tomorrow," declares Noel Barber in *Sinister Twilight*. For successful members of the European community, the Tanglin Club appears to have been one of the pillars of social life in Singapore. Most references to the club in the late thirties reflect a lively and relaxed atmosphere. "It was a cheerful place and unlike the SCC did not have that 'waiter-please-remove-this-gentleman-he's-been-dead-for-three-days' sort of atmosphere," according to a former Tanglin Club member Anthony Hill in his *Diversion in Malaya*. The club had "every form of minor relaxation one would want. There were twelve lawn tennis courts and three squash courts; a small swimming pool, a well-furnished reading and writing room and a good library. There were billiards and bridge. You could get a good game of bridge almost any time and the committee arranged duplicate matches once a month."

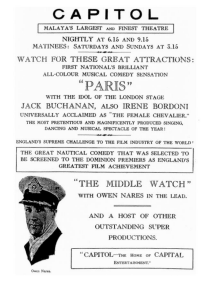

Sea View Hotel at Tanjong Katong, c 1906 — Paul Yap collection, N.A.

...if sport was an addiction, dancing was a passion...

Further north, for the healthy and fit, the Malayan peninsula offered beautiful and varied fauna: rhinoceros, elephant, wild cattle, tiger, leopard and clouded leopard, sambar deer, and many species of birds, especially the resplendent argus pheasant; the pursuit of elephant and *seladang* (buffalo) also afforded magnificent sport and the trophies obtainable were considered to well repay an enthusiastic hunter for his trouble. Conservation was first recommended in 1927 but no effective implementation of the recommendations was initiated. Trips to the game reserves — where hunting was disallowed — to photograph big game was also possible and, as country where game could be hunted was not far from these, photography and sport could be combined. If sport was an addiction, dancing was a passion — at the Raffles Hotel, at the Sea View Hotel and at the Tanglin Club where, from 1936, regular dances were held in the spacious open-air ballroom. Even before the war years, Lionel Griffith-Jones relates in *That's My Lot*, "young expatriate girls were not plentiful. They were vastly outnumbered by young expatriate bachelors, healthily libidinous, mostly impecunious. The girls would likely be fresh out of finishing school in Europe, living with Mum and Dad in some sumptuous company house, thoroughly well-heeled, and, despite their comparatively tender years, used to the good, that is expensive, things in life." As the number of military officers increased, there was always a considerable crowd of male 'wallflowers' on dance nights, and it was unkindly remarked that even the plainest young lady could be assured that her programme would be filled within minutes of her arrival at the club.

After a happy five years as the district officer of Ulu Kelantan in Malaya, Andrew Gilmour, who joined the colonial service after serving in World War I, took badly to life as a junior in the Singapore colonial secretariat to which he was posted in 1936: "while it was not a little galling to serve several masters and have one's work heavily criticised and draft despatches almost re-written by arbiters of literary style with their own ideas of what would please the Colonial Office, the main trouble was finance. Bereft of the up-country advantages of a rent-free house, kebuns, a prisoner as *tukang ayer*, a reasonable car allowance and the absence of temptations to spend money in clubs, hotels, restaurants or cinemas, and with children to educate, we found we could not live on a salary under $800 a month. The Cricket Club and Swimming Club, which I had joined in the 20's, were our only resorts; but I could not afford a new cricket bat or tennis racket. I never bought a new book for years and we ran an elderly Standard car (finally traded in for $138 when we bought a new Chevrolet two months before the Japanese invasion).

"Many of my colleagues were in equal straits and, at last, government agreed to a Cost of Living enquiry. Sir Atholl Mac-Gregor, Chief Justice in Hong Kong (afterwards a fellow-internee in Stanley Camp), came down to Singapore and, by a fortunate chance, took Lady Mac-Gregor to see a film on his first evening and told one of my colleagues that he was immediately prejudiced in our favour when he found that seats in the cinema cost as much (or more) in Straits dollars as he was accustomed to pay in Hong Kong dollars. His final recommendation, which was accepted, was no cost of living or married allowance, but quite a substantial education allowance for up to two children at a time. This made a spot of social life just possible, and, fortified by what my wife (firstly by a slip of the tongue and later out of mischief) called the MacGregor 'entertainment' allowance, we took the plunge and put our names up for Tanglin Club. The young generation might be amused to learn that I was 40 before I joined Tanglin Club and 50 before I felt able to join the Singapore Club," states Andrew Gilmour in *An Eastern Cadet's Anecdotage*. In a recent letter, S.F.T.B. 'Joe' Lever, chairman of the Singapore International Chamber of Commerce in 1970 and a former committee member of the club who was made an honorary life member in 1971, provided a recollection of a somewhat similar experience. In an amusing after-dinner address at the annual Tanglin ball in the mid-fifties, the governor Sir Robert Black revealed that during "his pre-war career as a rather irresponsible and certainly impecunious civil servant unable to live on his means, mainly through high living, he was 'posted' for non-payment of his monthly club dues. He considered himself most fortunate to be still a member of the club, let alone the guest of honour that evening."

The Tanglin Club Singapore

Tanglin Club was founded in 1865 in a small building which is still to-day part of the present Club.

The Club has passed through various vicissitudes and in 1912 was saved from closing by 4 votes. Quite recently 1933, after the slump, finances were again low but due to the energetic action of the new young committee Tanglin Club to-day is very strong.

The amenities of the Club include a swimming pool with circulating water, two squash courts, nine tennis courts and a bowls lawn.

Dancing every Saturday night to he Club's own Band is very popular and there is often the added attraction of a Cabaret.

Sunday morning swimming parties are very popular too.

The present membership including ladies is about 700.

Entry from King George V Silver Jubilee Souvenir Programme, May 1935

AN ODE TO TANGLIN CLUB
AND DANCING.

In days of yore, so goes the lore,
They used to dance at Tanglin,
When party girls with winsome curls
From apron strings were danglin',
And Mothers proud remarked out loud,
"How nicely Maud is dancing;
"With look demure, complexion pure,
"She's really quite entrancing."
The minuet you see and yet
You sense a something missing,
You wonder why, until they cry,
"Now in the ring they're kissing."
Oh! happy days now lost in haze—
Oh! how the times have altered;
Thus will you grieve, and still believe
Terpsichore has flatered.
But is this true, I ask of you,
Are we with ragtime sated?
The Gaby Glide, the Chaplin Slide,
Are these all overrated?
Perhaps you may with reason say
They are most energetic,
But modern life with ceaseless strife
Makes everyone athletic.
Our Grandmas talked, our Mammas walked;
This was all they desired,
But girls to-day with footballs play,
Yet none of them get tired.
So can you ask, when called to task
For criticising dancers,
"Why does that man play catch-as-can
"With partners in the Lancers?
"As for that minx, I'm sure she thinks
"She'll never have a tumble,
"Yet up she goes right off her toes;
"She's treated like a dumb-bell."
No. Times must change, and 'tis not strange
That people's tastes are changing,
So we must think that we're the link
'Twixt past and future ranging.
The past, we know, was rather slow,
For then they danced the two-step,
But now we're sure that never more
We'll think to dance the goose-step.

R.L.D. Wodehouse, The Straits & States Annual, 1919

By the 1930's, 'meet you at the Tanglin' had become the password for Saturday entertainment for members. Marion 'Pom' Whittington, who returned to the club in 1980 after a 20-year absence, recounted that "one of the Saturday routines of the younger generation in those days was to go to the club and lunch, swim, play tennis, have another swim then get all dressed up — you'd have brought your evening dress and everything else — and carry on." The club was quite prepared for this and there were amahs on hand to press the gentlemen's jackets and the ladies' dresses.

...which threatened to jeopardise the ballroom floor... In 1938 new dance crazes, such as the palais glide and the Lambeth walk, which caused the whole building to sway as dancers stomped to the music in unison threatened to jeopardise the ballroom floor. The problem was solved by the placement of half a dozen six-inch square teak posts beneath the dance floor in the changing rooms below. Gentlemen greatly enjoyed dancing without stiff collars and dinner jackets, customary at lido evenings; cool and comfortable in trousers and open-necked shirts, "it was quite a treat to see them dancing so untiringly the whole evening, and certainly a pleasure not to hear their awful groans about the stupidity

Bored Cynic : Honi soit qui Palais de Danse !

Straits Produce, April, 1926

"In those days before the war, we all wore stiff shirts with stand-up collars. When I went dancing, and I was an energetic dancer, I used to take two collars, and rub the insides of the collars with candlewax to deter their wilting. I also used to start by softening the bottom of my stiff shirt front with my shaving brush so that it didn't pouch when I sat down." [John Chippindale] [70th Anniversary Ball — <u>The Straits Times</u>, September 24, 1935]

"Another highlight of last week was the debut of Nick's Tanglin Six, the new band for the Tanglin Club. They started last Saturday and nearly everyone of the hundreds of people dancing there, myself included, remarked how very good they were. They definitely put life into their playing and all the tunes, no matter whether they were waltzes, fox-trots, rhumbas, tangos or anything else, were put over with such 'yumph' that you simply had to dance." [<u>The Sunday Tribune</u>, May 14, 1939.] In the late 1930's a group of musicians called Nick's Versatile Six arrived in Singapore from the Galle Face Hotel in Colombo. Innocent Mark Nick and three others of his band were White Russians who had reached South-East Asia via Siberia and Shang-hai. The band initially played two nights a week: Wednesdays, which was informal (jacket and tie), and Saturdays, which was formal (dinner jackets). After World War II, a new shell-shaped bandstand was constructed in the ballroom and the first cocktail bar was fitted into the room immediately behind. In early 1951, after the original group broke up, two of its pre-war members, the talented Curtis brothers Cecil and Laurie, formed the Tanglin Club band.

of men's evening attire," reports *The Sunday Tribune* of August 13, 1939, of one such occasion. Those who chose to go to the 'other' centre of Saturday night activities — the Raffles Hotel — to dine and dance, would adjourn after the Raffles closed at midnight to the Tanglin Club, about the only place that stayed open till 3 A.M. and offered snacks after midnight. However, club rules regarding guests were strict. Maureen Clarke, who was active with the Cheshire Homes organisation and the SPCA, an accomplished actress with the Singapore Amateur Drama Club and a member of the Stage Club for over thirty years, remembered one Saturday night when "we turned up with a friend who wasn't a member and were told to leave: guests were only allowed on Wednesdays."

...it would be almost impossible to coax it down again... The sartorial regulations at the Tanglin Club were equally unwavering — suits after 6 P.M. anywhere on the club premises, and dinner jackets for weekend dining and dancing; ladies had to wear long dresses. White tie and tails were mandatory at the Tanglin ball, an elegant affair regarded by many as the highlight of Singapore's social calendar, and formal dress was required on Christmas Eve

New Year's Eve, 1932 — Courtesy of Pamela Roper-Caldbeck

and Boxing Day night. Despite these rules, the club was a closely-knit and friendly one and 'Pom' Whittington recalled how diners who had booked a table would always spend some time at the bar to mingle with everybody there, even if they did not know them. The fancy dress ball on New Year's Eve, a tradition that continued for many years, however, "was a hilarious show," narrates Anthony Hill. "One year, eleven of us went dressed as a mixed (very mixed) cricket team of the Hambledon vintage. My W.G. Grace beard caught fire when somebody lit a cigarette near me; my eyebrows survived, though they remembered the occasion for a long time afterwards." In another year a daring young lady who had planned to go dressed as a jockey, with a commendable attempt at realism, tried to borrow a horse to ride up into the ballroom and was only dissuaded when it was explained that while the horse may be happy to ascend the stairs, it would be almost impossible to coax it down again. *The Sunday Tribune* of January 7, 1940, describes the hit of that New Year's Eve ball at the Tanglin Club — Bill Howell as Hitler: "His make-up was extraordinarily good and so was the impersonation of the Fuehrer to which he treated us during the course of the evening. This 'topical allusion' was further emphasised by the British barrage balloon provided by two army officers who came dressed as blimps...."

A Traditional Victorian Schoolmistress

Anne Laugharne Phillips Griffith-Jones, born in 1890 into a distinguished Welsh family in Pembrokeshire, was a welfare officer at a munitions factory in Wales during World War I for which she was awarded the M.B.E.. In 1923 she came to Singapore to spend a three-month holiday with her brother, O.P. Griffith-Jones, a well-known local stockbroker, and found life here so pleasant she decided to stay on and assist Lillian Newton, O.P.'s sister-in-law, in running a private school (in those days most expatriate children returned to the United Kingdom to finish their education in boarding establishments, a practice entailing long sea voyages and endless periods of separation from parents). Miss Griff, as she came to be affectionately known, had no teaching qualifications, though by all accounts she personified the traditional Victorian school mistress and had a disciplinary and austere disposition that belied a warm-hearted caring nature.

When Lillian Newton returned to England in 1924, Miss Griff took over some of her pupils and in 1925, with the club's permission and the help of Mollie Faiers, opened Tanglin Day School in two attap huts in the Tanglin Club grounds; among the first five pupils was her nephew 'Lilo' Griffith-Jones. As neither teacher could play music, the staff was quickly increased to three. The day school provided organised primary level schooling for European expatriate children and was a great success. Within a few years the attap huts could hardly accommodate the fifty pupils and the Tanglin Club generously stretched its rules and offered the use of the exclusive

men's bar, normally out of bounds to women and children. School assembly was held in the ballroom and, Laurette Shearman recalled, always began with 'All Things Bright and Beautiful'; her sister Hazel Booker remembered having "to get into a long line and hold our elbows on the hips and keep our shoulders well back, then walk into the main hall for prayers. Miss Griff was most particular about the elbows."

The main staircase entrance into the club left a larger than life impression on the small pupils. Dr. Charles Wilson, an early pupil, was certain "it reached nearly to heaven," and was amazed to discover on returning to the club in 1946 just how small it was. Jo Essery felt the same when, many years later, she brought her husband to the club especially to show him the giant staircase. The ritual of dismissal too is not forgotten by former pupils: the children sat on the 'jolly hard' front steps of the Tanglin Club and as each car pulled in a teacher would call the child as the syce rushed from the car, took Missy's or Master's wicker school basket, opened the car door and deposited child and basket into the safe-keeping of the amah waiting in the back seat.

In 1934, at O.P.'s suggestion, Miss Griff opened a Tanglin School in the Cameron Highlands, a boarding school with 150 pupils and 22 qualified teachers recruited from England. The story of the Tanglin schools until the Japanese occupation, through the Emergency and the changed conditions in Singapore and Malaya, is one which would inspire any educator. In Singapore the teachers were employed from the resident expatriate

Charles Wilson riding to Tanglin School on his jennet from his home in Goodwood Hill, c 1927 — Courtesy of Dr. Charles B. Wilson

Tanglin School pupils outside the attap hut, 1926 — Miss Griff's photograph album, courtesy of Julia Griffith-Jones

community and, over the years, included Dr. Charles Wilson's mother, O.P.'s daughter-in-law (Eric's wife) Pat, and O.P.'s daughter Gwen Pickering, who gave dancing lessons, a forerunner of the British Association ballet school. Swimming classes for pupils whose parents were members of the Tanglin Club were held three times a week, organised initially by the school and later by the B.E.A., before regular coaching by the club was introduced; among the instructors were Isabel Ferrie, Ann Nederkoorn and Nan Sandford.

Miss Griff was interned by the Japanese in World War II and, while 'in the bag' (Changi Prison and Sime Road Camp), displayed the same qualities of organisation and leadership which were a feature of her normal everyday life. In 1958 she retired to a small bungalow near Brinchang in the Cameron Highlands; she was conferred the O.B.E. for services to education and, in 1962, the PJK (*Pingat Jasa Kebaktian*) by the Sultan of Pahang for meritorious service. She continued to correspond with former pupils; Renée Parrish whose daughter attended the school in the Cameron Highlands recalled with affection the later years when Miss Griff, surrounded by her cats, made everyone welcome: "tea was always served in the best British tradition with a silver service and immaculate linen. Her humble cottage was a little bit of England, tucked away in the hills of Malaya." Veronica Goodban, the current headmistress, called on Miss Griff in 1971 and found her still up-to-date with the changes in expatriate education in Singapore then affected by the removal of the British Forces. In 1973 Miss Griff died in Ipoh Hospital, aged 83, after suffering in

Miss Griff, (seated sixth from left) with staff and students of the Tanglin School in the Tanglin Club ballroom, c 1927 — Courtesy of Laurette Shearman

her later years from painful arthritis; she is buried at Tapah in the foothills of the highlands she loved.

In 1953 after Miss Griff retired, the British European Association purchased the private company Tanglin School Limited for $20,000 — by then the school occupied two locations with enrolment in excess of three hundred pupils. In 1961 the junior section of Tanglin School occupied MATHERAN, a property leased from the Hongkong and Shanghai Bank at the junction of Tanglin and Jervois roads, and the school was converted into a non-profit education trust, Tanglin Trust Limited, controlled by a board of governors. After her retirement, Miss Griff visited the new school and shared some of her memories of the early days of the school where when "the rain beat in

on one side of the hut the five pupils picked up their desks and put them on the other side." In 1981 the Tanglin School moved to the present site in Portsdown Road, amalgamating with the two other trust schools, Raeburn Park and Weyhill Preparatory. Today Tanglin School boasts an enrolment of 1,200 pupils of 42 nationalities, an international staff of 62 teachers of whom 24 are recruited from abroad, and 28 Singaporean assistant-teachers. Dr. Charles Wilson, a school consultant doctor in the 1950's, maintains that "to talk about Tanglin School without associating it with Miss Griff would be unthinkable; it would be like talking of the City Council without mentioning the Mayor."

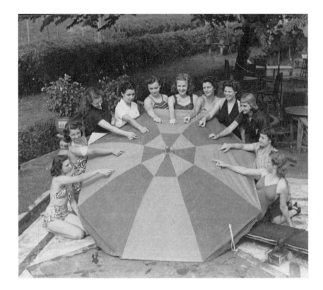

Some of the 'swans' relaxing by the Tanglin Club pool after rehearsing for 'The Circus Comes To Town', a music hall production held at the Raffles Hotel in August 1939 to raise funds for the Children's Aid Society's new home for the destitute youngsters in their care. An outstanding success, the show was reviewed as being the most lavish production of the century. [Rehearsal morning at Tanglin Club, 1939 — Courtesy of Isabel Ferrie]

In September 1939 war broke out in Europe; in June 1940 news arrived of Dunkirk and the fall of France. Three months later the Japanese had occupied northern Indo-China; to achieve their goal of establishing their 'greater East Asia co-prosperity sphere', Japanese ambitions included control of the port of Singapore. As the thirties drew to a close in Singapore, there was still a hectic gaiety about the life led by many Europeans and the presence of increasing numbers of servicemen and news of gathering war clouds over Europe did little to dispel the sense of well-being enjoyed as a result of the economic boom due to the increased world demand for more rubber, more oil and more tin. Labour unrest in the form of strikes supported by communists who sought to undermine the British war effort petered out from September 1940 with the effort to consolidate an anti-Japanese front.

...are you about to go home?

From 1939 to 1941, with the steady build-up of the British armed services, Tanglin Club facilities were offered to officers, many of whom were regarded as an asset to the life of the club. To deal with the more high-spirited among them, a team of chuckers-out was recruited from the tallest members of the club; 'Tiny' (J.M.) Mason (president, 1954) was the shortest at six foot six inches; the tallest was 'Panjang' (P.D.) Lawson at six foot seven inches. Three or four chuckers-out were on duty each Saturday, and most problems were solved by inquiring of the offender: "Are you about to go home?"

First inspection of volunteer nurses by the governor Sir Shenton Thomas, 1939 — The Straits Times Annual 1939

Following exhibition flights from 1911, on December 4, 1919, the first aircraft, a Vickers Vimy three-engined bi-plane under the command of Captain Ross Smith en route from England to Australia, landed at the old racecourse. In 1925 the Royal Air Force appeared for the first time, and in 1928 settled permanently at Seletar. Both Charles Kingsford Smith and Amy Johnson landed briefly in 1930. When the first commercial air flight to Singapore for Imperial Airways touched down at Seletar Air Base in December 1933 it opened a new era for South-East Asia — Singapore was now within a week's travelling time of the United Kingdom. The importance of Singapore as a centre for air traffic was soon established and the opening of the Kallang Airport, the first civil aerodrome, in 1937, with the adjoining seaplane base provided air services for Wearne's Air Services, Imperial Airways, Qantas Empire Airways, Royal Dutch and Royal Dutch Indies Airways. In 1939, when Tanglin Club member Cynthia Koek made her first air trip to England with 23 other passengers the journey took 5 days. [RAF fly-past, 1935, H.M. King George V Silver Jubilee photograph album — N.L.]

...the beginning of the policy of acceptance of Asian members...

"In 1939 and 1940 as a Member of the Club, I was nominated by Head Quarters Malaya Command (then in Fort Canning) to be the Forces Representative for the Club's Election Committee. My principal task was to confirm and assure the Committee that individual candidates for election from the Forces were suitable persons of the proper rank to be elected as Members of the Tanglin Club. This task was comparatively simple before the arrival in Singapore of the first war-time reinforcements of the British Garrison. These reinforcements, known as Force EMU, consisted principally of the 12th Indian Infantry Brigade together with units from supporting arms. Before this time, the only Non-European member of the Club, as far as I can remember, was His Highness, the Sultan of Johore. I do not think that the Rules precluded other Non-Europeans from membership; the facts are that they were just not elected and the Asian ladies and gentlemen who were seen in the Club from time to time were present only as Guests. Before the arrival of Force EMU, the Indian Officers of the Malayan Garrison were 'Viceroy Commissioned Officers' whose rank did not qualify them for election as members of the Club. But Force EMU contained a number of 'King's Commissioned Officers' whose status was considerably higher than that of the 'Viceroy Commissioned Officers'; in fact, the Indian 'King's

The Jagawallah With The Fantastic Memory

It is well after Saturday midnight in the year 1935. "The cars parked outside the Tanglin Club stretch all the way down Stevens Road into Orchard Road. Saturdays are dance nights and the Club is open until 3 A.M., closing promptly at 10 P.M. the rest of the week. People are beginning to leave... the men in evening dress, the ladies in long gowns. They have been dancing to top tunes of the year, like Irving Berlin's 'Cheek to Cheek'. Some have returned from UK leave and are full of stories about the Silver Jubilee celebrations. The Silver Jubilee of King George V and Queen Mary, that is. Now they wait on the front steps, as their cars are summoned by the jaga. The young Indian night jaga calls out the numbers in Malay to four lads who wait at the ready from 11 P.M. to 3 A.M. on Saturdays. They cycle along the road, spotting numbers and waking drivers. For this 4-hour spell of duty each boy earns 40 cents. As the last lingering 'goodnights' are said, the last cars drive off, the young jaga does his last round to see all is in order, then goes to bed, tucked away behind the Downstairs Bar." [From the Tanglin Club newsletter, September 1978.]

The story of Ram Surat Rai, the Number One Jaga known to generations of club members as Ram, begins when he and a friend took a train from a small town in Uttar Pradesh to Calcutta and sailed for Singapore where his elder brother was a jaga at the Tanglin Club. Ram remembered vividly the day of his arrival: his ship docked at 10:30 A.M.; by 8 P.M. he was at work, appointed night jaga at the Tanglin Club with a salary of $18 a month and wearing a khaki uni-

Ram Surat Rai, 1977 — T.C.

form with a green stripe. That was February 10, 1935, the year Sir Andrew Caldecott was club president. Four days after he started work the manager sent for him and discovered he was a 'Hindi only' man. As Malay was the *lingua franca* of Singapore, he was asked to spend two hours each evening, from 8 P.M. to 10 P.M., in the company of the Malay drivers while they waited for their tuans at the club: in three months he was fluent. (Drivers in those days earned between $12 and $15 per month and were on call 24 hours, seven days a week.) Ram remembered several things about the club before the war: the small pool; the sloping ground at the back of the club (near the present Draycott Drive entrance) that was covered with lallang and fruit trees like durian, mangosteen and rambutan; the long, low attap-roofed portion along the front — where the library and reading room were situated in the 1950's — which

was once used as the Tanglin School. There were two, sometimes three, English lady teachers who would ask him to keep an eye on the children and stop them running out on the road: two hours' work on schooldays for $8 a month. Occasionally, when a former pupil turned up at the club, there were joyful reunions.

The year 1939 was a proud one for Ram. When his elder brother (who retired in 1960) went to India on six months' leave, Ram replaced him at the front entrance as jaga of the Tanglin Club for the first time; that young Indian jaga remained at the club until his death in November 1981. A brass plaque in his memory was installed on one of the balustrade pillars at the top of the main entrance staircase of the present clubhouse where members still summon his presence with their favourite anecdotes about his fantastic memory for members' names and car numbers.

In 1921 the committee of imperial defence in London accepted as policy the building of a naval base in the East; in February 1923 the cabinet approved the siting in the north-east of the island colony of Singapore. The base was opened on February 14, 1938. [The King George VI graving dock — British Malaya, March 1938]

Commissioned Officers' ranked equally in all respects with the European Officers and some of the Indian Gentlemen concerned soon expressed their wish to become Members of the Tanglin Club. It then became my task to explain their position to the members of the Committee and to persuade the Committee that in all respects these gentlemen were suitable to become members of Tanglin Club. It was mentioned, for example, during the discussions that in protocol they outranked many of the existing members of the club. An example of one of the Officers concerned was a Captain K.S. Thimmaya, who subsequently represented India as a member of the Supreme Allied Commander Admiral Lord Louis Mountbatten's Staff during the Japanese Surrender and the Re-occupation of Singapore. He eventually rose to the rank of General and became Commander-in-Chief of the Indian Army. After his retirement, he was appointed Commander-in-Chief of the United Nations Forces in the Middle East where he unfortunately died. "After much discussion it was accepted that the Indian 'King's Commissioned Officers' could be elected and become Members of Tanglin Club and this was I believe the beginning of the policy of acceptance of Asian Members of the Club. I may say that I am still proud of being involved in that change of policy; if it had not happened I doubt if the Tanglin Club would today exist in Singapore." [Lt. Col. H.M.J. Jensen in a letter of May 25, 1990.]

The RASC Malaya marchpast during the birthday parade for King George VI held at Farrer Park in 1940; Lt. Col. Jensen is the officer in charge of the detachment — Courtesy of Lt. Col. H.M.J. Jensen

1915 HEWAN, The Hon. E.D.: Previously listed in Part Two.

1916 SIMS, William Arthur, (born 1875, London, England)  entered the service of the Commercial Union Assurance Company in February 1894 as a junior in the foreign fire department; sent to Hong Kong in 1900 as assistant branch manager; appointed manager of the company's Eastern branch in Singapore in 1904 where the areas under his control included the Straits Settlements, the Malayan peninsula and the Dutch East Indies. A municipal commissioner, Justice of the Peace, treasurer of the Singapore Swimming Club and secretary and treasurer of the Singapore Automobile Club. Retired in 1926. Remembered by Sims Avenue.

1917 1918 BRADDELL, Sir Roland St. John: Previously listed in Part Two.

1919 1920 CARVER, Gilbert **1923*** Squarey, (born 1879, England) qualified  as a solicitor in 1903, a cousin of C.I. Carver arrived in the Straits Settlements in 1905 and joined the law firm of Donaldson & Burkinshaw. Saw active service as a Captain in the 1st Cheshire Regiment, wounded on the Western Front in October 1917. Enjoyed yachting and tennis; member

of the Singapore Club, committee member of the Singapore Automobile Club; Hon. Sec. of Straits Settlements Assn. Married daughter of Mr. Justice Law, chief judicial commissioner of the F.M.S.

1921 1922 HARRINGTON, A.G., was an analyst with the muni-  cipality and a long-serving Tanglin Club committee member; lived at THURLE HOUSE in Cavenagh Road.

1923* 1924 GRIFFITH-JONES, **1929 1930** Oswald Phillips, **1931 1938*** (born 1882 Aberystwyth, Wales) educated at University  College, London; arrived in Penang in 1904 to join the merchant house of Sandilands Buttery; later moved to Nestlé and Anglo-Swiss Milk Products Limited in Singapore. After World War I joined Saunders & Macphail, exchange brokers, as a partner. Was a municipal commissioner for 20 years, a president of the Singapore Cricket Club and a committee member of the Bukit Golf Club and the Turf Club. A keen tennis player, 'brilliant cricketer and rugby player'; O.P. died of pneumonia in 1938 aged 56 years after a cricket match played in the rain. In 1950 Edith, O.P.'s widow, was made a life member of the Tanglin Club, the first lady member to receive this honour in her own right (the club bye-laws had to be rewritten to allow this).

1925* JELF, Sir Arthur Selborne, (born 1876), a graduate of  Oxford University, entered the FMS government service as a cadet 1899 and passed in 1902. Held posts as assistant district officer, assistant secretary to the resident, assistant collector of land revenue, chairman of the sanitary board in Kinta, Ipoh, Perak. Seconded for military service, 1917; acting under-secretary to the government of the FMS, 1920; director of the political intelligence bureau of the Straits Settlements, 1921; acting controller of labour, Straits Settlements and FMS, 1924. Left the Malayan Civil Service when appointed the British resident in Jamaica where he was knighted.

1925* FULCHER, Ernest William Popplewell, (born 1884, Norfolk, England) ar-  rived in Singapore in 1906 and was appointed assistant municipal electrical engineer and later municipal electrical engineer. Commissioned as Second Lieutenant in the 3rd Norfolk Regiment; seconded to R.E. Signals in 1915 and saw service in France, Egypt, Mesopotamia and North West Frontier; awarded the military MBE, 1921. A keen footballer and golf, tennis and squash racquets player.

1926 ELDER, Dr. Edward Alexander, (born 1882, Edinburgh,  Scotland) graduated with M.A., B.Sc., M.B., and F.R.C.S. and arrived in Singapore 1910. Appointed municipal commissioner, 1923. Enjoyed tennis, golf, billiards; a member of the Singapore Club.

1927 MARGOLIOUTH, L.C., was a manager of the South British Insurance Company and a municipal commissioner whose wife was a reputed singer. Remembered by Margoliouth Road.

1928 1940 GODWIN, Harold **1941** Sam, (born 1888, London, England) was managing direc-  tor of Godwin Holgate & Co, 1928, then Holgate & Co., which later became Anglo French & Bendixsens Ltd. Interned in Changi Prison during Japanese Occupation; joined Borneo Company after World War II as manager of the rubber department; retired in Singapore, 1957.

1932 SALMOND, Henry B., was a manager and divisional electrician, Electric Department of Eastern Extension Telegraph Australasia and China Company Limited; a committee member and captain of Keppel Golf Club.

1933 HOLLAND, Charles, started his career with the Hongkong and Shanghai Bank in Shanghai in 1908. Worked in Peking, then again in Shanghai and Kobe before arriving in Singapore in 1929 as an accountant with the bank. Left in 1933 for Batavia, then went to Yokohama as manager until he retired to England.

1934 HAWKESWOOD, H.W., was manager and chief buyer of the General Rubber Company of America.

1935 CALDECOTT, Sir  Andrew, (born 1884) obtained B.A. from Oxford University and arrived in 1901. Became a cadet in the FMS government service, 1907; acting district officer in Jelebu, 1911, and in Kuala Pilah, 1912; deputy controller of labour, 1913; acting assistant secretary to the chief secretary FMS, 1914 (was seconded for special duty in connection with the British Empire Exhibition in England in 1923); colonial secretary of the Straits Settlements; governor of Hong Kong and Ceylon. His memory is honoured by Caldecott Hill and Andrew Road; Olive Road honours his wife.

1936 1937 BATEMAN, Osborne Robert Sacheverel, (born 1887, England) arrived in Seremban in 1912 then joined Gattey to form Gattey and Bateman chartered accountants. 'Jo' was secretary of the Singapore Chamber of Commerce 1914–1916, and the firm of Gattey and Bateman (later Cooper Brothers) ran the administration of the chamber from 1916 to 1958. Described by a former partner Charles Tresise as having an Harrovian style, "always good company, but like many of his era a little sad about the unfulfilled promises of Edwardian times." A keen tennis, squash and golf player and especially interested in hockey — he set up the Singapore Hockey Association of which he was president in 1931; donated The Bateman Cup for squash competition. Interned in Changi Prison during World War II where his wife Angela, also an internee, organised art classes.

1938* 1939 HOLYOAK, Thomas  Henry, (born 1890, England) served in France in World War I; was the head of McAlister & Company; the step-father of Eric Griffith-Jones' wife, Pat. With Barton-Wright of Shell, 'Joe' escaped from Singapore in 1941 in a rowboat stolen from the Rowing Club. Returned to Singapore after World War II; a keen hockey and tennis player, member of the Singapore and Turf Club, he later retired to England.

DARK DAYS,
GREAT DAYS

The Tanglin Club New Year's Eve ball, 1956 — T.C.

Asia Insurance Building and Ocean Building, Collyer Quay, c 1953 — A.O.

Despite the outbreak of war in Europe, Singapore in early 1941 was still imbued with an atmosphere of ease and plenty; the only distress of the mercantile community was the introduction of income tax in February. The belief in the invincibility of the colony was so widespread that all except the Japanese and some British military commanders were lulled into a sense of security. The troops enjoyed soft living conditions and most Europeans continued to work hard, devoting their leisure time to civil defence duties even though the reality of war seemed remote. The theme song of the time, 'There'll Always Be An England', well reflected the prevalent feeling that, while Britain was battling for survival, Singapore was merely a sympathetic but faraway onlooker. In the confused uncertainty of 1941, political rather than strategic considerations influenced British defence decisions to favour Russian appeals for help over Australia's demands for a build-up of military strength in Malaya and Singapore. At the time, Singapore and Malaya were dangerously vulnerable to attack; they had few planes, no battleships, no aircraft carriers, no heavy cruisers and no submarines. British service chiefs recommended sending aircraft and a fleet of four ageing battleships to the East, to be supplemented by two more ships in early 1942. The British prime minister, Winston Churchill, decided instead to send spare tanks and fighter planes to Russia and to dispatch the new battleship HMS PRINCE OF WALES, accompanied by the veteran cruiser HMS REPULSE and a modern aircraft-carrier HMS INDOMITABLE, to Singapore; the force arrived without the valuable contribution of the aircraft-carrier which had run aground in Jamaica. As the two vessels sailed proudly up the Johore Strait to the naval base on December 2, 1941, the governor Sir Shenton Thomas, the Commander-in-Chief Sir Robert Brooke-Popham, Lieutenant-General Arthur Percival, a British cabinet minister Duff Cooper, air force and naval commanders and many dignitaries were there to meet them and the base was reportedly like Portsmouth in Navy Week. By the end of the first week in December, the air was alive with expectancy as servicemen were recalled to duty, sailors summoned back to their ships, and the naval base blacked out.

...a crippling surprise attack... Appreciating that their success in establishing a firm foothold in the Malayan peninsula depended on a crippling surprise attack, during the night and morning of December 7, and 8, 1941, Japanese troops landed at Singora in Southern Thailand, with ancillary landings at Patani and Kota Bharu, and the first bombs were dropped on Singapore. Within the span of the same few hours, Japanese forces destroyed

the American fleet in Pearl Harbour and invaded Hong Kong and the Philippines. Admiral Sir Tom Phillips, faced with the necessity of removing his fleet from its exposed position in Singapore, decided to head north to intercept any further invading forces, despite the fact that the RAF could not provide air cover — up to this time no battleship at sea had been crippled or even seriously damaged by air attack. With four destroyers as escort, the two British ships set out in the early hours of December 9, 1941, making a wide sweep beyond the Natunas before proceeding north towards the Gulf of Thailand. At about 10:15 A.M. on December 10 they were spotted by a single Japanese reconnaissance plane returning to base from a southward sweep. In just under an hour the ships were attacked by both high-level and torpedo bombers; by afternoon they were sunk, the Commander-in-Chief of the British Eastern Fleet was dead and the Japanese had control of the sea and air. Out of the 1,309 persons on board HMS REPULSE, 513 were lost; of the 1,612 on HMS PRINCE OF WALES 327 did not survive. The next day a lone Japanese bomber flew over the area and dropped a wreath.

Impossible To Pretend That Life Was Normal

The sinking of HMS REPULSE and HMS PRINCE OF WALES did more to devastate British morale and to exhilarate the Japanese than any other incident in the Far East. Pamela Hickley, who joined the club as a junior member in 1936 and in 1990 was the longest-standing lady member resident in Singapore, remembered service members of the Tanglin Club being in very low spirits when, as a member of the St. John's Ambulance Corps, she and other lady members helped to treat the casualties. Still, civilians continued to maintain a façade of unreal calm, a sense that their island 'fortress' was defended on all sides although their eyes could tell them it was not. In *Tales of the South China Seas*, the recollections of Ann, Elizabeth, Pippa and Susan — the four daughters of Mark John Kennaway, a rubber planter in Malaya — of the weeks before the fall of Singapore in February 1942 are typical of that mood. Ann remembered going to the Raffles Hotel quite often; "there was always dancing on Wednesday nights and Saturday nights to tunes that had been hit tunes six months ago in Britain like 'In the Mood' or 'Begin the Beguine'. Jerry and I had been at the Tanglin Club all day, sitting in the sun by the pool, as we usually did on a Sunday, and in the evening we went to the cinema. Four hours later we heard the sirens; they woke us up." Elizabeth recounted how "everybody was saying: Oh well it's only a practice, the street lights are on. We could look over the town and see the lights of the cinema going round and round coloured: *The Road to Rio*, with Dorothy Lamour, Bob Hope and Bing Crosby." Pippa

Machine-gun pillbox in Raffles Place, January 1942 — World at War — Fall of Singapore

described "seeing Japanese planes circling round our garden and waving to them thinking that they were our planes and being horrified to discover that they were Japanese.... Despite the increasing frequency of the air raids my sister Susan and I managed to enjoy ourselves. We swam a great deal at the Tanglin Club and the Swimming Club. I honestly believe that my mother was the one person in Singapore who was quite certain it was going to fall." In *Spotlight on Singapore* Denis Russell-Roberts, a Tanglin Club member who arrived in Singapore from war-torn Malaya in early February 1942, found "a little spot of paradise" where there was no food rationing nor immediate sense of danger. He spent the first day of his leave being fitted for silk pyjamas,

The Straits Times, January, 1942

Evacuation of British women and children, 1942 — Imperial War Museum, U.K.

Officer's curfew pass, 1942 — courtesy of 'Buck' Buckeridge

shopping at Robinsons and lunching at the Cricket Club between air raids, and then "in the evening we all went to the Tanglin Club to swim, and here we had an animated session of high-balls in the bar with a number of old friends." T.P.M. Lewis, a headmaster of Clifford School in Malaya, reached Singapore on Saturday January 31 and writes in *Changi: The Lost Years*, "when I visited the Tanglin Club the next day, which was Sunday, very few appeared to realise the gravity of the situation and were frankly sceptical when I told them that the Japanese were already in Batu Pahat." A few days later it became impossible to pretend that life would return to normal.

Eye-witness and survivors' reports of battles at The Gap, Alexandra, Bukit Timah and MacRitchie Reservoir which filtered through during the days before 15

February all spelt out a progression that left little doubt that the front line was coming closer. B.C.J. 'Buck' Buckeridge, who joined the Tanglin Club in 1947, recalled that these "meant little change for us in the Fire Brigade whose front had been spread all over the town for a month or more, but was now hardening into those hard cores of fire which engulfed whole areas — Havelock Road, the Harbour Board, Beach Road. Fires were still burning in a dozen other places too, but it was in these concentrated conflagrations that the shells were falling and our struggle became harder as men and water became fewer and less. We had long stopped trying to drive fire engines through littered scarred streets where shell holes and bomb craters, filled with water from broken mains, made the going difficult enough without the accom-

panying bombardment, and were now merely trying to replace men tired out with men less tired out. Bombing and shelling were continuous and getting worse though that was hardly possible. One shell pierced the wall of our flat and reduced my wife Lucy's piano to a heap of spillikins. An enormous crater appeared at the junction of Hill Street and Coleman Street, right outside our Fire Brigade gate which had become our only entrance and exit because our big red Fire Brigade doors had been bunded to protect the fire engines — which had never had time to be in them since the hostilities warmed up! All light and power was off, but supplies were restored within the hour. Telephones went off too, but Telephone Headquarters was just across the road so it wasn't even necessary to inform them — communications were soon re-established. And so the Fire Brigade, like the Windmill Theatre in bomb-blitzed London, 'never closed'. The noise, the litter, the deserted derelict look of Singapore was quite indescribable."

The Straits Times, January, 1942

After the first bombing there were few air raids on Singapore throughout the rest of December. By mid-January 1942, the Malayan campaign reached a critical stage and Churchill was warned that Singapore could not hold out once Johore was lost. Thousands of Commonwealth forces poured in. In the second half of January the air raids on Singapore were intensified; often there would be three air raids in one night and three more by day. While the main targets were the airfields, many bombs fell in the town causing terrible casualties in the crowded streets. In spite of the situation every attempt was made to keep the Tanglin Club open. Brij Nath Rai, who retired in 1987 and whose daughter Savitri now works in the club office, came to Singapore in 1940 and began work at the club as a messenger boy. Less than a year later he became an assistant jaga under his brother-in-law Ram Surat Rai. In the weeks before the fall of Singapore the club continued to function, though Brij Nath remembers helping to set up rows of beds on the verandah and a storage area for medical supplies. According to Ram, four doctors who had escaped from Kuala Lumpur ahead of the invaders sought refuge in the club and stayed in the downstairs bar in readiness until they realised that the situation was hopeless and disappeared. By this time the staff was severely depleted and any of them still on duty went each Monday to the home of club president Harold Godwin in Orange Grove Road to receive their wages.

...dangerous reading for prisoners of war... Immediately before the fall of Singapore on February 15 — Chinese New Year of 1942 — the club was prepared for use as a convalescent depot for the Malayan Armed Service and an evacuee centre. Unlike similar areas in the Cricket Club and St. Andrew's Cathedral, the casualty area — prepared perhaps by the ladies subcommittee which had been formed recently — was never used because events moved so quickly, Not all the tennis courts were open as 'they couldn't get the tukangs and kebuns to come any longer, and just because of a bit of bombing in some parts of the city and dockyards.' The governor had ordered the destruction of the rubber stocks, the tin-smelting plant on Pulau Brani and the massive stocks of alcohol — some 1,500,000 bottles of spirits and 60,000 gallons of *samsu* — which Singapore held as supplier to the whole of South-East Asia. On Black Friday February 13, 1942, the president of the Tanglin Club telephoned Ram to say that some members would come to smash and pour away every single bottle of spirits and beer there was in store — which was quite a few. Club member Ian May disclosed that his father had gone to the club and smashed all the bar stocks, except

for the bottle he took with him to Changi Prison. Later one evening, when a couple of hundred Indian soldiers appeared, with no arms and no leaders, thirsty and starving, Ram remembered the cases of soft drinks stored under the ballroom and invited them to help themselves before they vanished into the night. That was the end of the Tanglin Club, as members knew it, for more than three years. There remains a further incident recounted by Noel Barber in his *Sinister Twilight*. When Tanglin Club member Christopher Dawson, then secretary for defence, was allowed out of custody at Katong on a foraging expedition, he was given a special sticker for his car and ordered to report to the club, where a Japanese officer would examine everything he had collected, before returning to camp. "Dawson, prompted by a feeling that this would be a long, long internment, gathered together all the books he could find from the houses of friends, and towards evening presented himself at the Tanglin Club. The Japanese officer carefully scrutinised each book, finding nothing contraband, until his eye lit on one word in a suspicious title. Carefully he examined the book over and over again. He knew the implications of that secret service word on the title page — and flatly refused Dawson permission to take along P. G. Wodehouse's *The Code of the Woosters*."

...the corruption
was widespread...
During the Japanese occupation the Tanglin Club was used as a Japanese officers' club and as premises for a propaganda unit which extolled the concept of the 'greater East Asia co-prosperity sphere'. The club was also used to store rations and weaponry; food stored on the premises could be obtained by those who held special Japanese ration cards. Unlike many of the others, Brij Nath remained at the club employed by the Japanese as a storekeeper, a position that gave access to generous bonuses

Banana money, used during Japanese occupation

RAF Dakota spraying Singapore city with D.D.T. in a postwar clean-up campaign, 1945 — A.O.

of food supplies but which he was nonetheless quite happy to give up when he resumed his role as jaga after the Tanglin Club reopened. Under the British Military Administration (often referred to as the 'black market administration') which ruled the colony from the Japanese surrender in September 1945 until March 31, 1946, the Tanglin Club — once considered an extension of Government House, so exclusive was its membership — was run by the NAAFI (Navy, Army and Air Force Institutes) for the benefit of the services, including the women officers on Admiral Lord Mountbatten's staff. Some Tanglin Club junior staff worked for the NAAFI but senior and clerical staff refused; in the prevailing atmosphere of corruption and dishonesty many worried that employment by the NAAFI would disadvantage their chances of re-employment when the Tanglin Club resumed operations. A past president disclosed, "when we got back in March 1946 we were allowed to use the 'club' and I remember that if you wanted a gin and tonic you had to order the gin in a separate glass and test to see it really was gin. The corruption was widespread."

Preoccupied With Survival

In 1941 the Tanglin Club was full of men in uniform. As the fighting came nearer, the soldiers went off to the front. Air raids and shelling from Johore were the order of the day; Ram Surat Rai found it increasingly difficult to get to and from work, so he and his family moved into the vacant servants' quarters at the club. The jungle behind the club was used as an Australian artillery battery. On his rounds one day, Ram heard a shell land and searched until he saw a small fire downstairs at the back of the club which he doused with buckets of water from the swimming pool. With the fall of Singapore and the Tanglin Club closed, Ram and his family waited fearfully for developments. Soon after, a group of 12 Japanese soldiers, one of them a sergeant, showed up; Ram could only convey by signs that there was no one and nothing inside. A few days later a large car drove in with a Japanese officer and a Ceylonese interpreter. When matters were explained, he gave Ram an impressive-looking authorisation in Japanese — which would have been on rice paper with a large red chop — to be shown to anyone who tried to enter: the Tanglin Club was to be opened for use as a Japanese officers' club. The tennis courts were dug up for rows of vegetables tended by Javanese gardeners brought in by the Japanese and the swimming pool was stocked with ornamental fish. Ram picked up some Japanese and was able to supervise workmen around town so the family was able to eat. Though he never knew why, the club was closed on the 8, 18, and 28 of each month. Responding to the query in the October 1978 newsletter article 'Ram Remembers', club member K.

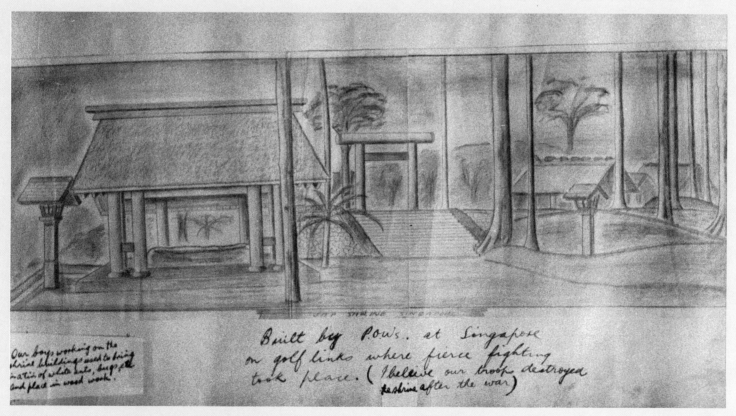

Sketch of Japanese shinto temple constructed at MacRitchie Reservoir by 20,000 prisoners of war used as forced labour, c 1943 — Courtesy of Vern Roach, 8th Division Association

Yasukawa wrote: "It was because the Pacific War broke out on December 8, 1941, and the then Military Government of Japan ordered the nation to have a simple meal on the three days of the month which had number 8 in sympathy with the soldiers fighting on the front. Restaurants were naturally requested to close on those '8' days."

The Japanese occupation of Singapore lasted three and a half years. On the second morning after the British surrender the European population was assembled on the Padang, inspected, questioned for hours, and sent for internment. The civilians, about 2,000 men and 300 women and children, went to Changi Prison and Sime Road Camp. Later, many internees and prisoners of war were sent to build the notorious 'death railway' designed to link Siam with occupied Burma and thousands died of disease and malnutrition. The Asian population suffered massacres and persecution, property confiscation, misgovernment, unemployment, malnutrition and disease, especially tuberculosis and malaria. In late 1943 prisoners of war were used to build an airfield at Changi. Singapore, renamed Syonan or Light of the South, was designated the capital of Japan's southern region; in view of its strategic and economic importance, the Japanese intended to keep Syonan as a permanent Japanese colony.

Singapore was preoccupied with survival; the basic foodstuff, rice, was in short supply because imports from Burma had dried up and the Japanese were hoarding stocks in preparation for further military campaigns. A self-sufficiency campaign encouraged the local population to grow their own food; veg-

etable plots and tapioca plants appeared in front gardens. A superficial industrialisation campaign promoted twine and rope production from pineapple fibre, methylated spirits from tapioca and ammunitions on a small scale. Japanese propaganda and documentary films sought to end western colonial materialism and instil Asian consciousness and a pride in Asian culture; the emperor cult was stressed and a one-minute silence was observed on the emperor's birthday; clocks were put forward two hours in line with Tokyo time. The statue of Raffles was removed; the two main department stores, Robinsons and John Little, were exclusively for Japanese customers, and only Japanese could travel in certain lifts in office buildings. A perpetual state of tension and fear pervaded the island.

As the fortunes of war turned against Japan, the value of paper money — known as bananas or coconuts because the notes bore plant designs — became worthless. Bribery and corruption flourished in an atmosphere of greed and speculation. Cafés, amusement parks, gambling establishments and cinemas were crowded with Japanese, black marketeers and collaborators; two of the three 'entertainment worlds' had been reopened, mainly for gambling. At the end of 1944 essential services, such as water, gas and electricity had broken down and hospitals were out of drugs and equipment. By July 1945 Allied planes were flying overhead and the liberation of Singapore was merely a matter of time; on August 6 and 9 the Americans dropped atomic bombs on Hiroshima and Nagasaki in Japan. On September 5, 1945, when British warships arrived, Commonwealth

Cathay Building, Mountbatten's headquarters, with the Ladies Lawn Tennis Club in foreground, 1946 — A.O.

troops landed to a tumultuous welcome; the three-mile route from the Empire dock to the Cathay building was lined with cheering crowds, waving British, American, Russian and Kuomintang flags. On September 12, 1945, five Japanese generals and two admirals led the delegation which climbed the steps of the Municipal Building to surrender formally to Admiral Lord Louis Mountbatten, Supreme Allied Commander, South-East Asia.

Membership cards introduced after the war were numbered: Freddie Kemlo held Card Number 1, John Phillips Card Number 2 and, in 1990, Arnold Thorne still holds Card Number 3. Postwar members who contributed to the re-establishment of the club included Gordon Strickland, Donald Stewart, W.L. Stewart, M.R. Swain, Gwen Pickering, Richard New, J.A. Grant, G.D. Prockter, A.G. Shafe, Bill Day, Vivian Bath, J.C. Gransden, A.A. Ewing, D.K. Anderson, E.C. Cooper, W.S. Hoseason, F.G. Lundon, T.B. Rogers, Nigel Morris, John Pickering, Charles Withers-Payne, Freddie Kemlo, Jack West, H.C. Hopkins, 'Tiny' Mason, John Phillips, Arnold Thorne, D.E.L. Anderson, F.G. Livingstone, Brian Bridgwood, C.P. Taylor, Professor Dyer, Robin Isherwood, Graham Hay, W.H. 'Pim' Drooglever, Francis Graham, 'L.V.' Taylor, Robert Foulger, A.C. Smith and R.A. Haines.

[Membership card — Courtesy of Arnold Thorne]

The men who gathered in the dining room of the Singapore Club on May 21, 1946, faced a daunting task: to reinstate the Tanglin Club, an institution founded seventy-five years earlier as a premier establishment — like the 'forty good men and true' who had met in 1865 — to meet the wants of the Britishers residing in the colony. Under the direction of Freddie Kemlo, a committee comprising pre-war members Arnold Thorne, John Phillips, Charles Withers-Payne, Leonard Knight and L.V. Taylor was able to report within a month that, despite such problems as obtaining the de-requisition (effective from August 15, 1946) from the British Military Administration, property damage, and the lack of transport, food and even ladies in the colony, the club could open in August or September. There were almost immediately additions to the committee: Leonard Knight was transferred up-country and replaced by Nigel Morris; in July Jack West was invited to join; in August police commissioner Robert Foulger assumed the position of vice-president after Dr. Sandy Elder was unable to accept due to business commitments; and Group Captain G. C. Bladon was appointed the services representative. The committee made claims of $40,000 for denial of liquor stocks to the enemy and a further $50,000 to the war damage commission for damage to property and for its use as a convalescent depot and an evacuee centre. [In 1953 the amount was finally settled for a total of $53,599.]

...elected by the counting of white balls...

The dedication of the postwar committee paid off. Koh Siang Mong (brother of the present assistant librarian James Koh), who was employed as an assistant receptionist when the club resumed operations, remaining at the desk for forty years, remembered how all the club employees, from waiters to the gardeners and the *tukang ayer* Hin Ah Sim, who had been with the club since 1927, did their share of cleaning and repairing the damaged fittings and fixtures. Considerable time and work had to be put into the matter of de-requisition, largely the responsibility of H.C. 'Hoppy' Hopkins; the responsibility for repair and replacement of property was undertaken by Jack West, the question of membership by Arnold Thorne, swimming pool maintenance by 'L.V.' Taylor, W.R. New and W.L. Stewart, and the setting up of the kitchen and redecoration of the premises by the ladies subcommittee. A separate election committee was also appointed, a practice followed for many years, and approval of applicants was decided by the counting of white balls (black balls represented non-approval), a procedure still upheld by the general committee today. Despite the difficulties faced, the club reopened informally on Sunday, September 1, 1946, with 182 ordinary members, including 127 pre-war registered members, 23 lady members and provision for up to 300 service members. The latter category was a dominant feature of membership that coloured the atmosphere of the club until independence.

...never fooled into giving rights to impostors... Compiling the membership list was no mean task as it seemed that all records had disappeared during the war, but chief clerk Siam Siang Eng was "never fooled into giving rights to imposters," related Arnold Thorne, a pre-war committee member, the first postwar honorary secretary and president 1950, 1953. "As soon as we took back the club the old Staff turned up and were invaluable. When it came to re-registering someone as a member it was necessary to confirm their pre-war membership. Many who had not been members attempted to qualify. We devised a method which gave Curreem [club steward since the 1930's] a chance to see the man. He knew many by sight but was not infallible. The applicant was asked for a specimen signature, ostensibly for registration in the office but in fact to show the Chinese clerk whose job it had been to sort out the bar chits each day — one glance at the signature was enough to prove membership or otherwise. On one occasion Curreem recognised the applicant but not the name, and the signature was not accepted though we all thought Cohen of the Singapore Harbour Board had been a pre-war member. It turned out that he had changed his name during the war, and the clerk immediately recognised a specimen of the pre-war signature." During this regeneration period the committee agreed to employ a full-time club secretary. Many military personnel who were being demobilised were keen to stay on and find work in Singapore, still regarded as a 'jolly, good place and one of the best stations in the East'; the club offered a three-year contract at $400 per month, free quarters and food, and a leave passage. By 1947 the post was filled by E.A. Chard, followed by Lieutenant-Colonel C.F. Seston, Colonel R.E. Kenny and then A.H. 'Tony' d'A. Willis who remained until 1961.

...joyous but not too extravagant... Due to rationing, a cash coupon system was in force until 1948. Coupons were issued only to members holding cards — obtained by re-registering and paying preferably six months subscription in advance — and handed over with their signed chits. The club's dining facilities opened with a limited bill of fare. Table d'hôte or à la carte

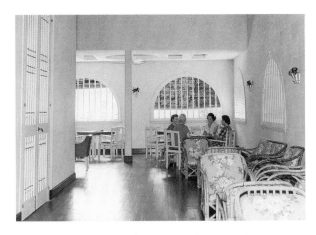

Despite frequent blackouts, regular Tuesday evening bridge parties after the war were organised by Alice Eber in August 1947. Lady members, dressed for the evening in patio frocks, sat at tables set on the verandah. These rather formal gatherings included some well-known players, notably Nelle Gilmour and Maisie Wilson. Ladies' bridge mornings were also enjoyed on the verandah. On June 3, 1952, "the question of payment of Bridge winnings was raised. The Secretary explained that many members, particularly their wives, preferred to receive their winnings by cheque rather than by credit in their (husband's) account. It was agreed to leave this matter as it stands." In 1955 the Walnut Room was made available for bridge on Thursday mornings and evenings. Rubber bridge was played for 20 cents and 25 cents per 100 points, all players being able to cut in. When the Walnut Room was transformed into the Tavern, all card players were requested to use the reading room which proved to be an unpopular move as readers naturally objected to the noise. For years there was a request for a card room. [The verandah, 1949 — T.C.]

meals were served at the usual times: on Saturday nights a special dinner was served for $2.50, on other nights a more simple dinner was $2.25; daily tiffins were available at $1.75 and Sunday's ma mee tiffin was the speciality at $2.25. Due to the shortages which still prevailed in Singapore, a circular was sent to members warning them not to eat more than $2.50 worth of food at any one sitting. As Christmas approached in 1946, an attempt was made to celebrate the occasion in a joyous but not too extravagant fashion. The committee suggested decorations but, at the same time, advised that "Members must not expect nor does the Committee think it desirable under present conditions, for decorations and functions to be on a pre-war scale." Traditional events such as the annual Tanglin ball, the New Year's Eve ball and children's party were not held because of the food and drink shortages and the lack of suitable clothes, but special dinner dances were held on Christmas Eve, Boxing Day, and New Year's Eve; 475 suppers were served at the latter function.

...the new card index system... The first postwar AGM held at the Tanglin Club on April 18, 1947, seven months after the reopening of the club, was attended by about 50 ordinary members and a few lady and service members. Many had been pre-war members — some had been interned, some had survived the 'death railway', some had miraculously escaped. At the meeting entrance fees were respectively set at $100, $50, $40 and $25 for ordinary, up-country, service and lady members. Members were reminded that if their wives had returned to Singapore they were liable for an additional one dollar per month subscription: "the committee would be obliged if members who have not already done so would advise the Treasurer of the date of return of their wives to Singapore, so that their accounts can be adjusted and membership cards made out." At the election committee meeting of October 6, 1950, the membership figures of the club — including active, honorary, up-country, country and non-active members, and those pending election — "as obtained from the new Card-Index system" were read as: 1,325 male and 941 female ordinary members; 296 male and 194 female service members; 200 lady members.

The High Jinks Of Members

"With the rationing of whisky the most regrettable practice has been resorted to by a few Members, of ordering doubles. After the bar boys had been instructed to serve single, i.e. stengah whiskies only, these individuals then proceeded to order three or four drinks at a time. Your Committee believe that the vast majority of members would prefer not to be associated with individuals who persist in this kind of behaviour. Should there be any further occurrences of this nature the Committee seeks the co-operation of members in bringing them to their attention. If after investigation the reports are substantiated, your committee will not hesitate to call for the resignation of the member or members concerned, under Rule 56." [Circular to members, 1947.]

In May 1947 a system was introduced whereby members lucky enough to have their own supply of whisky could hand in their own bottles at the bar, have the value credited against their accounts, and then sign for their stengahs in the usual way. The supply of liquor continued to be a preoccupation and after many complaints 'that a few Members were in the habit of consuming a large portion of the small daily Scotch ration in the mornings' the committee decided that no Scotch whisky would be made available before 5 P.M. From the reopening of the club members were often reminded that 'residents of Singapore and Johore Bahru may not be introduced as guests, except on occasions declared by the Committee as guest-nights. As from the June 1, 1947, until further notice, the first Wednesday of

The Tanglin Club viewed from Stevens Road, 1949 — T.C.

every month is declared a guest-night. Scotch whiskey will not be served on these nights so long as rationing is necessary.' At a meeting on March 15, 1948, it was further decided that, "a Committee Member should be on duty at the Club on Saturday Nights for the purpose of vetting persons using the Club, and that a roster be prepared and the name of the Committee Member in attendance at the Club be prominently displayed at the Club Entrance. Carried unanimously." By this time the bar turnover was reported as in excess of a quarter of a million dollars.

Bar prices went up in 1950 as a result of higher customs duties causing the usual flood of complaints from members. The price of a Pimms No.1 cup was increased from 75 cents to 90 cents and it was recommended that the bar use its cheaper South African brandy for mixing the ever

popular brandy and dry ginger; whisky cost 75 cents and a whisky soda 90 cents. In June 1950 the club announced price increases for port, sherry, brandy and liqueurs due to the purchase of new English glassware: the glasses were larger and held more liquid refreshment. Long Hin Tuan, who was a general bar assistant in 1951 (in later years he worked on bar rotation, serving beer and Scotch in the quiet exclusivity of the men's bar one day and Coca-Cola and 7-Up at the poolside the next, before he was assigned to the Churchill Room in 1985), recalled that the choice of mixed drinks was limited; stengahs, pink gins and beers — all available for less than a dollar — were the most popularly requested until the opening of the cocktail bar in 1954 when manhattans, Martinis and Bloody Marys were increasingly in demand. At the 1955 AGM "Mr. M.J. Cotton asked why the Club did not provide draught beer. Mr Mason replied that the Bar Committee member, Mr. Rushworth, had gone into the whole question last year and had decided against it. Mr. Prockter suggested that some importer of draught beer might be prepared to let the Club have three months free trial!" At a committee meeting on May 31, 1955, "it was suggested as a trial to provide salted nuts and chips at lunch time and from 7 P.M.," which has thereafter been enjoyed as a customary provision.

For a short time, on account of 'the condition of a few members,' all club bars were closed on Sundays from 3 P.M. to 6 P.M. The high jinks of some members at the time is illustrated in an incident following the introduction of one-way streets and road markings policed by the traffic police. A single white line down

Stevens Road made parking along the grass verge an expensive option. One Sunday, a day which was generally particularly congested, two young members who showed up, flagrantly parked, took out some black paint from the boot and painted out the line opposite their car, then boldly proceeded into the club to fill up on beer and curry tiffin. Reeling out some time later they again opened the boot, took out some white paint and painted back a rather crooked replacement.

No Other Kind Of Life

In *A Family of Ginger Griffins* Pamela Lattimer vividly describes the colonial ambience of the early postwar years. "Singapore was an hierarchical society from the Governor representing His Majesty down to the little Chinese women coolies who could be seen working on the buildings in their black tunics and trousers with red or white cloth headgear. After H.E. came the Chief Justice, the Commanders-in-Chief of the three Armed Services, the Vice-Chancellor of the University, the Colonial Secretary, Heads of Government Departments and of firms such as ICI, Shell and Dunlop. Then there were the Tuan Besars (Heads) of the big import and export Houses, the Chinese millionaires and representatives of American and European companies; all on one small island. Standing on the side lines was Malcolm Macdonald, Special Commissioner for South East Asia, with his Foreign Office Staff.

"We had been used to leading a pleasant social life in Fiji, for our first three years at least, but it was nothing on the scale we now experienced. A cousin of mine told me they could have accepted invitations for every night of the week, sometimes twice over. There was also much entertaining at restaurants, hotels and clubs which was too expensive for most government officials. Each expatriate community had its own club, in addition to the clubs which catered for particular interests, though many were overcrowded by accepting officers of the Services as temporary members. Some of the clubs were in very pleasant situations with little to remind one of the immediate proximity of a great city. One club stood out, the Tanglin. It was so English, and I imagine it was much like the clubs in India before the war. Membership was sought after. There was a swimming pool which our children tolerated, preferring the large, noisier Swimming Club as nothing so indecorous as a scream was ever heard at the Tanglin. The 'boys', club servants, moved quietly about almost like shadows. I would sometimes wander inside to read the English papers feeling almost like an interloper, and sit in one of the spacious rooms where even the ceiling fans seemed to rotate in a stately manner. I would watch the bridge fours who had been playing most of the morning, some of whom would continue after a club curry tiffin. They played with the calm assurance of people who had never lived any other kind of life.

"Towards the end of the year, the colony celebrated the wedding of Princess Elizabeth to Prince Philip, and made a great evening occasion of it which continued all night. Chinese dragons are no novelty now, but this was our first sight of one and it was a magnificent beast, something like thirty metres long. The overhead wires of the tramlines had to be removed to allow the endless procession of floats to get through. I had never seen anything like this before, not such fireworks, and I was quite as dazzled as the children."

The ballroom decorated for the 1953 Coronation ball — T.C.

At a committee meeting on August 25, 1952, it was suggested that a 'Teenagers Dance' might be held in the Club before the older children returned to the U.K. Mr. Rushworth and Mr. Oldham agreed to arrange the details. School holidays were often the occasion for family reunions. "We flew Ann out to Singapore for the summer of 1950. Arthur had been able to see Ann when he flew home each year for the Glaxo Export Conference, but I had not seen her for two years. In those days Glaxo did not fly children out during the holidays, not even after two years. But I was earning money at Tanglin [School] and saved up to pay for the flight. We stood waiting at the arrivals gate, sick with excitement. When we saw her we hardly recognised her; we had left a child at school and now she had grown tall and was so self-assured. All the parents who met that plane must have had the same feeling. That summer of 1950 in Singapore was magic. The children who flew out all got together and had swimming parties at the Swimming Club, tennis parties at Tanglin and launch picnics out to islands. They had a wonderful time and by the time they had to go back to England, we were all so exhausted from the fetching and carrying that it wasn't too hard to let them go. In March 1951, Arthur and I flew home with Judy, to settle her into Berkhamstead. It was two years before we saw either of the girls again." [Helen Scrimgeour in Hilary Williams' The Beginnings of Glaxo in China.] [Mrs. Dee assists at a Teenage Dance, 1950's — T.C.]

Children's Christmas party, 1950's — T.C.

One of the dramatic changes that took place immediately after the war was the gradual relaxing of the rules regarding children's use of the club. Whilst members were still being reminded that children were not allowed in the ballroom 'and amongst the instruments belonging to the band,' the hours during which they could use the pool were extended several times in 1947. During the school holidays, the ballroom was used for games and indoor sports. Children's swimming galas were family affairs with many events involving parents and children together. Swimming events were competitive, although requiring only a single length or breadth to be covered, 'not the gruelling three or more lengths in the fancy strokes of later years.' Diving events were popular features and in 1958 the Danish Olympic games champion J. Gjerding judged the older children's competition. In May 1948 there was a further extension of pool hours, together with the exciting news that 'the kiddies can now get their lunch served at the pool, and we have bought a really big consignment of ice-cream.' The relaxation of rules allowed children to swim until 6 P.M. on weekdays and until 12 P.M. on Saturdays, Sundays and public holidays with a consolation that they could be accompanied by a nurse or amah and enjoy lunch at the pool-side of the ballroom.

"Mr. P.F. Kavanagh asked why the Committee had found it necessary to alter the Bye-Laws by reducing the hours in which children were allowed to be in the Club. He pointed out that Members with children were now put to considerable inconvenience in removing their children from the Club at so early an hour as 12:30 P.M. on Saturdays, Sundays and public holidays. This meant in effect that on the sole days on which fathers were able to be with their children they could neither enjoy a lunch-time drink with their friends nor give their children lunch at the Club. In his view the amended Bye-Law while it favoured unmarried Members had not caused any increase in attendance by these people. In fact from 12:30 P.M. the Swimming Pool and area were virtually empty. The President replied that the Pool was there for the enjoyment of all Members and the original Bye-Law had in the opinion of his Committee over-favoured parents with children. Many cases of lack of control of children had been reported to the Committee and as the Club was for Members and not their children the Committee had felt it imperative to curtail the children's hours at the Club for the greater benefit of other Members." [AGM 1959.] On Sunday mornings, one of the times when children were allowed to swim, a bell at 12:30 P.M. was the signal for all minors to leave the water and, indeed, the club premises. Returning to the club one Sunday in the mid-1970's, a former member was heard to remark loudly at 12:45 P.M.: 'Isn't it about time they rang the bell so we can all get a decent swim?' [The swimming pool, 1949 — T.C.]

...pool frolics for adults only...

Annual swimming galas and lido afternoons organised exclusively for adults had been a regular feature before the war and continued to be popular once the pool reopened, especially in the 1950's. The frolics began around 7 P.M. with events like cork bobbing, lighted candle and cigarette races, walking the greasy boom, oyster diving, pillow fights and Adam & Eve apple races. Nothing dampened the enthusiasm of members, as was apparent in 1951 when the gala was cancelled due to bad weather — participants simply 'adjourned for the eats and dancing already planned for the latter part of the evening.' Between events there were demonstrations of exhibition diving by Mrs. Marr and crazy diving by the Sawdust Brothers. During the aquatic events the club band was in attendance to provide suitable instrumental sound effects. A popular item on the programme was the 'Miss Tanglin' competition in which competitors walked to the end of the springboard, curtsied and paraded along the diving stage for the judges to vet their figures before pushing each 'maiden' into the pool. The highlight of the evening was the flame dive: all the lights in the ballroom and pool were turned off as the diver plunged from the diving stage into ignited petrol flaming on the surface of the water. Before supper the pool was opened for general 'frolics'; after bathing costumes were exchanged for informal evening wear the band led a march to the tune of a conga round the pool and up the main stairway to the ballroom where a barbecue supper was followed by dancing. Prizes in the form of drink chits were distributed later in the evening. As the pool remained open until midnight, quite a few people ended their evening of frolics, fully clothed, in the pool.

...a second-hand lamp from Sungei Road... With the problem in the supply of electricity in the postwar years, a novel system was found to light the swimming pool by suspending a second-hand cluster-type lamp purchased from Sungei Road from a large tree behind the pool. Black-outs, however, were frequent — even the 1949 AGM was held by candlelight. In an effort to conserve electricity all light bulbs were changed from 40-watt to 25-watt. In a 1950 meeting to discuss the air-conditioning of the bar and the billiard room, members were informed that electricity was restricted for such use from 6 P.M. to 10 P.M. and that, in any case, the club could not afford to air-condition these at that time. It was not until the new power station was in operation in 1952 that the committee decided to seek official clearance to air-condition the restaurant, which was still to all intents a part of the ballroom and lacked any intimate atmosphere.

The ballroom, 1949 — T.C.

In 1946 it was reported that Professor W.E. Dyer, a professor of history at Raffles College who had entertained fellow-internees at Changi Prison with history lectures, would once again accept the position of librarian and make recommendations to reconstitute the library; Chew Poh Gee who had joined as the assistant librarian in 1935, also returned. Shelves were constructed by the public works department and, by September 1947, 670 books had been catalogued. Professor Alexander Oppenheim, who survived the 'death railway', and Professor Brian Harrison, who had been captured during the war on the beach of the Yacht Club and interned at Changi prison, were two other members assisting on the project. Invited to return from Ireland in 1946 to re-establish Raffles College, Professor Harrison found that transport was non-existent and the only accommodation available to him was a dilapidated hut on the grounds of the Goodwood Park Hotel. The Tanglin Club was "in the most pathetic state; used as an Officers' Mess during the war, and then by the NAAFI, a mess it certainly was"; the library shelves had been used for a bar, the building was a cockroach paradise. Professor Harrison took charge of book orders, simultaneously developing his special interest in South-East Asian history. Frequent appeals were made for members to donate their old books and committee members were asked to join book societies at the expense of the club as a means of acquiring further reading material. In 1951 members were asked to approve a one-dollar monthly subscription to a library fund. The popularity of new books over old was such that in May 1952 the borrowing of books less than three months old was restricted to one per member — older and shabbier volumes could be borrowed two at a time. In spite of the punitive regulations, late returns of new books were very common and the income from library fines in that year amounted to the phenomenally high total of $1,749 — more than twice the income then generated by the billiard room. When James Koh Mong Seng started work as assistant librarian in 1951, both the library and the reading room occupied one long room, separated by only a thin partition. Smoking was permitted in the reading room but members had to be reminded to exercise caution after several cushions were damaged by burning cigarette ends. Later in the fifties the area was extended, and with air-conditioning installed the books no longer suffered from mould and mildew. For the first time, a separate, quiet area was set aside for reading, though on special occasions such as the annual Tanglin Club ball it was used as a venue for pre-dinner drinks and the tranquillity of the area shattered.

The first postwar committee worked with a will to repair the recreational facilities and the records of minutes of this time detail the severity of the problems. Material was found to cover one of the two billiard tables. The lawn tennis courts were, not surprisingly, in poor condition, having been cultivated with tapioca and okra and the Golf Club agreed to provide grass and black earth to repair them; the four hard tennis courts were in reasonable repair. During the occupation the squash courts had been used as store rooms. Originally entered by descending a ladder worked by a pulley system, the Japanese had cut holes in the sides of the walls to provide easier access which caused recurring problems with dampness; two courts could be used but repairs to the third court were necessary. It was agreed to purchase badminton equipment and prepare ground; the old lawn bowling green became the lower-tier tennis courts. The swimming pool presented major problems: the pumping and filtration equipment was old and worn, the chlorination apparatus obsolete and the wooden steps into the pool that had been cemented over by the Japanese were constantly slimy and impossible to clear. The pool could not be emptied because water was not available to refill it and for over a year was continually being patched up.

In September 1947 Freddie Kemlo wrote to members giving an account of the progress made in the year of reopening: the tennis and squash courts had been "rehabilitated and re-equipped"; the club had been completely outfitted with new furniture, cutlery and crockery; the men's bar had been restored and the club was completely repainted. Interest on debentures from February 1942 to date had been paid off, and the purchase of outstanding debenture holdings was practically completed. Members were also informed that the committee was proposing a programme to "extend the amenities of the Club" which involved enlarging the car park, extending the swimming pool by 15 feet, removing the pumping plant from beneath the club to a site on the Stevens Road side of the pool and providing a lawn between the pool and the new dressing rooms to be built on the Stevens Road boundary. "Of this programme the resiting of the pumping plant and the building of the car park can be regarded as essential, and the cost will amount to approximately $30,000 — or about half of the total cost. The pool will never function properly while the plant remains where it is. Irksome restrictions on the use of the pool will remain, while there is the ever present fear of a breakdown in the chlorinating arrangements which might necessitate the emptying of the bath, in which event we should not be permitted by the municipality to obtain the water to refill it. The pool is already overcrowded on holidays, and its lengthening will remedy this. It will also provide an opportunity for catering more adequately for children and the provision of a segregated area for them. There are also certain defects in the present pool which can only be remedied by lengthening." Subsequently, the dressing rooms, which were his idea, were often called 'Kemlo's cabins'. The scheme was eventually approved by the municipality in 1950 and the total cost estimated at $60,000.

"Mr. [Francis] Graham then said, 'I am one of the oldest members of the Club and I have seen the Club on the financial rocks twice — I do not want to see it on the financial rocks a third time....' To deal with Mr. Graham's comments, this Committee is fully aware that on two previous occasions this Club has been on the rocks, but they put forward the suggestion that one of the reasons why this Club was on the rocks, on at least one of those occasions, was due to the fact that it had, immediately before that occurred, not adopted a progressive policy. It was years behind the times, its conditions were unattractive to the people likely to use it in those days, and consequently it went down. In those days it was perfectly correct to say that the majority of the revenue of the Club came from the bar, to-day from subscriptions, the rest comes from people using the Club. To-day people have all sorts of other places in the town where they can go and get the same things that they get in this Club. If we do not keep up to date in our furnishings and decorations, and, far more important, in our service of those amenities, we will not keep the business." [Committee meeting April 20, 1950.] [Aerial view of the Tanglin Club, 1949 — T.C.]

At the 1949 AGM the debate resumed: should the club be overhauled or rebuilt? Again a subcommittee was appointed to investigate the alternatives, and on September 9, 1950, the president reported that the building had another ten years life and recommended renovation and refurbishment rather than reconstruction. In particular, the billiard room and men's bar were to be reduced in size to create a small, intimate dining room with a long bar running the length of the room. The committee was also authorised to obtain plans for a secretary's bungalow on the tennis court next to Stevens Road for which a $42,000 estimate was later submitted. An alternative suggestion, seriously considered in 1950, was to build bachelors' quarters, including a secretary's flat, but this was thought to only benefit a few members. The servants' quarters estimated at $45,000, formerly on land later exchanged with Tan Chee Boon for a block behind the clubhouse, and the new bungalow were completed in 1951. With foresight the plans had been changed to build on the land occupied by the tennis courts nearest to Stevens Road. In June 1955, a committee meeting reported that Tan Chee Boon "was agreeable to hire the area behind the squash courts facing Stevens Road to the Club for use as a carpark at a nominal rent. It was agreed to ask him to accept a rent of one dollar per annum." A further 16,000 sq. ft. of land at the rear of the club near the carpark was acquired from Guthries.

At the AGM on March 27, 1953, retiring president Freddie Kemlo included in his address, 'The Future', an additional proposal that the club either build on the land behind the existing premises, or sell

Passageway leading to the library, 1949 — T.C.

its entire land and move further out of town. In April 1954 the club committee decided that plans for major redevelopment or rebuilding of the club should be left for two to three years. However an immediate start was made on the conversion of the billiard room into an air-conditioned grill restaurant, renovation of the kitchen, an extension for the band and a small dance floor in a part of the main bar. After discussion approval was given for the expenditure of up to $100,000 for the renovations.

In the early 1950's the sole eating area in the club, known simply as the restaurant, served predominantly European fare: special Saturday dinners cost $3.50;

a barbecue meal of a steak or two chops with chips, roll and coffee was $2.50; a snack lunch of salad, fruit, roll and coffee went for a dollar; satay was ten cents a stick. In August 1954 the committee confirmed that approval had been granted to the firm of James Cubitt, Leonard Manasseh and Partners to proceed with their plans to design a new air-conditioned restaurant to accommodate up to 150 diners. A suggestion to include a cocktail lounge in the new air-conditioned restaurant was dropped because of the expense. Although 'progress was somewhat hindered by a London dock strike which held up much of the equipment ordered from the U.K.' the new res-

Air-conditioned billiard room with braziers, 1954 — T.C.

taurant was opened in November 1954 and named the Chandelier Room — more in keeping with the décor and style than Orchid Room, a name originally proposed. Goh Sin Fatt, now a barman, who joined as a waiter in 1952 and served in the newly-opened restaurant, remembered the introduction of exotic continental and local specialities. Although the Chandelier Room was immediately popular, the committee expressed dissatisfaction with the décor and lighting; subsequently another firm was engaged to repair the new plastering and paintwork, and some of the outstanding fees owing to the original architects and contractors were retained. On March 27, 1956, a quote of some $16,300 was accepted from Messrs. Swan and Maclaren,

architects, to convert the card room into an air-conditioned function room with walnut veneer panelling intended to be used also as an additional dining room for private parties. It was completed by June 1956 and named the Walnut Room.

In 1957 a panel of architects co-opted from members decided to redesign the area between the ballroom and the air-conditioned Chandelier Room opened in 1954. The new room was to be air-conditioned with space for about 50 diners and connected to the Chandelier Room, as a 'club within a club.' The new room and bar included an elliptical dance floor under a correspondingly recessed ceiling across the short access of the room, with a band platform between two archways leading to the new ballroom. On special

occasions these could be opened to join the two areas. The estimated cost of the project was $100,000, including 'the high cost of the additional air-conditioning equipment.'

The new room — boasting an expensive carpet specially made in England — and bar was opened on November 22, 1957, the night of the annual Tanglin ball, and was well-received by the members. It had, however, yet to be named: one suggestion was the Brocatelle, after the upholstery of the chairs and settees, no doubt influenced by the W.S. Gilbert quotation carried in the menu for the night: 'It isn't so much what's on the table that matters, as what's on the chairs.' A bottle of Black Label whisky was offered as the prize for a suitable name which

The Churchill Room, 1957 — T.C.

should have 'home or London associations.' Six members suggested the Churchill Room and lots had to be drawn for the prize, finally won by A.T. de B. Wilmot. The new Churchill Room was an instant success, so successful in fact that the kitchen could hardly cope. A special circular was sent to members explaining the situation and urging their cooperation, such as asking large dinner parties to order a set menu rather than à la carte. Despite being 8,000 miles away, Sir Winston Churchill himself was not totally unaware of the room named in his honour: in 1957, the club president Dr. R. Calderwood had written to request a signed photograph of Sir Winston which he collected and presented to the club in September 1958 with Churchill's best wishes; the present whereabouts of this, unfortunately, is not known. The present head waiter Liang Sia Heng, who joined

the club in 1953, has been in the Churchill Room since 1958.

Renovation of the premises continued from 1959 to 1965. A major project was the renovation and instalment of air-conditioning for the library and reading room. The construction of men's changing rooms was completed in June 1959 at a cost of $42,892. The former rooms became a staff dormitory and, to the distress of the snooker players, billiards was dropped from club activities to allow additional staff to be billeted in that room. A major work in 1960 was the construction of a new car park for 45 cars behind the flower garden at the back of the club at a cost of $15,000; later this became the site of the new clubhouse. The pool terrace was developed in 1961 at a cost of $42,000, including a snack area, improved bar facilities and a covered staircase to the main building.

"Members were not attracted to the Club by the vast empty Ballroom in the earlier part of the evening and went to dine and dance at other places of entertainment coming to Tanglin only when these places had closed. The Committee felt that with Malayanisation, etc, unless action was taken quickly the Club might be out of business. They concluded that Members wanted facilities to eat and drink and to dance at the same time in pleasant surroundings which must be air-conditioned, and that these facilities should be provided on a better scale than anywhere else in Town. The Committee therefore sought the advice of three qualified architects who were members of the Club — Messrs. Brundle and Cobley, who had since left the Colony, and Mr. Koren. It was impossible to give the Ballroom a London nightclub atmosphere but after some thought it was considered practicable to convert the old Main Bar to this purpose. Mr. Koren was asked to prepare plans and when these were ready the proposition was put to Members in a Circular. The response was most encouraging, tenders were called for and the work was put in hand. The result has been the Churchill Room."
[AGM 1958.]

"Colonel Kenny is unfortunately not with us today as your Committee agreed to release him for service in Perak for the Anti-Bandit Month." [AGM 1950 observing the absence of the club secretary]

Party for servicemen, August 1952 — T.C.

Arriving in Singapore in 1948, John Gauntlett met and knew few people outside the Tanglin Barracks where he was stationed. "Whilst on the troopship outward bound to Singapore I had studied a book entitled *Spoken Malay (Phonetics)* just in case that few, if any, of the Island population spoke English! Mr. D.E.L. Anderson, then of Shell, proposed me for Membership of the Tanglin Club, where I originally made contact with local European residents. Some time later I met a brother-officer from another troopship and took him for lunch at the Club, of which I was justly proud. Over a pre-meal drink, I enquired from my guest as to what he thought of the place, with its swimming pool, tennis courts, dance floor, library, etc. To which question he replied: It's all right, Old Boy, but there are too many Civilians around! (He did not, of course, know that members of H.M. Forces enjoyed special privileges insofar as Entrance Fees and Monthly Subscriptions were concerned)."

With emergency regulations in force from 1948 to 1953, British forces continued to be based in Singapore where the Tanglin Club hosted functions for NCOs and servicemen from the Royal Navy, Army and Air Force. Some were on anti-terrorist missions in Malaya for up to three years, others had not been back to England since D-day. Many of the regiments, some raised in the seventeenth century, had served the Empire heroically in the past and previously had been stationed in Singapore. To name but a few, the Tanglin Club played host to men from Honeywood's Dragoons (the 11th Hussars) of the Charge of the Light Brigade at Balaclava in the Crimea; the 1st Battalion, the Royal West Kent Regiment, who had served for a time as marines under Lord Nelson and, in 1953, were congratulated by General Templar for their 'score' of one hundred terrorists during a three-year counter-insurgency operation in Malaya; the 2nd Battalion, the Royal Welsh Fusiliers, who served in Malaya during the state of emergency and also in Singapore during the riots of 1956. Members of the club were unstinting in the hospitality offered to servicemen and also patients from the British Military Hospital. Servicemen, usually over a hundred at a time, turned out in full force for an evening of free food, beer — the military authorities instructed that no spirits were to be served — and cigarettes; swimming, darts, billiards and dancing. Club members helped to organise the games and man the bar and their wives to serve the food, and daughters volunteered as dancing partners as their contribution to the war effort. By 10:30 P.M. the men boarded the transport provided to return to base. The cost of these functions was entirely funded by voluntary contribution — some members had a standing order with the club office that their accounts be debited a specified amount for each party.

...subscriptions that allowed officers to enter on the cheap... Officers residing in Singapore could join the club as service members; selected senior service officers were invited to make use of the club as honorary members during their stay in Singapore whilst others were admitted as visiting members. On one occasion a serviceman, said to have been a lieutenant-colonel, took exception to a private in uniform entering the club. As the private was in fact a club member and prominent government official who had just finished his daily stint with the Volunteers, the officer was told in no uncertain terms that it was that private's subscription that allowed army officers to enter 'on the cheap'. [The Singapore Volunteers had been involved in the defence of the island in World War II. In 1963, when Singapore was part of Malaysia, the Corps was designated the 10th Battalion Territory Army; with independence in 1965 it was redesignated the 10th People's Defence Force and subsequently renamed the 101st PDF in 1974.] It was only at a meeting on August 29, 1960, that it was pointed out: "the time had come for the Club to raise the Entrance Fee for Services members. The fee had been kept low in earlier times as the Services had been comparatively poorly paid

and they were only resident in Singapore for a 3-year tour at the most. The latter premise might still apply though it was becoming noticeable that many officers were returning to Singapore for a second and third tour due to the reduction in the number of overseas establishments. On the other hand, the Services were now very much better paid and they could afford to pay a higher entrance fee. The Services entrance fee was last raised, from $40 to $50 in 1951 at the same time as the Ordinary members' entrance fee was raised from $100 to $150. The Services had therefore gained a considerable advantage over the civilians."

...the club remained closed for three days... In December 1950 the annual Tanglin Club ball and New Year's Eve ball were postponed due to the Maria Hertogh riots. The government had decided to return to her mother in Holland a thirteen-year-old Dutch Eurasian girl, Maria Hertogh, who had lost contact with her interned parents during the Japanese occupation, been brought up by a Muslim family and married a Muslim. "Stirred up by leaders of the Malay Nationalist Party and by the Muslim press, Malays, Indonesians and Indian Muslims in Singapore protested violently against the government's action. The Commissioner of Police allowed the situation to get out of hand; Europeans and Eurasians were attacked indiscriminately, and 18 people were killed and 173 injured in two days of rioting," documents C.M. Turnbull. Ken Gould, president 1968, disclosed: "I had been a Service member of the Club from the time I was posted to my Regiment in Singapore in June 1940 until the surrender in February 1942. When I returned after the war as an assistant in Rodyk & Davidson I was too junior to be a member and did not re-join until I became a partner in 1953. I made full use of the Club for the next 20 years until returning to England in 1973. I was Counsel acting for the Dutch Government in the case and had tried very hard to persuade them to fly the girl out of Singapore when the Court initially ordered that she be placed in their care, but they did not do so, with the results that are now history." During the riots three truck-loads of slogan-shouting rioters drew up at the Tanglin Club. The quick-thinking club secretary Tony Willis, hurriedly shepherded those present into the liquor store below and padlocked the door. Seeing the cars parked outside the rioters burst in to be told by the jagas that all had gone home; infuriated, they smashed up glasses and other club fixtures before finally leaving. As the yelling died away in the distance the members returned home and the club remained closed for three days. The committee decided that a reward of $100 be shared by the three jagas.

A Suitable Baby Grand Was Found

Dancing at the Tanglin Club may not have evoked the same passion after the war as in the thirties, but an immediate concern of the postwar committee had been to locate all of the incomparable Nick's Versatile Six. At first, Tebneff and Koodravsev, still in Singapore, formed a temporary group which included Lammerts and two others and played six nights a week for $2,000 per month. They received an advance of $400 to purchase instruments and $30 to buy sheet music. Great efforts went into finding a piano and a budget of $4,000 was finally approved when a suitable baby grand was found. Dancing past it one evening, Lester Goodman recognised it as his own which had disappeared during the war and re-claimed it. Through advertisements, the Curtis brothers, Cecil and Laurie, were

located in the United Kingdom and were also delighted to return to play in the club band. Tebneff on violin was the band leader with Lammerts on violin and sax-ophone, Koodravsev on clarinet, Laurie on drums and Cecil, who became band leader when Tebneff left in 1951, on piano. Another decade of musical enter-tainment was ushered in with the now renamed Tanglin Club Band. On one oc-casion the Curtis brothers submitted their resignation which caused such consterna-tion that members willingly accepted an increase in the monthly subscriptions to pay for them to stay. Various changes in the band occurred as members took leave; Tairoff, who had been with Radio Malaya's orchestra for some time, joined as a full-timer in 1951, and when Tebneff resigned Kleinmann and Moran stepped

in. Occasionally the club hosted special band benefit nights to augment their wages and leave fares, and salary condi-tions were maintained by the provision of a band kitty fund, later called the band passage fund, into which fees from out-side engagements were lodged. The band continued to be in demand at other venues, notably at the RAF Officers' Club

"Mr. Kinsey referred to complaints re-ceived that the Band played too much South American music and he would in-struct them to play fewer sambas and rhumbas. He had also stressed this point in his recent letter to the Curtis brothers. He would also cut out the Mexican Shuf-fle as it might damage the supports to the floor, and the Tango which few members could dance." [Committee meeting Au-gust 27, 1951.] "Mr. Shepherd reviewed various complaints regarding the perfor-mance of the Band and illustrated how difficult it was to suit all tastes. It was agreed that the type of music played by the Band should be more lively and that a little Scottish dance music might be re-in-troduced." [Committee meeting June 26, 1961.] [Above: Cecil and Laurie, 1950's — T.C.; Left: band in costume, New Year's Eve ball, 1956 — T.C.]

at Changi, and for studio recordings. At a committee meeting on March 28, 1955, "Mr. Henton tabled a letter from Mr. Coupland of The Gramophone Co. Ltd. asking permission to engage the Band to record in their Studios. The Band were agreeable to do this subject to the Club's normal 'Outside Engagement' terms...." The club refused, however, to allow band members to give music lessons on the premises. Substitute bands like the Royal Hampshire Dance Band and the Noone Collars Band also appeared during this period.

The Curtis brothers performed until their retirement from Singapore in 1958. Tairoff, the new band leader, Koodravsev and Lammerts were joined by Gomes from the Cockpit Hotel on piano, Topaz from the Seaview Hotel on drums, and Krempl on double bass and piano. The band now appeared in a new uniform of grey coats with maroon bow-ties and handkerchiefs. At a Wednesday dance on August 26, 1959, Ruby Wah made her début as a singer and was acclaimed as 'quite fantastic.' With her mother always in attendance as chaperone, she performed at the club until her farewell night on April 27, 1963. Later that year, when a new era was proclaimed, "a letter was tabled from Radio Singapore requesting the services of Mr. Tairoff, the Band Leader, between 9:30 P.M. and 10:30 P.M. on the night of August 30, 1963, the eve of the birth of Malaysia. This was granted." [Meeting August 2, 1963.] Many singers and performers have been on the club stage but the Tanglin Club Band under Curtis and later Tairoff is still remembered as about the finest.

Singer Ruby Wah entertains, 1950's — T.C.

Charleston ball, 1956 — T.C.

The Best Possible In Modern Bad Taste

More than thirty years after its publication, there is still a waiting list at the club library for *A Lion in the Sun*, a Singapore-based romantic drama by former club member Gerry M. Glaskin, in which the Tanglin Club is characterised as a charming place of old-world atmosphere where the "modern comfort of air-conditioning had been installed... with the interior décor in... about the best possible in modern bad taste. An enormous bar curved in and out like seclusive bays, around which members clustered in groups as though each curve of the bar was a semi-circular table, a convenient arrangement until the club was overcrowded (as inevitably it was later in the evening) and people were ... three and four deep. [There were] reading and billiard rooms, the squash courts and swim-ming pool... where the mems and missies planned luncheons, coffee mornings, bridge-mornings, mah-jongg mornings, charity fêtes and bazaars, tea parties in the afternoons, more cocktails and din-ners, and dining-and-dancing for future evenings.

"After an excellent dinner, we danced to the music of the orchestra which played on a dais with walls made into the shape of a feinted shell. There were five or six in the orchestra altogether. When I had first heard them, I had quite enjoyed their music; but by this time I had come to realise that their repertoire was rather re-stricted. After several evenings at the club, one came to know exactly what time it was by the tunes they were play-ing, most of them resurrected from the era shortly after the First World War. After

Fondly remembered gala occasions of the colonial period in the fifties and sixties such as elaborate fiestas, cabarets and theme parties, include the Balinese, Latin Quarter and lido nights, February fiestas, Grand National and Derby nights and scavenger hunts — all enthusiastically or-ganised by members. At the Easter dinner fashion parade members were 'expected to wear their smarter clothes' while models from Ruth Warner's modelling agency showed the latest styles; on at least one occasion this was compèred by Johnnie Johnson, swimming instructor and pio-neer of the coralarium at Sentosa with Jack Fisher. [Above & left: February Fiesta, 1955 — T.C.; Opposite page, top: February Fiesta, 1955 — T.C.; left: Easter Fashion Parade, April, 1958 — T.C.; right: Hugo Pigou, February Fiesta, 1955 — T.C.]

such old-time tunes as 'Show Me the Way to Go Home', 'Little Black-Eyed Susan' and 'If You Know Susie' it was almost a shock to hear a comparatively modern number like 'Goodnight, Sweetheart' wind up the evening before 'The King' brought everyone to a stiff, chest-pointing standstill. Then with either the hauteur of aristocracy departing from a court ball, or the buffoonery of public schoolboys at an end-of-term dance, members crowded to the entrance foyer and waited on the brass-railed stairs while their cars were called by numbers in Malay. As the cars drove up one after the other, Malay syces erasing either sleep or the last card-game from their eyes, there were more Goodnights and See-you-soons and Don't-forget-to-call-me-soons.

"Then all who were left in the club were the obstinate hard-drinkers, a bachelor or a grass-widower with his wife 'at home' in the U.K. to look after the children's schooling; a few desperate couples determined not to finish the evening without a frolic in the swimming pool, with much chaff and splashing and horseplay, declared intentions about sex and bodies that never went further than bawdy remarks. Then there were the silent boys impassively clearing the tables and bar and the dance floor — duties they had commenced with the playing of 'Goodnight, Sweetheart', ignoring the National Anthem as something that, at best, was symbolic of things too remote and alien to have any meaning for them, or, at the worst, a symbol of a wealthy and privileged race that, though once ruling over them like conquerors, had only recently restored themselves after defeat and subjugation by the Japanese."

Christmas ball, 1950's — Courtesy of Arnold and Sue Thorne

During the fifties the club consolidated its finances and continued to build up membership. The band was a focal point of attraction; though their wages and salary bill constituted half the expenses of the club, members considered the price worth it. By September 1950 membership stood at 1,309 ordinary members — including 13 life and honorary members — and the waiting list was temporarily closed for the first time since the war. In June 1952 the committee decided it was time to withdraw the facility of permitting pre-war members to rejoin the club without election and on payment of an absentee fee of $25. Later, ordinary members' monthly subscriptions went up to $10, service members' to $10 and lady members' to $3 to offset the cost of the club's projects and renovations; up-country members had to pay $18 per annum.

...hankies tied on the backs of chairs... In September 1950 additional attractions for members included the Tanglin Trio which provided light orchestral music at lunch-time. The younger members subcommittee, formed in 1951 to run entertainment programmes, enjoyed their first success with a leap year dance in February 1952. On a Sunday night in January 1953 a new form of entertainment was initiated — not quite in the tradition of smoking

Decoration of the club for special occasions was the responsibility of the ladies subcommittee. A regular arrangement with Qantas Airways ensured a supply of fresh flowers for the ballroom as needed; these were flown into Singapore the previous night, stored in the refrigerators and, as the evening of the ball progressed, the blooms would open, releasing their perfume into the tropical night air. At the 1953 AGM, "Mr. K.D. Matthewson asked whether it would not be better for the Ladies Committee to be elected. Mr. Kemlo explained that the Ladies Committee was purely an advisory committee and had no executive power. It was the tradition to leave the choosing of her Ladies Committee to the new President's wife, who was automatically chairman. He hesitated to suggest telling the chairman whom she should choose." At the earlier 1951 AGM, in reply to a question from "Mr. MacDougal whether Lady Members were entitled to vote, the President replied that they were not entitled to vote, nor were wives, Service Members or Ordinary Members whose accounts were not in credit. (Loud laughter.)" [In 1974 the sole female candidate for the Tanglin Club committee was proposed at the AGM when Inez Quitzow, a life member — and therefore eligible for nomination irrespective of sex — stood unsuccessfully for election.] [The Tanglin Club Band, early 1950's — Courtesy of Arnold and Sue Thorne]

concerts or gramophone parties — which brought a new technology and recreation into the club. Four hundred and fifty members turned up to watch *Kind Hearts and Coronets* and *The Years Between*. Despite the crowd and heat — it was necessary to turn off the fans, which drowned the soundtrack — the cinema's popularity was such that it became necessary to reserve seating by a hanky tied on the back of the chair. Socially, the club was humming, so much so that the superintendent of police had to write to the president complaining about members' syces sounding their automobile horns on Wednesday and Saturday nights in the vicinity of the club in contravention of the Sounding of Horn Rules 1950, which prohibited sounding horns between 6 P.M. and 6 A.M. in the municipal area. Within the clubhouse, however, decorum was upheld : "A request from Mr. J. Stogden to hold a [Old Harrovian] party in the Club on Friday, July 9 was accepted, subject to the usual terms, and to use the piano provided there were no bawdy songs." [Committee meeting June 8, 1954.] Stringent standards of discretion continued to be the order of the day. "A letter was tabled from Mrs. Doris Geddes complaining of the Secretary's letter regarding her introduction of two visitors to the Club one Sunday night [during a dance competition]. It transpired that her 'visitors' were a professional dancing couple currently engaged at Raffles Hotel [and therefore, according to club rules, deemed Singapore residents] . The Committee upheld the Secretary's view that they could not be termed as genuine visitors." [Committee meeting February 28, 1955.]

From the mid-1950's concerted efforts had to be made to attract members to the club on Friday and Saturday nights to counter the cut-throat competition from the smart new establishments springing up in Singapore which offered dining and cabaret shows in the early part of the evening. Following the reopening of the club after the war, contract catering was used, the club taking a commission of 12.5 per cent on the first $6000 and 15 per cent on profit in excess of that, but the system was a failure. Various efforts to improve the restaurant facilities were made, including the employment of a succession of stewards and caterers — Fernando from the E & O Hotel in Penang, Miss de Mornay of Robinson's Catering Service and Jacobs, a professional chef from the Capitol Restaurant. Expert opinion was sought from De Vries, manager of the Capitol, and Gachnang, superintendent of the Singapore Club. For years, the Tanglin Club restaurant subcommittee confronted problems caused by acquisitive cooks and dubious accounting, with supplies purchased on club credit and resold for profit on the side, and difficulties on the part of senior staff in maintaining discipline. The issue, a continuing thorn for the club, was resolved in December 1951 when George Goldsack, whose reputation had been established at the Runnymede and Europe hotels, assumed the position of restaurant manager on a salaried basis of $800 per month including free meals and accommodation on the club premises. About this time, Mrs. Dorothy Dee, a previous housekeeper, returned and took charge of the daily

"Mr. Craig informed the Committee of the damage and filth caused by the cats in the Club during the strike. It was unanimously decided that the entire cat population of the Club must be eliminated." [Committee meeting December 2, 1962.]

running of the club. In addition to being housekeeper, 'Mem' Dee also supervised the kitchen in the absence of the manager, the security patrols and the gardens, and was also the assistant secretary until her retirement in 1964. In March 1954 dining facilities were transformed with the engagement of Guilio Giacomo Attias, who had worked previously at the E & O Hotel in Penang and at Raffles Hotel, as club steward. All internal staff except clerks, tambies and amahs were under his supervision. The restaurant atmosphere improved enormously, the quality of the food was immediately better and the staff increasingly efficient; though sadly lacking in keeping good accounts, Attias was extremely popular and well-liked for his personal service until he left in 1964. Robert Lim Jew Kum then became food and beverage manager, leaving in 1981.

...one cook had stabbed another... During the last part of the 1950's the situation of labour unrest in Singapore became more pronounced. Recalling a Saturday evening of chaos in the kitchen, Tony Willis, who occupied the club bungalow near the tennis courts, recounted: "I was laid low with mumps and in bed when Attias telephoned to say that one cook had stabbed another and there was chaos in the kitchen so could I come over. My wife said certainly not, so I suggested that Mr. Donald McKenzie, Committee Member (Catering) be called. So Don McKenzie went over to the Club and found bedlam in the kitchen, blood everywhere, cooks and 'boys' shouting, police arresting the attacker, ambulancemen carrying off the victim. In the midst of all the turmoil, Attias turned to Don McKenzie and said: Sir, we are getting terribly short of waiter trays, would you order some more!" In October 1960, after the industrial arbitration court was set up to abolish labour exploitation through freely negotiated collective agreements, the threat of strike action by the staff was averted by negotiation. The following year the club decided that the union demands were unreasonable and, despite negotiation with the ministry of labour, failed to reach a compromise. *The Straits Times* of March 17, 1962, informs: "About 110 employees of the Tanglin Club in Stevens Road went on strike... the second within a week. The employees, members of the Singapore Catering Services and Workers Trade Union, walked out just before 4 P.M. The union yesterday had served the club with a 24-hour strike ultimatum to settle its claims for more pay and better terms of service." The strike continued for 109 days, until July 1, 1962, and a pattern of demand and negotiation was set that has continued to dominate staff relations to the present day.

Mr Attias, New Year's Eve, 1955 — T.C.

133

Busy Condemning Colonialism

On September 22, 1951, Singapore was proclaimed a city. The Royal Charter conferring city status was presented to T.P.F. McNeice, the president of the municipal council which, thenceforth, became the city council. In April 1948 a legislative council had replaced the advisory council established in 1945, though both the 1948 and 1951 elections resulted in only token local representation in the council without affecting British colonial control. In October 1953 the British colonial office appointed a constitutional commission headed by Sir George Rendel which, in February 1954, recommended a legislative assembly of thirty-two members, twenty-five of which would be elected for a 4-year term; of the other seven members, three would be British officials and four would be unofficials nominated by the governor. Control of external affairs, defence, internal security, the civil service, finance and law would still remain in British hands. In his introduction to *From Early Days*, the story of the Singapore International Chamber of Commerce, Alex Josey, a Tanglin Club member from 1947, writes, "the last Chamber member to sit on the Legislative Council was Sir Ewen Fergusson. He served from 1946 until 1955. Though the Chamber's privilege to elect a representative was abolished, the Rendel Constitution made provision for the governor to nominate unelected representatives. A British businessman, a banker, Mr G.A.P. Sutherland, served briefly in the last session of the old Legislative Council. He held no mandate from any person or group. He said he considered himself spokesman for all expatriates in Singa-

"Tanglin Club is a purely social Club and it is inadvisable, at the present time, that it should be associated in anyone's mind with a political body as this could be a potential source of embarrassment. After some discussion Mr. A.F. Thorne, who is also President of the British European Association, informed the Committee that he would make arrangements to hold the BEA Meetings in future at some place other than Tanglin Club." [Committee meeting July 29, 1957.] [BFA barbecue at the Tanglin Club, April 1960 — The Beam, May 1961]

pore. In the heat of debate he was sometimes referred to, by contending politicians, all busy condemning colonialism, as the Member for the Tanglin Club, (then an exclusive expatriates club), a description which Sutherland found offensive, and he sought the protection of the speaker. Sutherland welcomed self-government, but deplored the unseemly haste. He warned that the constitutional crisis which had been created, 'while

providing something of a spectacle and ephemeral fame for our orators,' was doing Singapore and its trade, 'which is the life-blood of the place,' no good at all. Sutherland did not speak for the Chamber, but there were many apprehensive members of the Chamber who shared his view. Fortunately the crisis did not last long, and trade soon picked up again."

In the run-up to the elections for the legislative assembly scheduled for April 1955 new political parties were formed. In late 1954 the Labour Front, led by David Marshall, stood for immediate independence and merger with Malaya. In November 1954 the People's Action Party committed itself to the removal of British colonialism and the establishment of an independent non-communist Malaya, including Singapore. In February 1955 some members of the Singapore Chinese Chamber of Commerce founded the Democratic Party. The elections on April 2 resulted in a Labour Front victory; David Marshall, Singapore's first native-born chief minister, formed a coalition government with the United Malay National Organisation-Malayan Chinese Association alliance. Having fought with the Volunteers during World War II, Marshall now entered a different fray as he battled the colonial government over respective powers.

In October 1955 emergency regulations were replaced by the Preservation of Public Security Ordinance; until 1959 the governments of first Marshall, then Lim Yew Hock faced serious challenges from the communist united front in the form of communist-instigated strikes and student unrest. Of the nearly four hundred strikes

during this period barely one-third were in support of better working conditions and wages; the rest were sympathy strikes or demands for the release of detained trade union leaders. The insurgency of the 1950's also involved a spate of violent acts in Singapore starting with the attempted assassination of the governor Sir Franklin Gimson in April 1950. Later a rubber factory was destroyed, transport disrupted and vehicles burnt; subversive materials were found in some Chinese schools. In October 1956 British and Gurkha troops were brought in from Johore to help put down the riots in the communist-led campaign of agitation. At the Tanglin Club a concern for security measures led to several suggestions by the police that the perimeter fencing be improved. There must have been much nervousness in the club as the British

business community was running scared of a possible communist takeover in Singapore. The British European Association, later the British Association of Singapore, was conceived in 1956 primarily as a form of European self-protection in light of the changing political and economic situation. A contemporary club president, Arnold Thorne, drafted the aims and objectives of the association and was chairman from 1956 to 1959.

In April 1956 the Merdeka Talks for full internal self-government were held in London and, after the failure of this mission, Marshall resigned. A second round of constitutional talks was held in March 1957; in April 1958 a third all-party mission went to London and on 28 May an agreement was finally signed which provided for a constitution for a state of Singapore with full powers of internal

The Coronation Ball on Wednesday June 3, 1953, was a grand affair celebrated by 400 members. Ten thousand dollars was spent on decorations alone, which included vistas of London and caricatures of committee members prepared by Barbara Fairbanks (wife of club member Gough) assisted by a subcommittee. There were divided opinions over the dress code for the occasion with one group insisting it should be formal — tails, mess kit or shell jackets — and the other that it should be evening dress. Eventually a compromise was reached allowing both, but recommending formal attire if possible. There were many counter-attractions in Singapore, both European and Asian, arranged for the Coronation week. The Tanglin Club organised a gala ball, a dance, a children's party and swimming gala, an international cocktail party for members and guests (including Asian friends), and a party for children of staff members. On the night of Tuesday June 2, Coronation Day, the Tanglin Club Band played at the Government House ball; they were also booked for the Royal Golf Club ball on Friday. [Coronation decorations at the Tanglin Club, 1953 — T.C.]

self-government. In August 1958 the British parliament changed the status of the island from a colony to a state. In the general elections of June 1959, assisted by its role in the running of the city council, the People's Action Party (PAP) led by Lee Kuan Yew was victorious and on June 5, 1959, the 36-year-old Lee was sworn in as prime minister. The new government faced formidable problems; serious un-employment, an acute housing shortage, a need to implement an education policy, concern with external affairs and a need to industrialize were all matters of para-mount concern as the government sought to attract foreign multi-national invest-ments to the island. In July 1961 the $30-million Shell oil refinery, the first in Singapore, was opened on Pulau Bukum.

The political events of the years 1961-65 concerned the proposed federation of Malaysia constituted by Malaya, Singa-pore, British North Borneo, Sarawak and Brunei. In February 1962 a commission of inquiry found that a majority in British North Borneo and Sarawak were in fa-vour of joining Malaysia. In Singapore, a government white paper issued on No-vember 16, 1961, spelt out the terms of power and status within the federation. Finally on July 6, 1962, the referendum bill containing three options for merger was passed in the legislative assembly and on September 2, 1962, 90 per cent of the

624,000 registered citizens voted, with 71 per cent in favour of the PAP merger option. The Malaysia Agreement was concluded in July 1963 and the Federation of Malaysia scheduled to come into being on August 31, 1963; the prime minister Tunku Abdul Rahman decided to defer implementation of the agreement to Sep-tember 16 because of objections on the part of Indonesia's President Sukarno who saw the federation as a menace to his concept for a united Malay world and had initiated an armed confrontation against the new entity on January 20, 1963. The three-year campaign brought physical vi-olence, the seizure of Singapore fishing boats, bomb explosions, and damage to trade links with Indonesians. The task of dealing with Indonesian attacks and ha-rassment was mainly undertaken by Brit-ish forces which numbered about 50,000 men at the height of the confrontation and also successfully deterred aggression on a larger scale.

On August 31, 1963, Lee declared Singapore's freedom unilaterally and, in the fifteen days before merger, called a snap election. The result looked doubtful as the PAP had lost much of the mass support it commanded in 1959. It had, however, achieved its main political goals of independence from colonial rule and merger with the federation. It had also brought material benefits to large num-bers of people in the form of a better livelihood and some redistribution of na-tional income through social services, housing, education, health facilities, and relatively peaceful industrial relations. A network of community centres which be-came important instruments of govern-ment and consolidated PAP power also provided recreation facilities, literacy

"The President reported that a delay had occurred in the supply of the pictures of the Yang Di Pertuan Agong and the Raja Permaisuri Agong, due to printing diffi-culties in Kuala Lumpur. A delay of ap-proximately 3 months was expected. As soon as the pictures were received they would be framed and hung in the Foyer. The Yang Di Pertuan Negara's picture will be hung in the Ballroom and that of Her Majesty The Queen in the Reading Room." [Committee meeting October, 28, 1963.]

classes, wireless and television, the latter launched on February 15, 1963, for the masses (the government controlled all broadcasting). The election result was a clear victory for the PAP, the first Singa-pore election to swing away from the Left, and the political situation in Singapore appeared more stable than at any time since 1955. Lee promised to turn Singa-pore into the "New York of Malaysia, the industrial base of an affluent and just society." However, relations with the central Malaysian government were a growing source of concern. In the context of industrialisation, Singapore, with its lack of resources, was unwilling to aban-don its free port status while the rest of the federation was reluctant to lower tariff barriers to competition from Singa-pore industry. Despite a promise not to contest the 1964 federal elections, the PAP changed tactics and entered Malay-sian federal politics, an intervention which eventually proved fatal to Singapore's membership in the Federation of Malaysia.

"Our President, Mr Justice Knight, has asked... that I read his speech: Ladies & Gentlemen — In the first place I must say how very sorry I am not to be with you tonight but what with 'Merdeka' and 'Malayanisation' it would appear that my future in Singapore is very far from secure and it has thus become necessary that I should hawk my rapidly decaying charms around the city of London as soon as possible, in the hopes of persuading some misguided chap to give me a job." [Vice-president E.I. Henton at the 1957 AGM.]

'Polo' Prockter, the governor Sir Robert Black and Eric Henton, Tanglin ball, 1957 — T.C.

Throughout the postwar colonial years, the annual Tanglin Club ball continued its tradition as a major highlight in Singapore's social diary. According to Ken Gould, before such gala occasions the old ballroom structure had to be inspected by engineers to certify that it was sound and strong enough to withstand the strains which enthusiastic members were sure to impose. Tony Willis recalled that in the early fifties it was a wonderful sight to behold some very elegant well-dressed lady members sweeping into the ballroom decked out in their gowns and party finery; the men donned their full dinner or mess dress, minus decorations. Running the length of the ballroom were long dining tables, colourfully decorated with floral centrepieces and trimmings along the edges. During the colonial years the governor and his wife were by tradition the guests-of-honour. The programme was ritualistic in its consistency; members arrived by 10 P.M. and at 10:15 P.M. the guests of honour were met at the bottom of the red-carpeted stairs by the club president and the rest of the committee. Despite the air of formality it was never a dull affair; dancing and drinking went on into the wee hours of the morning ending with a breakfast. For a few dollars, about 500 members had an evening to remember. The Tanglin Club's New Year's Eve ball, another members only affair, enjoyed a more colourful tradition. For as far back as members remember, it had been a fancy dress extravaganza with good music, an enormous cold buffet and, after midnight, a hearty supper of bacon and eggs, sausages, or even kippers. At 11 P.M. the parade would

'Bugis' Street, 1950's — Courtesy of Nizar Ahamed

start, with the judges meticulously scrutinising each participant for the awarding of prizes for the best dressed lady and gentleman, as well as for the most original fancy dress for individuals and couples. In later years the parade became increasingly elaborate as members turned up in entire troupes, sometimes of ten or more people, prompting the introduction of team entries. Even the band entered into the spirit of things dressed as jesters, scholars, coolies and Santas.

...weird signatures on the chits... The New Year's Eve ball reached its peak years in the mid-1950's when, as the notion of fancy dress grew to include stage props, it was common practice for spectators to line Stevens Road to view the parade as members entered the club. In 1956 the parade before the judges became so congested that the organisers had to introduce traffic control: teams were called first, one at a time, to cross the ballroom, followed by couples, then individuals. As space was extremely limited, those with extensive properties had to remove them to the back garden or swimming pool area immediately after their presentation was over. The judges were staggered by the breath-taking presentations which included Napoleon and his Court, Anna and the King of Siam and The Vikings complete with longboat. In 1964 the first prize went to a cricket team, King Willow, which had participants dressed as cricket positions. There was no shortage of original entries, like the team which walked onto the dance floor — two ladies dressed in bright orange stood at either side while the rest,

Judges at the New Year's Eve ball, 1956 — T.C.

dressed alternately in all-black and all-white, lay down on the floor on their backs — as a zebra crossing. As to be expected, with the increased time taken for the judging over the years, the organisers were always hard-pressed to finish before midnight brought in the new year. Predictably, staff would be faced with weird signatures on the chits, such as Tarzan, King Tut and various other characters to be seen during the evening. Eventually, the committee would have to issue appeals to members to own up so that billings could be made out. Numerous long-standing members still regret the demise of those 'real' fancy dress evenings.

...resenting this tyranny of the tie... At a meeting on August 25, 1952, "Mr. Clark reported that a Service member ... had deliberately refused to put on a coat after 8 P.M. on Friday, August 22 after he had been approached by the Head Boy and later by himself and that considerable embarrassment had been caused." Throughout the 1950's the club's dress code was continually broken by a small number of members; typically, the secretary was requested to write to transgressors who were seen dancing in day dress on Saturday nights despite the bye-law that evening dress was essential. Gentlemen were reminded in the monthly circulars that they and their guests must wear coats and ties in the cocktail bar, restaurant, ballroom, reading room and lounge after 8 P.M. Tanglin Club member Mary Cowe was embarrassed on one occasion when the manager tapped her on the shoulder as she was dancing with a partner who was smartly dressed in a lounge suit and tie and requested that she leave the floor with her 'improperly attired' guest. In 1959, on his last visit, enroute to Japan for the opening of an exhibition in his honour in 1959, Somerset Maugham found Singapore greatly changed and felt a stranger in the place to which he was so mythically linked. His parting shot at the Tanglin Club, where the manager of the Raffles Hotel had taken him for a drink, was occasioned by "a fuss that he was 'improperly dressed' in his bush jacket and Maugham, resenting this tyranny of the tie, gazed contemptuously over his glass at the assembled company; in a voice pitched high enough for everyone to hear, he declared: Observing these people, I am no longer surprised that there is such a scarcity of domestic servants back home in England." In the 1960's the sartorial standards of the Tanglin Club began to clash with the dictates of fashion, style and culture. Committee members held different views on the subject of the ladies' dress code, a matter which gave many headaches to one later president who ruled that trouser-suits — which included Asian national dress — no matter how elegant, were unacceptable.

Their Skill In Pouring Tea

In the minutes of the first postwar AGM in 1947, the first matter to be addressed by the president Freddie Kemlo concerned nationality and membership: a local newspaper had advocated internationalising the club, criticizing its restricted membership. Although Kemlo favoured an international club, "he failed to see why this club should be selected, pointed out that other communities have their exclusive clubs, and emphasised that the restriction of membership of this club to Europeans in no way denotes any lack of respect or affection for our Asiatic or Eurasian friends." He suggested, however, that members should consider seriously the question of the introduction of guests of different nationalities. On the question of vetting members it was proposed, in a committee meeting on March 7, 1949, that "in future the wives of applicants for Membership of this Club should attend with their Husbands on Election Committee Night, and that any Member marrying

"It was decided to invite to become Honorary Members the following gentlemen: Lord Killearn (Special Commissioner for S.E.A.), Mr. Malcolm MacDonald (Governor-General, Malayan Union and Singapore), Sir Edward Gent (Governor, Malayan Union), Sir Franklin Gimson (Governor, Singapore), Mr. P.A.B. McKerron (Colonial Secretary, Singapore), Mr. Justice C.M. Murray-Aynsley (Chief Justice, Singapore), Maj. General L.H. Cox (G.O.C. Singapore)." [Committee meeting August 9, 1946.]

after election should seek re-election. A Married Member who applies for Membership before his wife arrives in the Colony should present his Wife to the Election Committee at the first meeting of that Committee after her arrival in the Colony." The ladies subcommittee played a not insignificant role in interviewing the wives of prospective members, 'more to check the colour of their skin than their skill in pouring tea,' remarked a ladies subcommittee chairman of the fifties. After the war, it is rumoured, a Eurasian lady was made member of the Tanglin Club so that she could spot any candidates of mixed race who might try to pass themselves off as European. In *This Was Singapore* Ronald McKie informs, "the Eurasian is not allowed into the four main white clubs in Singapore, and I doubt whether he would want to enter them; he is seldom seen in any of the three big hotels....The European who marries a Eurasian is ostracized....He will probably keep his membership of European clubs, but his wife will not be allowed into them and will not be accepted or invited to the homes of his European friends or business associates."

In August 1946 the committee had addressed the question of Indian officers applying for service membership and decided that, while no rule could be made to prohibit this, proposed applicants should be informed that they were likely to be the only Asiatic members of the club. On May 5, 1947, the committee recorded the view "that there should be no objection to the introduction of Asiatics as guests on the less popular evenings provided that adequate safeguards could

"Mr. Gransden warned the General Committee that the Election Sub-Committee should be asked to exercise the greatest care in the election of candidates to the Club. Agreed." [Committee meeting December 29, 1952.]

be introduced to control the number and quality introduced." In September 1948 the question of Asian guests was raised again and answered to the effect that there was "nothing whatever which prevented an Asian Lady or Gentleman being introduced into the Club as Guests, nor indeed for Membership. The Committee has carefully checked the Rules, including the Secretary's Copy of the old Pre-War Rules, where no evidence could be found which has the intention of excluding Asian Guests." In October 1948 "it was agreed that there was no objection to any Asian Lady or Gentleman being introduced as Guests under the Orders for Guests, and that there was nothing in that rule which was new." At a committee meeting on January 23, 1950, "arising out of an enquiry by a member, it was held that there was no objection to an Asian Guest of a member using the Swimming Pool on a Guest Day."

In 1946 Malcolm MacDonald, the Commissioner-General of Malaya, had come to Singapore and found only a small minority who felt that the Chinese, for example, with their ancient civilisation could be regarded as absolute equals. In John Drysdale's *Struggle for Success* he discloses: "I knew it was going to be

A section of the Chandelier Room and bar, 1954 — T.C.

something like that but it was much worse than I thought... [non-whites] couldn't even join the Tanglin Club and so on, and this was one of the other things which I was determined to do everything I could to stop," an attitude evidently held in contempt by many of his compatriots; Mac-Donald did not accept the offer of honorary membership at the Tanglin Club. Drysdale also interviewed Tan Sri Tan Chin Tuan, a former chief executive of the Overseas Chinese Banking Corporation and a senior unofficial of the exec-

"The Committee take great pleasure in recording the gift by Mr. W.L. Clark of a portrait of Her Majesty The Queen. The portrait has been hung in the Main Lounge." [Committee meeting 1952.]

utive and legislative councils in the 1950's, who related an occasion when Sir Franklin Gimson had invited him, the Chinese consul-general and their wives to dinner at Government House. After dinner, it was suggested that they attend a function at the Tanglin Club which had been given due notice of the governor's impending arrival together with his guests. "When we walked in, we saw eyebrows raised at the presence of non-Europeans in the governor's party. Subsequently, the committee had the temerity to write to the governor to point out his contravention of the bye-laws of their club. Since then, I have never been to the club and when the racial restriction was removed, declined one of the first invitations to join it." The minutes of an October 1946 meeting at the club referring to this particular occasion read, "there is no Rule prohibiting the introduc-

tion of Chinese guests; that traditionally it has never been the custom of the Club to introduce such guests; that the Election Committee had expressed the view that an application for membership by an Asiatic would be unlikely to succeed; that the Committee would deprecate the introduction of such guests until the principle has been authorised by a General Meeting of Members." At the 1959 AGM "Mr. B.R. Lowick asked if the Committee was departing from its past practice by permitting the introduction of Associate Members. Mr. Thorne replied that there was nothing in the Rules precluding other nationalities from joining the Club — in fact there were many non-British members — and the question of regularising the rules for the election of non-British members was now under discussion by the Meeting."

Commentators on the social world of the British in their pre-war colonies have observed that institutions like the Shanghai Club, Selangor Club and Tanglin Club provided an exclusive setting for the intercourse of those in positions of power. "In spite of the pretence of equality among members, there was an end of every long bar that was tacitly reserved for taipans and tuans, and here the exchanges of views and the veiled negotiations which affected the commercial and political policies governing colonies and concessions would often be transacted," comments George Woodcock in *The British in the Far East*. In *Tropic Temper* James Kirkup discloses his feelings: "though the Selangor Club now admits non-whites — which is why it is known as 'The Spotted Dog' — it still has, for me, a heavy atmosphere of colonial privilege. I would rather not belong to it for that reason. Yesterday afternoon, I walked down past the padang where the club was crowded with mems eating and smoking and nattering, watching their menfolk, in long white baggy shorts, punting a football about. There were also some Indians playing hockey, in vivid turbans. And some Malays, looking bird-frail beside the elephantine whites."

From its founding, the Tanglin Club embodied a complex of attitudes representing the most powerful interests and elements of the British population in the colony. By the end of the 1950's this exclusiveness had aroused some bitterness among Asians and the reluctance of the club to open its membership to all became a political issue. In his *Struggle For Success* Drysdale observes that for most members of the Tanglin Club at that time, a national or racial exclusivity in the form of a social club was seen as legal, enjoyable and wholly desirable as providing a meeting place for people with a similar cultural heritage. "Indeed, many members would have probably been distressed if they had learned that injury could be caused to the pride of non-members, as would be the case if unreasonable objections were advanced for the admittance of members' guests on the grounds such as racial discrimination." In 1950 Pandit Nehru visited Singapore and was given honorary membership of the Tanglin Club. J.L.M. 'Mike' Gorrie, a later member who was then private secretary to the governor, Sir Franklin Gimson, assisted the club in its liaison with this distinguished visitor.

Before political considerations in the wake of independence eventually led to the statutory opening of membership at the Tanglin Club, changed perceptions of certain features of colonial society were increasingly voiced. In *Struggle For Success* R.W. 'Bob' Lutton, an affectionately remembered chairman of the board of governors of the United World College, reflected on the transformation of his own attitudes. On his arrival in Singapore in 1955 to join Union Rubber Brokers he had believed in the general superiority of English institutions, but after about two years began to realise that England was not the fount of all that was good in the world: "I joined the Cricket Club, more or less the first day I arrived. I joined the Tanglin Club several years later, largely through embarrassment. I had been taken there as a guest so often that the 'boys' were bringing me the chit. But I did not like the Tanglin Club at that stage: I think perhaps it represented my general feeling. I enjoyed being in Singapore but I don't think I would have stayed in Singapore under a colonial society for anything like as long as I have." At the Tanglin Club, the stirrings of a different outlook were also being acknowledged. In a committee meeting on July 29, 1963, "Mr. Craig reminded the Committee that at the last meeting, Mr. Caldicott had suggested that the Tanglin Ball as such be discontinued and a Malaysia Ball be substituted and it had been agreed that the Committee should give this their serious consideration.... Mr. Caldicott explained his reasons for suggesting such a change in that circumstances had changed considerably. The Club was no longer a purely British Club and to change the Tanglin Ball to a Malaysia Ball would in his opinion be an encouragement to Asian Members. He considered that the Tanglin Ball was a symbol of colonialism and therefore an anachronism."

"The President referred to the incident on the night of Thursday, December 3, when a member, Mr. P.H.B. Dowson, had roughly handled Mr. Attias and two members of the Band for not playing the new State Anthem. In view of the incident mentioned above instructions had been given the following day to the Band Leader to play the State Anthem as well as 'The Queen' and this had been done every night from December 4 onwards. Mr Henton said that he had raised the question of playing the two Anthems and flying the two Flags with the U.K. Commissioner's Office who stated that although The Queen had approved the State Flag and Anthem no rules had yet been promulgated. The Commissioner's Office said there was no compulsion to fly the State Flag or play the Anthem but they thought it would be a courteous and civil gesture to do so. It was decided that as a courtesy to the State the opening bars of the State Anthem should be played every night followed by the first half of 'The Queen'. It was also agreed to continue flying the State Flag and the Union Jack at the entrance to the Club until further notice." [Committee meeting December 7, 1959.]

The last significant event in the years leading to the centenary of the Tanglin Club in 1965 concerned the opening of membership. Although the rules of the Tanglin Club did not specifically deny membership on the grounds of race, in practice the club was British. In 1959 the elected government decided to eliminate the advantage enjoyed by citizens of the United Kingdom and British colonies in their eligibility for Singapore citizenship. An amended citizenship bill passed in May 1960 disallowed dual nationality and made the period of residence to qualify for Singapore citizenship eight years for all applicants, including British subjects.

...in a reasonable time... Late in 1962 the government asked all major clubs to achieve at least 50 per cent Singaporean membership as soon as possible. On April 23, 1963, H.F.G. Leembruggen, on behalf of the prime minister, met the president of the club and "requested information regarding a change to the Rules of the Club whereby Asians or any male resident of Singapore could become an Ordinary Member of the Tanglin Club." The change was incorporated into the membership rules, although at the time the club had a total membership of 4,250 and the committee could not guarantee an unlimited intake of new members as facilities were fully extended. At a committee meeting on August 2, 1963, "the Secretary reported that only that afternoon a telephone call had been received from the Prime Minister's Office requesting a break-down of our membership. It was proposed and unanimously agreed that it would be in the Club's interest if a full break-down of Club Members by nationalities was prepared. The Secretary was instructed to arrange for this to be carried and if the new list could not be made available in a reasonable time for the Prime Minister's office, then he should forward the usual list distinguishing between non-Asian and Asian Members." At a meeting on September 30, 1963. "the Secretary submitted details of the present Club membership broken down into nationalities. This showed that there are 22 different nationalities in the Club and that our Asian membership stood at a total of 30 males and females as at 31st August 1963." Among the first Singaporean members to take advantage of the change in membership rules were Dr. Yeo Chee Peng, Tan Eng Han, Koh Eng Yam, U.S. Chan and C.K. Sng; of the Singaporeans who had joined prior to 1963, the earliest was Shaw Vee Meng.

1940 1941 GODWIN, Harold S.: Previously listed in Part Three.

[There were no presidents for the years 1942-45.]

1946 1947 1952 KEMLO, Frederick J., (born London) arrived in Singapore in the late 1920's and became chairman of Harrison and Crosfield. Was a recognised authority on rubber marketing and grading and

chairman of the Singapore Chamber of Commerce Rubber Association, 1947; a member of the Raffles College Council, 1947. An amateur actor with the Island Committee which raised funds for the Malaya Patriotic Fund, was considered a versatile and experienced performer in Gilbert and Sullivan productions, especially *HMS Pinafore* and *Yeomen of the Guard*, and played with Noel Coward when the latter was in Singapore; produced *Journey's End*; a regular weekly reader of the midday news bulletin. A few weeks after addressing the 1953 A.G.M. as retiring president, died in the Comet air disaster over Calcutta in May of that year, aged 48 years.

1948 HOPKINS, Hubert Carew, (born 1892, England) entered the service of the Standard Chartered Bank in London in 1912 aged 20 years; transferred to Kuala Lumpur in 1919 and

then Singapore in 1920. Appointed to Hong Kong in 1932 and transferred to Shanghai in 1937 where he was interned in 1943. After liberation returned to Hong Kong, then Singapore where he was a director until his departure in July 1949. 'Hoppy' was a committee member of the Singapore Chamber of Commerce, 1947-48, and also played an important role in the re-establishment of the smelting business in Singapore which had been abused by the Japanese; was in charge of negotiations to de-requisition the Tanglin Club in 1946.

1949 WEST, Jack Victor, came to Singapore in 1934 with Asiatic Petroleum Company (later Shell) and became the chief accountant with Shell after the war. Served on the rent

assessment board, 1947, and as municipal commissioner, 1947.

1950 1953 THORNE, Arnold Forster, (born 1911, Penang) son of a Supreme Court Judge of Singapore and the Federation, joined Donaldson & Burkinshaw in Singapore in 1934. Was

sent to England at age 2 where he remained for schooling at Charterhouse, then Jesus College, Cambridge, before being admitted to the Bar of Lincoln's Inn, 1933. In Australia at outbreak of World War II, he returned to Singapore in January 1942 as a member of the SRAV, was interned at Changi Prison and worked on the 'death railway'.

Long-serving committee member and honorary secretary of the Tanglin Club, 1938; committee member of the Singapore Association; co-founded the British European Association in 1956; assisted in the establishment of Gleneagles Hospital. Retired to England in 1959 and served as a director of the World Wildlife Fund, 1967-76; is a member of the Royal Wimbledon Golf Club.

1951 RUSHWORTH, Eric Dudley, (born 1903, England) arrived in Singapore in 1923 and joined Mansfield & Co., the shipping agent for Alfred Holt Blue Funnel Line. Escaped to Australia

at the surrender of Singapore. Was president of Singapore Automobile Association. Retired to U.K. in 1954.

1954 MASON, John Metcalfe, (born 1908, Klang, Selangor) was the son of John Scott Mason, a district officer who became the British resident in Kelantan, then

the governor of British North Borneo (where he was killed in a riding accident); his mother remarried Sir William Taylor, a governor of the Federated Malay States in 1914. 'Tiny' was educated at Rugby School and Caius College, Cambridge, and came to Singapore in 1933 after working in Penang with Boustead and Co., serving in Kuala Lumpur and Singapore; he became chairman of the Far East in 1955. Joined the R.A.F.V.R. in 1940

and was a P.O.W. in Java throughout World War II. Was a nominated member of the federal legislative council in 1951 and of the Singapore legislative council some years later, and Commandant of the Volunteer Special Constabulary, 1950-58. Committee member of the Singapore Turf Club and a prominent race horse owner in Malaya, Singapore, England and South Africa. Returned to England in 1958 and served on the board of Edward Boustead & Co. Ltd.; also served on the committees of the Rubber Growers' Association and the British Association of Malaya and Singapore, and on the Council of the Malayan Commercial Association — he was president of the latter two. Retired in 1965 to Natal, South Africa.

1955 1958 HENTON, Eric Ivan, (born 1910, Auckland New Zealand) an alumnus of Auckland Grammar School, served as a major of the New Zealand Army during World War II in

the Solomons, Fiji and Italy. Arrived in Singapore in the 1930's and joined the Tanglin Club in 1935. A prominent figure in the insurance industry in Singapore, New Zealand and England, Eric was manager of Great Eastern Life Assurance Co., Singapore, and agent for New Zealand Insurance; retired to the UK in 1960 and resumed work for NZI in London. Pioneered the Tanglin Club weekly teenage dances during the summer holidays in the 1950's; was a president of the Singapore Gun Club and the Ex-Services Association of Singapore; a member of the Singapore Golf Club and a Justice of the Peace.

1956 KNIGHT, Justice Clifford, served as magistrate and later as a puisne judge in several colonies in Africa before arriving in Singapore where he sat on the bench of the Supreme Court for six years until 1958 when he returned to England. Served on committees, tribunals and commissions of inquiry; especially concerned with reformative training and the Prisoners Aid Society, and with his wife assisted the R.S.P.C.A.

1957 CALDERWOOD, Dr. Robert, (born 1909, Glasgow, Scotland) qualified with M.B., Ch.B., D.P.H. and D.P.M. from Glasgow University, arrived in Malaya in 1936 and worked as a health officer in Kuala Lumpur, Ipoh, Cameron Highlands and Penang before coming to Singapore in 1939. Was interned in Changi Prison and arrested by the *Kempeitai* for involvement in obtaining materials for a secret radio (with Sir Robert Scott) and sentenced to solitary confinement; rescued during the Japanese surrender by Dr. Cammie Bain. Subsequently worked in Malacca where his wife, also a doctor, was responsible for maternal and child health programmes. Promoted to officer in charge of the Singapore General Hospital, then chief medical officer, Singapore. Returned to England in 1959 and worked with the ministry of health in Liverpool until retiring in 1974; enjoys golf, bridge, reading and gardening.

1959 PICKERING, John Bryce, (born 1906, Singapore) was educated in England at Westminster School, joined the Eastern staff of Guthrie & Co. in London in 1925 and was posted to Penang in 1927. Married Gwen Griffith-Jones and was in Singapore in 1940-41, but on honeymoon leave in Australia when Singapore fell. Joined the RANVR, served in New Guinea, then seconded to Force 136 in Colombo. Returned to Guthries in Singapore, 1946, appointed a director, 1948 and in 1956 became local chairman and general manager; enjoyed tennis, squash, golf and photography; a member of the Singapore Swimming Club, the Singapore Cricket Club and the Bukit Timah Turf Club; retired to England in 1960.

1960 PARKER, Edward Anselm, (born 1908, England) arrived in Singapore with the army in January 1942, was interned as a P.O.W. and worked on the 'death railway'. 'Tim' returned to England to study law, where he was recruited by Donaldson & Burkinshaw in 1951 to assist the heavy work load resulting from the reconstruction of Singapore. Became a managing partner and retired in 1968 to England.

1961 BUTTROSE, Justice Murray, (born 1903, Australia) graduated from Adelaide University and was admitted to the Supreme Court of South Australia in 1927. Served with the RAEVR, 1940-1945. Began his career in Singapore in 1945 as Legal Adviser, Singapore District, during the British Military Administration after World War II and successfully prosecuted cases before the war crimes tribunals; in 1949 appointed Senior Crown Counsel; in 1951 and 1954 acted as puisne judge and elevated to the High Court bench in 1957. Described by A.P. Godwin, president of the Singapore Advocates and Solicitors Society, on the occasion of his retirement in 1968 as having had a long association with "the administration of justice in Singapore, an association which has extended over a period of change which witnessed the metamorphosis, by a series of interesting, important and legally significant developments, of Singapore into its present status as an independent Republic within the Commonwealth."

1962 HANNAY, William, (born 1910, Scotland) was educated at Fettes Edinburgh, joined Shell and later went east with Boustead & Company in 1933. 'Bill' was a Volunteer and was interned as a P.O.W. on Blakang Mati. Returned to Singapore served in up-country posts and later became chairman of Boustead & Co.; retired in 1963. Joined the club as one of the Hungry Hundred; enjoyed rugby and golf; a president of the Singapore Club and active Rotarian.

1963 CRAIG, John Harcourt, (born 1916, Cheshire, England) arrived in Singapore in December 1938 to joined Guthrie and Company. A member of the Royal Naval Volunteer Reserve, was captured by the Japanese and sent to Siam on the "death railway". Returned to Singapore in April 1946 and still remembers the accommodation at Raffles Hotel — six to a room and dehydrated food. After some months in Ipoh and Penang returned to Singapore; became chairman of Rheem Hume, Singapore, and managing director of Guthries; in 1966 was transferred to the U.S.A. with Rheem then to England with Rheem International. A member of the Institute of Export and fellow of the Institute of Directors; enjoys the theatre and gardening.

1964 SMYTH, Harold Norman, (born 1914, England) joined Alfred Holt & Co. on leaving Liverpool Collegiate School in 1932, then joined Mansfields in Singapore in 1936. Served with the RNVR throughout the war, first on minesweepers and patrol boats in Malaysian waters and later on convoy escorts in the Atlantic. Returned to Mansfields in 1945 and retired as Chairman in 1965. Chairman of Straits Steamship Co. Ltd.; Director of Malaysian Airways Ltd.; member of the Port of Singapore Authority. Lost his wife and a daughter in the 1953 Comet air tragedy. Enjoys swimming and golf and was a member of the Singapore Swimming Club and the Bukit Timah Golf Club.

A WORK OF ART,

A WORK OF TIME

The old and new clubhouses, March 1981 — T.C.

Assembly on the Padang for the First National Day parade, August 9, 1966 — N.A.

When Singapore proclaimed its independence on August 9, 1965, the island still retained its extraordinary role as 'turnstile of the occident and the orient.' To some political commentators, however, Singapore's existence as an independent state defied conventional concepts of politics and economics: a small island with nearly two million people and no mineral or agricultural resources, self-sufficient in neither food nor water and dependent on imported raw materials for its industry, did not seem destined to be viable as an independent state. Taking advantage of the favourable factors in the world economy in the mid-1960's and the island's own strategic location, the government embarked on a concerted export-oriented industrialisation drive; in conjunction with various incentive packages to encourage foreign capital investments and promote skills development, more infrastructural facilities were built and industrial estates created as opportunities for technical training became more widespread. By the end of 1967 the Singapore economy was beginning to reap the results of all these developments, augmented by the resumption of trade with Indonesia, the expansion of exports to Vietnam and increased earnings from tourism.

... you will survive and prosper here for a thousand years...

On July 13, 1966, the prime minister Lee Kuan Yew spoke to civil servants of his vision and aspiration for Singapore; survival, was not the question: "The question is — how well can we survive? What is required is a rugged, resolute, highly trained, highly disciplined community. You create such a community, and you will survive and prosper here for a thousand years. This is a lesson which other nations have learnt and which I hope we will learn in time." In August 1966 the governments of Singapore and Malaysia decided to have separate currencies; Singapore opted for a fully-convertible currency with 100 per cent backing in reserves and new currency was issued in June 1967. In 1968 the withdrawal of the British forces stationed in Singapore was announced: British military expenditure in Singapore amounted to about $489.9 million annually, or 15 per cent of the GNP, with about 40,000 people working directly for the forces and thousands more indirectly dependent on the British military presence; by 1971, however, the employment problems associated with the withdrawal were resolved. In 1969 Singapore celebrated the 150th anniversary of its founding with a National Day parade held at the Padang; Princess Alexandra and her husband Angus Ogilvy were among the distinguished foreign dignitaries and guests present at the occasion.

As the Tanglin Club approached its centenary in October 1965 the expectations of members were that, having survived enemy occupation and the turbulence of the pre-independence period, there need be no further anxiety about the continued existence of the club. With the declaration of Singapore's independence also came a general feeling that more should be done to attract Singaporean members who were uncomfortable with the colonial atmosphere which the clubhouse exuded. The incumbent committee decided that plans for redevelopment should be drawn up while, in the meantime, the building be completely redecorated and refurbished at a cost of $60,000 in time for the centenary ball.

...the whole future of the club was uncertain...

Plans to alter the club and give it the desired 'new look' had been delayed in large part because of continuing staff unrest and union intrigue. The small group of union activists who had initiated the strike action of 1962 (and later discovered to be on police records as suspected communist agitators) had been accepted back by the club, a disastrous move in hindsight as they continued to cause severe disruptions. On December 17, 1965, a union-enforced work to rule order went into effect without formal notice being given to the club after the newly-appointed club secretary Bill Kerr sacked the two waiters who were the principal union agitators on the grounds of abusive language and threatening gestures. Sometime later further staff problems arose, including the refusal of the Catering Workers' Union to accept a duty roster schedule which would have resulted in a huge overtime bill for the club. On January 12, 1966, at an extraordinary general meeting held at the Victoria Memorial Hall attended by 215 members, the club president Pat Caldicott, who had played an important role in settling previous labour crises, reported that "the difficulties of labour relations and the lack, until quite recently, of an effective Executive have made the whole future of the Club uncertain." Between 1962 and 1966 there had been over twenty meetings between union representatives, with Mike Gorrie, Douglas Beaton and Ken Gould patiently negotiating on behalf of the club. Eventually the club arrived at a compromise and from then on accepted union rules.

...the committee was empowered to proceed... In the early 1970's the committee had to address the problem of complete electrical rewiring of the premises. Being a largely wooden structure, the old clubhouse presented a fire hazard and expenditure on such invisible alterations as the replacement of floor and structural timbers, the air-conditioning and sprinkler systems, and the electrical re-wiring of the building was determined to cost in excess of $2 million. By this time the total membership of the club, including family members, had exceeded 5,000 and the demands of this number exceeded the capacities of club facilities, particularly the kitchens. On Monday July 29, 1974, an extraordinary general meeting was called. The club president Jim Heaton, fully aware of the antipathy among members to demolishing the familiar and well-loved old building, had, in order to convince them of the financial necessity of the proposal, posted summaries illustrating the monthly commitments required just to retain and maintain the existing premises over the following 10 years on the walls of the ballroom where the meeting was held. Members in attendance could not fail to see that the cost of electricity, sewerage works and basic maintenance would be approximately $1 million per year — after an initial upgrading expense of $3 million. By a vote of 109 in favour, 3 against, the committee was finally empowered to proceed with plans for the development and construction of a new clubhouse and amenities not to exceed $9.8 million. The delay in government approval of the project until 1977, while resulting in the disguised bonus of substantial accumulated funds that otherwise would have been borrowed, also caused an escalation in costs. The committee had to seek further approval from members for a new budget of $13,750,000 against which a loan of $5 million was arranged with a consortium of banks headed by the Hongkong and Shanghai Bank and paid off within five years.

An Ambitious Economic Strategy

"Singapore was unique among colonial countries in having independence thrust upon her unilaterally, her Prime Minister publicly lamenting in tears this 'moment of agony'," observes C.M. Turnbull.

On July 21, 1964, barely a year after the formation of Malaysia, the worsening communal atmosphere engendered by unresolved questions concerning Singapore's position in the federation and the continuing Indonesian policy of confrontation culminated in the outbreak of racially-motivated violence; the whole island was placed under curfew, twenty-two people were killed and hundreds injured. In September violence broke out again. The most serious incident of the confrontation years was a bomb explosion at Macdonald House on Orchard Road on March 10, 1965, which killed three people and injured thirty-three.

In June 1965, when the prime minister of Malaysia Tunku Abdul Rahman left for London to attend the Commonwealth Prime Ministers' Conference, ongoing efforts to resolve the differences between Singapore and Malaysia were initiated by the prime minister Lee Kuan Yew. When a compromise could not be reached, expulsion from Malaysia was seen as the only practicable solution. Singapore's independence was subsequently proclaimed in August and immediately recognised within the Commonwealth by Britain, Australia and New Zealand, and by the United States; in September Singapore was admitted to the United Nations.

With the separation from Malaysia, many businesses that had previously set up in Singapore were forced by the imposition of retaliatory tariffs and duties to relocate to Malaysia; simple aspects of transactions such as the hitherto routine crossing of the Causeway were suddenly mired in immigration restrictions, vehicle permits and entry quotas. Heralding an ambitious economic strategy, the Jurong Industrial Estate was inaugurated in the sixties, a concept promoted by Dr. Goh Keng Swee, a former first deputy prime minister and an honorary member of the Tanglin Club. Graham Bell, honorary treasurer 1990, is chairman and managing director of Crown Cork and Seal Singapore Company Limited, the first company listed on the register of the Jurong Town Corporation. Others among the first to establish a base in Singapore where they could take advantage of manufacturing facilities and tax incentives included National Iron and Steel Mills Limited and B.R.C. Weldmesh (SEA) Private Limited which opened factories in Jurong in 1964. According to Graham Bell, the area then "was mostly jungle with mangrove swamps, some kampongs and a few Chinese farmers." Henceforth, many Tanglin Club members whose direction from work to club had always been east to west now travelled west to east and, while a century ago some members had considered the Claymore district far out of town, they now traversed the whole island as part of their daily routine.

In June 1968 the fully government-owned Sembawang Shipyard Limited was formed to take over the King George VI

Jurong, a giant construction site, early 1960's — 20 years On — Jurong Town Corporation

George G. Thomson, who joined the Tanglin Club in 1953, came to Singapore in 1945 as a lieutenant-colonel in the military administration under Lord Mountbatten. An influential figure of the post-independence era, he was a director of the information services department and Lim Yew Hock's speechwriter until 1959. He was subsequently a director of the Singapore Civil Service Political Study Centre and a professor of South-East Asian studies at Nanyang University.

[George Thomson seated behind the prime minister Lee Kuan Yew, July 13, 1966 — Courtesy of the Ministry of Information and the Arts; Singapore skyline, 1989 — Courtesy of Urban Redevelopment Authority]

Dock at the Naval Base and to convert it for commercial use. Managed by the British Swan Hunter Group under Neville Watson, a Tanglin Club member, it began ship repairing operations on December 1, 1968, with over 3,000 workers retrenched by the Naval Base and by the 1970's was a highly successful and profitable company. Policies to develop Singapore as a financial and banking centre initiated in 1968 encouraged foreign banks to begin operations on the island and in November 1968 the Asian Dollar Market was established; exchange controls were liberalised and tax incentives introduced to promote the growth of banking activity and the expansion of financial expertise through training facilities. In mid-1968 the Economic Development Board was re-organised and the government's policy of attracting foreign industrial capital with generous incentives ultimately helped to achieve a miracle in industrialisation which provided full employment and raised the standard of living of all Singaporeans. Throughout Singapore's independence, the government has consistently consolidated efforts to attract foreign and local investment at various levels of its export-oriented industrialisation programmes; the government-owned Development Bank of Singapore has also played a significant role in facilitating manufacturing and development with long-term loans as well as direct investments. Attracted by a climate of industrial peace and political stability, investment capital and technical expertise have continued to flow into Singapore and, from what seemed like doubtful beginnings, today the robust economic life of the island nation is beyond doubt.

Poolside entrance to clubhouse, 1977 — T.C.

In 1971, the completion of the pullout of the British forces stationed in Singapore signalled the end of a tradition in membership and association extended by the Tanglin Club from its founding in 1865; at a special meeting of members on May 3, 1976, the category of service membership was deleted from the rules of the club. Hospitality continues to be extended, especially to naval personnel as plaques in the Tavern attest. In February 1976 the committee began to address the issue of internationalising the membership of the club. At a meeting of the membership and rules subcommittee in August 1978 the subject of the Singaporean composition of membership was seriously reviewed; at the time accounting for 40 per cent of the total membership, projections indicated it could reach 60 per cent within 3 years. [In 1976 Joseph Grimberg was the first Singaporean president of the club; in 1980 Thai Chee Ken was the first Asian Singaporean to be elected president.] Given the desire that the club maintain an international flavour, the subcommittee suggested it may be necessary to consider either a percentage limitation on the nationalities of members or the establishment of a new class or classes of membership such as term or corporate — the latter was subsequently rejected on the grounds that the committee would lose the right to vet individuals put up by a company; there was also a suggestion that the name of the club include the word international. In October 1978, when the membership of the club stood at 2,561 with 498 on the waiting list, it was proposed that membership applications be

Guest of honour Othman Wok, the minister for culture and social affairs, and chieftain J.L.M. Gorrie, St. Andrew's ball,
Tanglin Club, 1967 — Courtesy of Neill and Morag Aitken

temporarily closed while the latter be absorbed over the next 9 to 10 months so that the club would be in a better position to ratify the membership question. Subsequently, on February 20, 1979, the membership and rules subcommittee proposed a corporate membership — not exceeding 10 per cent of ordinary membership — and a new rule on nationality balance based on the criterion that no one nationality (citizenship as identified by passports) shall exceed 50 per cent of the total ordinary membership of the club; it was further agreed not to adopt the name Tanglin International Club.

...the rules
determining future
membership...

Amendments to the rules relating to restriction of membership were presented at the AGM on May 14, 1979. Club members overwhelmingly defeated the corporate membership proposal; after considerable discussion Mr. (later Justice) Lai Kew Chai proposed an amendment specifying the limit to membership of any one nationality at 51 per cent to remove the sting of possible discrimination: this was carried by a substantial majority. After approval from the Registrar of Societies the amendments to the rules determining the future membership of the Tanglin Club came into effect on August 1, 1979. In October 1985 priority for consideration to election for membership was introduced for children of members within 12 months of their attaining the age of 21 years, so long as this could be allocated within the 51 per cent nationality limit.

Maintaining The Dignity And Status

During 1966 and 1967 the foremost concern of the committee was planning for the future use of the club land and buildings. An invitation was issued to five leading Singapore architects to participate in a design competition for a new club complex. At an extraordinary general meeting on April 8, 1968, the architectural firm of Iverson Van Sitteren and Partners presented the design-winning plans by Charles Ho, a club member and later president, for a complete redevelopment within the guidelines for maintaining the dignity and status of the Tanglin Club as a premier social club which would appeal to younger prospective members: the proposal was voted out by 114 votes to 0 (of a total of 1,143 members only 114 attended the meeting). Other proposals intended to increase the social and recreational facilities of the club in the 1960's included one for a discothèque (provisionally dubbed The Snake Pit); a suggestion that the club buy a horse to be stabled at the Saddle Club for the convenience of members and another that a box be obtained for use by members at the Turf Club; and a request for a 28-foot cabin cruiser — all of which were rejected. In March 1970 a controversial proposal put to members to build a new swimming pool for use by adults only at a cost of $60,000 was also de-

The clubhouse, 1977 — T.C.

feated. In December 1968 members gave the committee approval to spend $165,000 on the renovation and refurbishing of the Churchill and Chandelier rooms; this work was completed in 1969. In 1971 a new squash court was built and, in December, work was completed on the transformation of the Walnut Room which had been poorly patronised for some time. With the installation of a new bar, wooden beams and even an inglenook fireplace, an English pub atmosphere was further evoked by naming the renovated room the Tavern; it was opened by club president Wal Waller on February 18, 1972, with a free 'happy hour'.

By this time it was evident that no further expansion was possible within the existing structure; while modifications over a hundred years had allowed the much-cherished clubhouse to accommodate the needs of members, the days of its capacity to remain relevant to emerging needs were numbered. Once again the chestnut of demolition appeared. A decision was taken to hold a referendum

Clubhouse entrance on Stevens Road, 1977 — T.C.

In 1979, with the assistance of Eric Jennings, the club acquired a reproduction of a portrait of Sir Stamford Raffles by G.F. Joseph painted in 1817 in England; the original, which hung in the dining room of Raffles' house, HIGH WOOD, in Hendon, London, is the property of the National Portrait Gallery in London. In 1984, reproductions made through the courtesy of Jack Drake of Aviemore, Scotland, of the miniatures in the collection of Mrs. M. Rosdew Drake, great-granddaughter of Captain Flint and Maryanne Raffles, were obtained of Lady Sophia Raffles (Sir Stamford's second wife), Maryanne Raffles (his favourite sister), and her husband Captain William Flint R.N. (Singapore's first harbour master). Also acquired was a reproduction of the Chalon portrait of Sir Stamford which hangs in the boardroom of the Zoological Society of London of which he was the first president. [The Rosdew Miniatures. Clockwise from top left, Sir Stamford Raffles, Lady Sophia Raffles, Captain William Flint R.N. and Maryanne Raffles — T.C.]

among the members on whether or not to rebuild the club and the issue of moving premises altogether was again introduced; however, a submission for new premises in Firestone Park, near Ridley Park, was rejected by the authorities due to the need to retain a green lung in the heart of the city. During 1974 plans were presented to the authorities proposing the sale of the tennis courts and manager's bungalow (on the site of the present squash courts) and the rezoning of the land for the development of an 18-storey residential apartment block on a site of 63,000 square feet (the total club land area being 243,743 square feet). Funds raised were to be applied to the rebuilding of the clubhouse, the design of which included squash courts underneath a car park and tennis courts on the top. These proposals were rejected on the grounds that noise from such amenities would disturb the neighbours.

Subsequently, the architectural firm of Raglan Squire and Partners was selected to propose a design that Wal Waller recalled was to include "an impressive en-

Tanglin Club pool, 1977 — T.C.

trance lobby with a grand staircase — the more to encourage proper dress!" In 1975 the complete new set of plans was submitted and approval to build finally granted on June 6, 1977, (one of the reasons for the delay being possible interference with development of the mass rapid transport system being planned for the island at that time). To finance the redevelopment the committee had proposed, in July 1974, a building levy surcharge of $6 for town and service members, and $4 for lady members; entrance fees were increased from $600 to $1,000. Owing to the delay, the accumulated revenue obtained from these together with funds from an increased membership — amounting to $1.6 million — enabled the club to proceed without the disposal of the tennis courts. Peter von Selkey of Raglan Squire, who designed the premises which would become a landmark in the Claymore district, took charge of the redevelopment at the request of Peter Holmes, a club member and partner in the same firm, in 1974; Albert Hong, another club member, assumed the role of partner in charge on the departure of Peter Holmes. The project manager for the reconstruction was John Ewing, a club member and later president, whose dedication in time and involvement over five years earned him the unstinting admiration and appreciation of the committee and club members. During the years of rebuilding, the various club committees devoted much of their personal time to the project, worrying about every detail — although they all subsequently denied any responsibility for the orange tiles in the men's lavatories, claiming to a man to have missed the particular meeting at which that colour was chosen.

The Verandah Restaurant, 1977 — T.C.

The architectural plans originally submitted for the new clubhouse had included the preservation of some features of the original building, notably the original porch; however these were denied by the planning authorities on grounds that the structure was of no architectural value. In *Singapore: A Guide to Buildings, Streets, Places* Tanglin Club member Peter Keys echoes the sentiments harboured by long-time members: "The earlier buildings of the Tanglin Club on this site were beautiful examples of the style of architecture of former days, when life had greater elegance and graciousness was a virtue....How they must have enjoyed sitting on the open verandahs under the punkahs as many have done long since. Much of this has changed abruptly with the demolition of the old buildings to make way for the present quarters. The new air-conditioned 4-storey building, in a pseudo-Chinese Spanish architectural style, is obviously popular, but lacks the splendid architectural qualities of its predecessor."

Clubhouse entrance on Draycott Drive, 1990 — T.C.

The building of the new clubhouse and amenities, carried out in phases to minimise disruptions and allow the continued operation of the club, was finished ahead of schedule at a final cost of $13,737,237. Phase I began in September 1977 with the building of the new squash courts which were opened by the club president Peter Tomkins on July 14, 1978. The new multi-storey car park which began Phase II was completed in April 1979. The building of the new clubhouse began on June 1, 1979, directly behind the original one; on completion in March 1981 the buildings were in such close proximity that members could stand on the verandah outside the new Tavern and touch the old clubhouse. The last major social function to be held in the old clubhouse was the November 1980 Tanglin Club ball, an occasion tinged with a degree of nostalgia marking the end of one era and the beginning of a new one. The club newsletter of December 1980 provides a rather understated account of that historic evening: "The last Tanglin Ball in the old Club was a full house and attended by over 230 members, the overflow being accommodated in the Tavern. The floor show for the evening was provided by The Shayne Twins and our thanks are due to Mr. Sonny Lien and the Mandarin Hotel for arranging their appearance. The evening ended on a nostalgic note with the Band playing 'Now is the Hour' followed by 'Auld Lang Syne'. Our thanks are also due to the Ladies' Sub-Committee for arranging the floral decorations for the Churchill Room which were once again beautifully done."

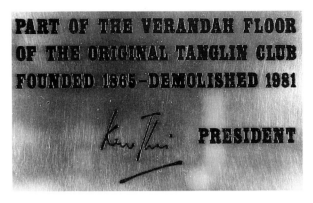

At the Closing Down Party on March 14, 1981, memorabilia from the old clubhouse were auctioned under the direction of John d'Arcy Kincaid; the $9,000 collected was donated to the Children's Charities Association of Singapore, to be divided equally among its 6 affiliates. Before the demolition of the old clubhouse, part of the verandah floor was cut into 12-inch strips which were polished, mounted with a brass plaque carrying the inscription 'Tanglin Club — Established 1865 — Demolished 1981' and the signature of Thai Chee Ken, president 1980, which sold for $50 each, the proceeds going towards the building fund. [Brass plaque attached to floorboard, 1981 — T.C.]

...under the timbered beams for the last time...

At the closing down party held on the night of Saturday March 14, 1981, the Tanglin Club members who entered the porch on Stevens Road and mounted the old staircase for the last time, trod in the footsteps of one hundred and sixteen years of history. Six hundred members gathered at the poolside, on the verandah, in the Churchill Room, the Raffles Room and the Tavern in casual attire — with, of course, the usual restrictions on jeans, T-shirts and flip-flops. With a sense of consolation, the age-old Tanglin nightmare was faced for the last time as several committee members were stationed underneath the verandah floor to ensure that it could withstand the heavy spirits at the occasion — there were very real fears that a final collapse could be imminent not from the stomping of the Lambeth walk but from the sheer weight of additional people. After a barbecue that included a roasted ox (donated by Fitzpatrick's) and non-stop dancing to the accompaniment of the club band and the 1st Battalion Royal New Zealand Infantry Regiment Band, at 3 A.M. the strains of 'Auld Lang Syne' resounded under the timbered beams for the last time.

...amidst congratulatory greetings and merrymaking...

On March 15 and 16 the Tanglin Club was closed; only the sound of frantic dismantling and moving of furniture and whispered pleas for sleep were to be heard as committee members readied the new clubhouse for its unofficial opening on Tuesday March 17. On March 16, 1981, at a pre-opening cocktail party attended by past presidents, committee members and others who had served on various subcommittees or in voluntary capacities, Dr. Leo Taylor unveiled a painting of the old clubhouse by Choo Keng Kwang, commissioned as a gift by some past presidents. On April 25, 1981, the new clubhouse was officially opened by E.W. Barker, then the minister for law and member for Tanglin. Briefly tracing the development of the area from its days of nutmeg plantations and tigers, Barker, an honorary member of the Tanglin Club, noted that the total value of property in Singapore in 1865 was roughly equivalent to the value of the new clubhouse. As members admired the new facilities and were treated to a gala programme including an appearance by West End cabaret entertainer Max Bygraves, all those involved in the development sighed in relief as their years of perseverance and hard work were nearly at an end. Peter von Selkey, the architect, still talks of a particularly unforgettable moment of that opening night. Five hours after the official opening, as he was enjoying a

The library catalogue now carries 13,000 entries of general fiction and non-fiction; 500 volumes are checked out each week, the most popular requests still being for novels set in old Singapore. The children's library, started in 1977 by Joanna Shaw and Bim Callis on the verandah in a corner of the ballroom, is a great attraction for young children who can change their library books after swimming lessons. Adjacent to the main library is a well-appointed Reading Room which stocks local and international newspapers and periodicals and where members can write and browse in tranquillity. In May 1978 the members' newsletter was changed from a cyclostyled circular to a magazine format and, under the direction of Alan Croll, Joanna Shaw and Marlene Rauwerda (who also produced the new format annual reports in 1982), acquired a more professional look. In addition to the monthly calendar informing members of all the facilities, promotions, social events, entertainment and sporting fixtures organised by or involving the Tanglin Club, the newsletter also contains members' contributions ranging from articles on travel, book reviews or other esoterica. [The Reading Room, 1981 — T.C.]

well-deserved beer amidst the congratulatory greetings and merrymaking of members experiencing the novelty of their surroundings at the new Tavern bar, there was an ear-splitting crash. The heavy wooden fire-rated door between the kitchen and bar had come off its hinges and landed on a few hundred stacked glasses. In the ensuing eerie silence every head turned to the architect whose expression mirrored his thoughts — *sic transit gloria...*

...features which
preserve...
One feature of the present clubhouse that alludes to former days is the retention on the front steps leading to the entrance on Draycott Drive of a portion of the brass rail that had been deemed essential to negotiating the steep steps of the entrance to the old clubhouse after a few stengahs. This, however, is not the only aspect recalling a semblance of club life of yesteryear; as the committee was to observe prematurely in 1980 before the opening of the new clubhouse: "There obviously will be more elbow room at the new bar and this should satisfy the regulars of the Tavern whose serious work of consuming ale is currently hampered by the occasional nudge and jostle which accelerates the flow of beer, but only down the shirt front." In 1987 members approved a plan to further enhance the clubhouse and facilities and a development in two stages was proposed. Phase I involved the redecorating and installing of a new sound and light system in the Churchill Room, the redevelopment of the main kitchen, the construction of a small satellite 'grill' kitchen at the back of the Tavern, the extension of the Tavern dining area into the area occupied by the Billiard Room and Fruit Machine Rooms, and the construction of a new Billiard Room, Card Room, Fruit Machine Room and the open-air Wet Bar on top of the Wheelhouse Restaurant. The main work to the interior of the clubhouse was completed before the end of 1988 and the Terrace Bar was opened on New Year's Eve; the Tavern lounge extension was opened by Chinese New Year 1989 and by April 1 the Wheelhouse Restaurant kitchen had been fully renovated; the Card Room and Billiard Room were completed at the end of January 1990. The development of Phase II, held in abeyance pending an appeal against redevelopment charges, involves the construction of a sports complex, including a modern gymnasium and the conversion of some of the tennis courts into a car park with new courts on the roof. As with all previous renovations and redevelopments, members of incumbent Tanglin Club committees are constantly involved with the maintenance, repair and remodelling of the property to ensure the magnificent manner in which the Tanglin Club is always presented.

The Tanglin Club staff, 1990 — T.C.

The first postwar financial report of the Tanglin Club which covered the 10-month period from September 1946 to July 1947 recorded a cash balance of $16,913 in the pre-war account with outstanding payments on debentures and interest thereon of $51,502, leaving a cash deficiency on start-up of $34,589. In ten months of operation after de-requisition the club earned a surplus of $78,908 from which it paid off $42,523 against the debentures and interest, and expended $73,663 on capital expenditure and rehabilitation expenses. A comparison between the finances of the club for the first full year of postwar operations from January 1, 1947, to January 31, 1948, with that for the year 1989-90 will illustrate the extent of the growth of a once surburban social institute in the out of town Claymore district. Total full-time staff strength as at January 1990 was 276.

	1947-1948	1989-1990
INCOME		
Members subscriptions	71,095	2,492,760
Interest Income	—	316,011
Profit from bar	90,650	847,370
Profit from restaurant	(19)	2,117,100
Revenue from:		
Squash courts	1,701	(51,070)
Tennis courts	2,949	(14,960)
Billiards	642	(13,870)
Scuba	—	(28,010)
Guest room rentals	—	461,270
Revenue from jackpot machines	—	1,483,200
Entrance fees	29,995	1,396,500
EXPENSES		
Wages & salaries	61,725	4,737,920
Band wages & expenses	31,742	222,400
Cinema & sound equipment	—	62,790
Electricity & water	9,650	628,400
Insurance	1,373	29,540
Repairs & upkeep	25,989	547,350
Property tax	1,244	140,260
Telephone & postage	2,100	37,140
Advertising & entertainment	925	13,030
Printing & stationery	6,934	59,890
Transport	671	6,590
Periodicals/Library	511	26,770
Dhoby	2,126	141,190
Interest	1,795	—
Audit fee	500	16,000
Miscellaneous expenses	7,682	92,000
ASSETS		
Freehold land & buildings	100,000	11,283,000
Library	1,000	—
Furniture & fittings	10,000	722,000
Current equipment & stocks	42,211	212,000
Sundry debtors	14,138	292,000
Cash at hand and on deposit	186	6,625,000
LIABILITIES		
Surplus account	89,918	19,900,000
Debentures outstanding	5,775	—
Bank overdraft	35,476	—
Sundry creditors	32,379	1,224,000
Members subs paid in advance plus credit balance	3,988	1,115,000

The Kemlo Ground For Divorce

After the interruption of the war, lawn tennis quickly picked up and became one of the most popular and well-organised sports at the Tanglin Club. The upper four clay courts were repaired, the lower four grass courts were restored with assistance from the Golf Club, which provided the grass, and the SCC which provided the roller, and two additional grass courts were laid. The first post-war tournament

Since the late nineteenth century the amount of lawn tennis played in Singapore was 'something astonishing!'. The earliest Singapore championship was held at the SCC in 1875, two years before Wimbledon and five years before the first American championships. In 1884 the Ladies' Lawn Tennis Club was established with seven courts at Dhoby Ghaut; ladies matches — for the McCabe Reay Cup — were inaugurated at the 1933 Colony v FMS tournament held at the Tanglin Club. Although matches held at the club may not have attracted the crowds they would have if played at the SCC or some other more central location, "there is no gainsaying the fact that they enjoyed universal interest and that Press reports were eagerly awaited," reports 'Rimau' in The Sunday Tribune June 11, 1933. Tennis was a popular late afternoon recreation and many bungalows boasted a private court; the 1936 Lawn Tennis Association of Malaya Handbook notes more than 500 courts in the Tanglin district. [Aerial view facing Scotts Road showing Tanglin Club clay courts, 1980 — T.C.]

mentioned in the minute book is the American Tournament for mixed doubles in April 1948. From 1949, and especially during the fifties, tournaments were run through the season in the form of friendly matches between the clubs — the SCC, Singapore Chinese Recreation Club, YMCA, Malay Sports Club and Hollandse Club. Tournaments were also organised with the Services, notably RAF teams from Seletar, Tengah and Changi, GHQ FARELF and REME. Since the 1950's members have participated in two major club events held annually, the Open Championship and the Handicap Tournament; other events included the gentlemen's Godown Doubles for the 1930 Griff Cup (discontinued in 1978) for partners from the same firm or in the same line of business or servicemen from the same headquarters. The courts were always fully booked, except during the rainy season when the clay courts were repaired and the grass courts allowed to rest. When the Tanglin Club won the 1953 Singapore Lawn Tennis Association (SLTA) Kliny Cup (first presented by D. Kleinman of the SCC in 1937) there was little doubt that it was the best of all the affiliates of the association. In 1955 several Tanglin Club members participated in the Singapore championships. At this time the Tanglin Club allowed the SLTA to use its courts and facilities for the Singapore Open Championship. Evening tennis matches were started in 1957 and flannel dances were a popular post-game programme of supper and dancing; it was customary for men only to play at peak times and ladies in the afternoons and there was no charge other than a $2 booking fee which was waived if the court was free.

A major attraction of the Tanglin Club from the fifties to the seventies continued to be the standard of tennis. Social games were popular and competitions flourished — in 1967 the Open Tournament attracted over 100 entries — but the great challenge was to be selected for the Tanglin Club team; Francis Chan and Dr. Koh Eng Yam were star performers on the courts and lady champions of county standard like Anne Garfick, Martha Young and Vivien Gwee had joined their ranks. In 1970 all the grass courts at the Tanglin Club were changed to clay but problems with maintenance seriously hampered the game; after frequent tropical rainstorms the courts remained soggy and wet for days — good drainage was considered too costly to install and new supplies of clay were frequently unavailable. Players were in two minds over this problem, with one group supported by the SLTA strongly in favour of retaining these last clay courts in the region, the loss of which would result in the Singapore championships being moved elsewhere. [Finally a majority voted for the change and eight first-class hard courts were constructed in 1981.] In 1971 the first resident coach Y.P. Lee arrived (the first tennis lessons were given in 1951 by Mrs. M.J. Lewis) and in the seventies promising young players were encouraged to play for the club; Tanglin Club champions Vivien Gwee, Lim Phi Lan and Teo Lay Lim also played for the national team. Excellent expatriate players included Vera Kaspers, Margaret Jones, Pippa Miall, Joke Kitovitz, Patrick O'Shea, Maurice Broom (the Australian Davis Cup player), Tom Chambers (the American clay court doubles champion), Wolfgang Roh, Robert Gilman and Carl

Knudsen (Davis Cup player for South Africa). Veterans' tournaments were started and People-to-People competitions, first played at the Tanglin Club in 1970, brought goodwill ambassadors from America to the courts in a spirit of friendship. The après-tennis spirit of the seventies also encouraged players to gather for seafood barbecues beside the pool and enter prize-winning teams at the fancy dress balls.

In 1976 the Singapore Open Clay Court Championship was hosted by the Tanglin Club on behalf of the SLTA (in pre-sponsor days the cost was borne by the club) and in the 1980's the club began to host charity and celebrity matches. With lighting installed on all the courts, evening clinics had been introduced and the cushioned all-weather Deco-turf surface enjoyed by all players. Tennis in the 1990's continues as an integral part of the club's sports programme and features friendly matches and tournaments at home and away. A more competitive spirit now replaces the social atmosphere of earlier days in matches for trophies of the club — at the annual Handicap Tournament the Kemlo Bowl for husband and wife teams has engendered such fierce competition that it is sometimes referred to as 'the Kemlo ground for divorce' — but certain traditions are still upheld, like Wimbledon Evening when players, suitably flannelled, enjoy strawberries and champagne in front of the live telecast of the final.

Matches For Visiting World-Class Players

Ladders for squash were reintroduced in 1947 and proved to be popular right from the start; an open ladies tournament began in 1956. In 1950, the club renewed its affiliation with the Squash Rackets Association of London. Postwar inter-club matches were played principally against the Police Training School, and military establishments who also had courts.

In 1971 a fourth court was constructed with an entrance through the back wall designed for the seven dwarves; players forced to duck-walk into this court complimented the designers for introducing com-

Even before the war, the Tanglin Club played a prominent role in squash rackets in Singapore in terms of facilities and players. In earlier years, the courts were as unique and daunting as any mechanical mind could devise. Entry to the three courts was over the back wall on a balanced ladder which was intended to descend and ascend at the touch of a finger, but which jammed frequently so that it was not uncommon to hear exhausted players pleading for help from passers-by. Lady squash players faced a unique problem as spelt out in the June 1950 circular: "Ladies visiting the Squash Courts are requested to use the exit from the Clubhouse at the end of the service corridor or take the path leading off the main staircase round the Reading Room. The Billiard Room and Men's bar and the exit therefrom is reserved for men only." As a consolation, the bye-laws were amended to let ladies play anytime on Wednesdays and Saturdays.

pulsory bending exercises prior to a game. By the mid-1970's squash in Singapore had become the rage and the Tanglin queues formed in the early mornings to book courts a week in advance. Sensitive to the increasing popularity of the sport the club built the first glass-backed court in Singapore. This fifth court, completed in 1974, which included a gallery for 50 spectators — though additional enthusiasts were known to swing from the rafters and roof — permitted a glimpse of some of the top world-class players who used Singapore as a stop-over and needed a practice court; the Tanglin Club then had the second largest squash complex in Asia.

The prestigious Singapore Open Championship, held at the club from 1970 to 1975 (in 1976 the Kallang Squash Complex was completed), has been instrumental in placing Singapore as one of the major world tournaments on the squash circuits in the Far East and Pacific, eventually surpassing even the Australian and New Zealand opens. Exhibition matches have included Qamar Zaman, Mohibullah Khan and Gogi Alaudin, players whose rise to the top ranks was witnessed by club members. Since 1976 the club has continued to host practice matches for visiting world-class players like Geoff Hunt, Jonah Barrington, Hiddy Jehan, Maqsood Ahmed, Bruce Brownlee, Murray Lilley, Heather McKay, Ali Aziz, Chris Dittmar, Chris Robertson, Rodney Martin and Brett Martin, some of whom have also held coaching clinics.

The first modern squash complex in Singapore — and still the largest of any private club — was opened at the Tanglin

Club by club president Peter Tomkins on July 14, 1978; built for $670,180, the complex boasted 8 courts, 2 of which were glass-backed with seating for 200 spectators. The squash complex now also serves as the booking centre for tennis, sells sports items and club souvenirs.

Leading lights in the development of squash in Singapore, all Tanglin Club members, included the first president of the Singapore Squash Rackets Association (SSRA), Eric Cooper, as well as subsequent SSRA presidents Richard Evans, Dr. Teoh Hoon Cheow and incumbent Dr. Eddy Jacobs; committee members of the SSRA have included club members Benny See, Hubert Hill, Norman Wee and Brigadier General Patrick Choy. In the early years of the East Asian and other regional team championships, the Singapore team included Tanglin Club members Malcolm Simons, Barry Thomson, Tan Eng Han, Eric Cooper, Hubert Hill, Peter Hill (the first and only professional Singaporean player on the international circuit), Lina Ong (who won the inaugural 1985 Asian Junior Championship), Lim Seok Hui (who won the National Women's title at 13 years and was the youngest player to represent Singapore at the East Asian Championship) and Sue Paton, a Rhodesian-born world-class player who competed in the men's league. In 1989 the club hosted the Australian and Swedish qualifying match in the World Team Championship. At present, of the 15 international referees given accreditation by the International Squash Rackets Federation, 3 are from Singapore; of these, Desmond Hill and Munir Shah are members of the Tanglin Club.

The social calendar of the Tanglin Club over the last twenty-five years has seen the passing of some cherished traditions and the evolution of new ones resulting from the different lifestyles and emphasis on leisure activities of contemporary generations of members. Wine appreciation dinners, always fully-booked, in the air-conditioned comfort of a banquet room are a far cry from the days of sipping stengahs and pahits while stretched out in a long chair on a fan-cooled verandah. Members' tastes have come a long way from the single preoccupation with the supply of whisky in the days of the 'whisky roster' when different whiskies appeared in rotation; wine, it seems, has ceased to be the arcane interest it was deemed to be, and the Tanglin Club wine cellar is one of the best in Singapore. The Tanglin Club kitchens now offer a standard of fare which rivals any institution in the city, and members who may gather over a meal to solve a murder mystery dine on the finest foods of the world, with fresh ingredients flown in daily to an island where in the twenties only local produce, augmented by a few imported items, graced the table. Sunday curry tiffin, a colonial tradition throughout the empire, is still available but is now followed by a few hours beside the pool perusing international newspapers available on the day of issue. Luncheon fashion parades attended by elegant lady members, where fine creations from local and inter-

Clubhouse viewed from the pool, 1990 — T.C.

national couture houses are presented, are quite different occasions from those of the fifties when expatriate women on home leave were identified by their 'real jewels and home-made clothes'; the ladies who gather at the club today also combine socialising with taking instruction on a wide variety of subjects like antique silver, investment planning, reflexology, tropical horticulture and Chinese brush painting. On Wednesdays, classic films out of early Hollywood which once brought members together under the fans on the verandah are now watched by a dedicated following of the silver screen in an air-conditioned theatr-ette; new release movies are screened on Saturday and Sunday evenings. The children's cinema on Friday afternoons offers not only Michael Jackson and *Ninja Turtles* but also the still-loved adventures of *Mickey Mouse* and *Popeye*. Children's parties now involve second and even third-generation members at Christmas, New Year and Hallowe'en festivities while teenagers transform the Wheelhouse into an up-beat discothèque at parties that keep the rhythm going into the early hours.

The Tanglin Club Dragon Boat Race team, 1978 — Courtesy of Helmut Fehse

...the games people continue to play... The spirit of the Tanglin tradition is nowhere more alive than in the games people continue to play. In 1967 bridge lessons on the verandah of the old clubhouse were resumed with fees donated to the Red Cross, and throughout the seventies organised social bridge in the Library on Wednesday evenings soared in popularity. Although continued requests for a permanent home went unheeded, 'profit before pleasure' players charged as they were moved to a redecorated storeroom in the new clubhouse. Finally, in 1989, the Card Room overlooking the pool was opened and members now play duplicate, social, team and charity bridge, the latter in aid of cancer research, and at inter-club league matches; the room is also used for chess, backgammon and mahjong with cards — traditional tiles are considered too noisy.

Over the years members have seen the Tanglin spirit in various games, especially cricket, lawn bowls, soccer and darts, wax and wane, and witnessed the introduction of new pastimes. One of the most active recreational programmes of the club is organized by the scuba diving section — originally registered in May 1975 as a special branch of the British Sub-Aqua Club — with Saturday afternoon dives on coral reefs off the Southern Islands, frequent weekend expeditions to the east coast of Malaysia during the peak diving season from mid-March to mid-October, and further afield 2 or 3 times a year. Another attempt to stimulate a new interest arose in 1978 with the first invitation from the Singapore Sports Council to compete in the annual dragon boat race. In true Tanglin tradition, members and staff gathered on the Esplanade on a breezy, hot Sunday morning with curry puffs and sandwiches, iced beer and chit books, and the club flag flying proudly to signify their presence; the team sported white caps bearing the club logo and specially ordered white shirts. At the starting gun binoculars were focused and the race took off, soon to prove that enthusiasm, will-power and insufficient free board were no match for months of practice. Six years later a more determined effort was mounted. Despite the encouraging attendance at practice meetings near the Changi Sailing Club, the pep talks and limbering exercises on the day, the enthusiastic club members who took readily to their task were defeated, allegedly by the wash of a passing freighter; to the cry of 'Men Overboard' the boat and members' spirits sank off the Bedok Jetty while the team swam ashore to commiserations and a certain amount of welcome beer.

In June 1981, when the Billiard Room in the new clubhouse was opened, trophies were dusted off and, after many years, the game reinstated as a club activity; following further club development, in 1988 players moved into the new Billiard Room above the Wheelhouse where new faces around the three tables in the once exclusively men's domain now include junior members and lady players at allocated times. No longer confined to playing on the Sepoy Lines, keen Tanglin golfers can now be seen teeing-off for monthly in-house games on any and every available course in Singapore and up-country; in 1987 the 1903 Withers Cup, a handsome trophy formerly competed for in lawn bowls, was adopted as the Tanglin Club Golf Handicap Challenge Trophy. Another traditional pastime, the five-dice game balut, once popular among executives of the older shipping agencies and trading houses and played throughout South-East Asia and Australasia, is still enjoyed by a few enthusiasts to rules established following those of the former Singapore Club. Family nights continue to be a popular event; at the first such occasion at the new clubhouse on September 4, 1981, various games perennially in vogue, like mummy wrapping, piggyback races and orange peeling contests, were played by 120 parents and children — not a single one of whom left before the national anthem was played. As with all other sporting activities of the club, the easy-going camaraderie of former times has been supplanted by a greater emphasis on winning and excellence, and the Tanglin swimming galas and competitions of today are far more competitive than the frolics of the forties. The annual October battle for 'The Pot' in which members chance life and limb against the SCC in various sports — squash, tennis, cricket, lawn bowls and snooker — harks back to a one-upmanship in existence even in the early days of the Tanglin Club. The Tanglin Club Trophy, a silver wine cooler presented to the SCC in November 1977 to mark its 125th anniversary — irreverently called The Pot, is held by the club winning a majority of the events, but remains in possession of the SCC. In 1990, its 125th year, the Tanglin Club finally triumphed over the SCC in cricket.

...still notable occasions in the Singapore social calendar...

The annual Tanglin ball, although no longer commencing with the ceremonial entrance of the governor, is still a notable occasion in the Singapore social calendar but now competes with other gala events held around the city throughout the year. The crowded New Year's Eve balls of the present are a mostly black-tie affair with little resemblance to the masquerades of former days, though, in the early hours of New Year's Day, members

The New Nation of November 6, 1972, informs: "The Tanglin Club intends to re-introduce black-tie nights on Saturdays in the Churchill Room. To start with this will be once a month. ...Once the symbol of British colonialism in Singapore, the old Tanglin had adjusted to the times and the membership now includes a large proportion of Asians as well as Europeans. Most of the diplomatic corps belong to it, as well as a fair number of Singapore Armed Forces officers. The officers will probably enjoy the chance to wear their attractive evening formal wear on these occasions. It's a fact that men like dressing up now and then, given half the chance." The dress code of the Tanglin has always distinguished it from many other private clubs in Singapore; on one occasion, Lord Snowdon, wearing a parson's-collared shirt and no tie, was denied admission. Well-known gallery owner and club member Della Butcher still delights in the memory of how she tested the dress code after hearing that Margo Gill, a guest who was dressed in a Punjabi suit, had been asked to sit inconspicuously in a corner and refrain from going onto the dance floor on January 19, 1970 — a newly-introduced bye-law banned ladies trouser suits or culottes in the Churchill Room and adjoining bars after 8 P.M. After dining at the Cockpit Hotel on January 25, Della Butcher went on to the Tanglin Club to dance, wearing an evening trouser suit of elephant crêpe, iridescent with sequins on lace, and a bell-shaped jacket which reached two inches above her knees. Arriving at the door, she unhooked and unzipped the trousers, so that when accosted by the committee member on duty for the evening she let them fall off and, to the great delight of members, entered the club wearing a most attractive mini-skirt and exclaimed for all to hear: "What sort of club is this where a lady must half-disrobe to get a drink!" In 1980, the 'impeccably dressed' actor Patrick Macnee was turned away from the dining room for "wearing a shirt, tie, a jacket and trousers. The jacket was oatmeal and the trousers beige. The difference in colour was infinitesimal." In his interview with The Straits Times of September 16, referring to "the essentially British character of the club and his previous faultlessly-dressed characterisation of John Steed in the television series, The Avengers, he added: It's poetic justice really."

can still enjoy the traditional 2 A.M. breakfast. Fancy dress is still occasionally donned at the Tanglin Club of the 1990's, though with far less abandon than in earlier times; Brazilian nights, Latin fiestas or other ever-popular theme events now provide the occasion for members to step from luxury cars designed for the twenty-first century in creative costumes specially hired for the evening, a somewhat different entrance from the enthusiastic amateurs of the 1860's who arrived by hackney carriage and enrobed for the stage. The Tanglin Club of today not only hosts a wide variety of events but also sponsors visiting entertainers and lecturers from Singapore and overseas. Concert evenings have seen performances by Singapore-born violinist Lee Pan Hon, members of the Singapore Symphony Orchestra, the Vienna Boys' Choir and opera singer Rosamund Illing, and sophisticated productions by local stage companies; cabaret evenings have featured Jack and Daphne Barker, Anita Sarawak, David Gray, Rolf Harris, The Supremes, Matt Munro and several West End entertainers, many of whom return regularly to Singapore and to the club. Guest speakers have included Sherpa Tenzing, who made the first ascent of Mount Everest with Sir Edmund Hillary, Captain Mike Hatcher, who discovered the Nanking cargo on the sunken Dutch East India tea clipper *The Geldermalsen*, and former members who hold court with talks of their early days in Singapore when club life was enjoyed at a more leisurely pace and elegance of dress was a sartorial requirement. Sharing the enjoyment and relaxation afforded by the entertainments and facilities offered by a premier social institute, the Tanglin Club in the 1990's continues to enrich the lives of its members.

The story of Singapore from 1945 through independence to the present is one of economic rehabilitation, self-discovery and self-expression. The change from colonialism to nationalism was achieved without any lasting bitterness against the expatriate whose skills are seen as a welcome and essential element in the national economy. In 1990 the island's population numbered 2.5 million people, comprising 77 per cent Chinese, 15 per cent Malay, 6 per cent Indian and 2 per cent of other extractions, all of whom subscribe to a mix of cultural beliefs. Raffles' little port of 1819, in an island just 41 kilometres long and 22 kilometres wide, has grown to be the second largest in the world, visited in 1990 by 45,000 ships. Huge shipyards and dry docks repair everything from island traders to vast tankers, and giant oil refineries tower over the islands scattered around the harbour. The historical entrepôt trade in the region's wealth in tin, rubber,

The foyer, 1981 — T.C.

coconut, oil, rice, timber, jute, spices and coffee continues alongside the hundreds of ships that now ride at anchor or glide in and out of extensive container wharves holding all manner of goods. Though the age-old abacus can still be seen, Singapore has become a computer-age city; telecommunications link boardrooms with stock exchanges around the world and the republic's banking system is one of the key international financial centres. The terminals at Changi International Airport are served by over 40 of the world's major airlines and ten million passengers pass through Singapore every year. Still, amidst the clamour of commerce in bustling bazaars, gleaming shopping centres and dramatic skyscrapers which top even Bukit Timah, the highest hill, and overlook quaint backlanes of shanty Chinese shop-houses, the green, green of Singapore still thrives.

...to conjure a vision of the future... In the district of Claymore, the Tanglin Club of the nineties is surrounded by a very different kind of jungle: the club now lies in the shadow of concrete and glass buildings which tower 30 storeys high, providing luxury condominiums and apartments with marble floors and costly appurtenances where thousands of residents of many nationalities enjoy the proximity of chic Orchard Road boutiques and world-class hotels and the convenience of down-town living. Scant vestige remains of the vivid green, undulating hills and the airy raised bungalows, though tiny enclaves such as Goodwood Hill and Ridley Park evoke the colonial days of the tuans besar. As at its formation in 1865, and throughout its development when the club attracted and catered to personalities who played a significant role in the history and development of the island colony, so now are high-ranking civil servants and members of the judiciary, tycoons of business and industry part of the membership of the Tanglin Club. Of approximately 5,500 members representing 56 nationalities, 51 per cent are involved in business and commerce, 8 per cent are in the medical profession, 7 per cent are bankers, 6.5 per cent are engineers, 5.5 per cent are lawyers, 5 per cent are accountants and the others include journalists, diplomats, surveyors, teachers and lecturers; the constant turnover of expatriate members provides a sound financial basis which ensures that there will never be another mortgagee sale of the Tanglin Club. To ensure that the club will constitute a source of friendship and influence for generations to come, its members will surely be faced with contemporary issues no differently than the members of one hundred and twenty-five years ago. Every one of those issues has as much reference to the evolution of a 'suburban social institute' founded in the early days

Viewed from a distance, the Tanglin Club (left foreground) now stands out against the sombre backdrop of tall buildings in the Claymore district of the 1990's — T.C.

of the colony as to the aspirations of previous generations of members. As the final decade of the twentieth century ushers in new challenges posed by the triumphant emergence of Eastern Europe from totalitarianism, the unsettling consequences of the crisis in the Persian Gulf and the rapidly changing and emerging role of South-East Asia in international affairs and business, so will the members of the Tanglin Club in the island of Singapore, like those 'forty good men' who first paved a way through the nutmeg plantations of Claymore, be faced with a challenge to conjure a vision inspired not by the past but by the future.

1965 1966

CALDICOTT, Thomas Patrick, (born 1924, Lincolnshire, England) served with the Royal Naval Volunteer Reserve, 1942-46, on Atlantic convoys as a navigator in motor torpedo-boats in the English Channel and the North Sea, and on minesweepers off the coast of Greece. 'Pat' arrived in Singapore in 1947 to join Mansfield and Co. Ltd. Singapore; was manager of the Penang office, 1955-57, then director of the company in Singapore. Appointed a director of Straits Steamship Co. Ltd. in 1961 and subsequently made managing director. With his wife Myra (formerly secretary to Arnold Thorne), lived at ARDEN in White House Park. Played rugby for Singapore and Penang; was chairman of the Singapore Maritime Employers Federation, 1963-66; a council member of the British European Association for 7 years and chairman, 1963-64; and a member of the Penang Port Commission. Left Singapore in 1969 to join the head office of Ocean Group in Liverpool and retired in 1983. A member of King George's Fund for Sailors and the Marine Society in England; enjoys sailing.

1967

BEATON, Douglas Alexander, (born 1931, Scotland) arrived in Singapore in 1957 as a chartered accountant with Ernst and Young and later became a senior partner. Was chairman of the Auditing Standards Committee; a committee member of the Singapore Society of Accountants; and a council member of the British Association of Singapore and their representative on the board of governors of the United World College. A member of the Singapore Town Club, Singapore Island Country Club, Singapore Cricket Club and British Club. Retired in 1989 and resides in England; enjoys golf and bridge.

1968

GOULD, Kenneth, (born 1919, England) joined the Territorial Army as a gunner and, at the outbreak of World War II, was posted to Singapore and was a service member of the Tanglin Club in 1940 (subsequently joining as an ordinary member in 1953). Interned in 1942 and sent to Siam to work on the 'death railway'. After completing his law qualifications in England, returned to Singapore in 1947 to join Rodyk and Davidson; became a partner in 1953 and a senior partner in 1957. Joined the Borneo Motors Group in 1962 and became chairman and managing director of Inchcape Berhad. Was vice-chairman, 1970-71, and chairman, 1971-73, of the Singapore International Chamber of Commerce; played cricket for Singapore. Retired to London in 1982 and is a trustee of the Oriental Club, London.

1969

ELIAS, Joseph Edward David, (born 1915, Java) arrived in Singapore as a child. A member of a well-known family — his father built the David Elias Buildings in Middle Road and his uncle constructed Amber Mansions (demolished in 1984 to make way for the MRT) on Orchard Road — was educated in Switzerland and then read law at Oriel College, Oxford, where he was a keen fencer and awarded Assassins Club colours. Admitted to the Inner Temple as a barrister and practised in London and Singapore. During World War II served in intelligence in India. In 1950 founded the law firm of Elias Brothers with his brother S.H.D. Elias. Retired in 1972 and resides in Spain; enjoys tennis and sailing.

1970

WALLER, Ernest George, (born 1924, Beijing, China) served with the Royal Australian Navy, 1942-46; worked as an agricultural survey officer in Ghana, 1948-52, then as an administrative officer in the Malayan Civil Service, 1952-62. During the Malayan Emergency his proficiency in Mandarin was useful in negotiating with terrorists, for which he was awarded the P.J.K. (Pahang). 'Wal' became a member of the Tanglin Club in 1963 when he arrived in Singapore and joined The Borneo Company as a personnel director; was subsequently a timber director with Inchcape Berhad, 1978, then with Burns Philp (Australia), 1981-82. In the 1970's chaired the special working committee to plan the future of the Tanglin Club. Retired to England in 1982 where he is now a business counsellor with the Department of Trade and Industry.

1971 1972

LAWTON, James William, (born 1922, England) was educated at the Adams Grammar School, Shropshire, and Aston University, Birmingham. Arrived in Singapore in 1950 as a chartered electrical engineer, worked with General Electric Company and became chairman for Singapore and Malaysia and of subsidiary companies in Thailand, Indonesia, Burma and Israel. 'Jim' was a fellow of the Institute of Electrical Engineers (United Kingdom, Singapore and Malaysia) and a keen boating and golf enthusiast. A member of the Republic of Singapore Yacht Club, Singapore Island Country Club, Sentosa Golf Club, the Oriental Club, London, and the Wrekin Golf Club. Retired to England in 1981.

1973

TAYLOR, Dr. Lionel Roland, (born 1912, Calcutta, India) graduated from the University of London and St. Bartholomew's Hospital Medical College as a qualified F.R.C.S. (Edin.), M.R.C.S. (Eng.) and L.R.C.P. (Lond.). 'Leo' joined the Royal Army Medical Corps in 1939 and arrived in Singapore in 1950. Set up his own surgical practice in 1954 and re-established St. Mary's Hospital (later the American Hospital). Joined the Tanglin Club in 1950 as a service member, then in 1955 as an ordinary member; also a member of the Singapore Cricket Club and Singapore Island Country Club, and an honorary member of the Town Club. Retired to England in 1982; enjoys golf, gardening and chess.

1974 1975  HEATON, James Rothwell, (born 1934, England) who works for the Standard Chartered Bank, joined the Tanglin Club when he came to Singapore in 1968 and was a driving force behind the redevelopment of the club. After leaving Singapore, 'Jim' managed the bank's branches in Canada, New York and California, and assumed responsibilities for their operations in East Africa before returning to London. A keen tennis player, plays for the Hale Tennis Club, U.K.

1976 1977  GRIMBERG, Joseph, (born 1933, Singapore) was educated in England at Mill Hill School and Cambridge University, and admitted as an advocate and solicitor in Singapore in 1957. Was the senior partner of Drew and Napier from 1967 to 1987, when he was appointed to the High Court bench as a judicial commissioner. Has subsequently returned to Drew and Napier as a consultant. 'Joe' has played rugby for Singapore and All-Malaya, and rugby, cricket and hockey for the Singapore Cricket Club. Also a member of the Singapore Island Country Club and Town Club.

1978 1979  TOMKINS, Peter Gerard Linton, (born 1934, England) spent his childhood in India where his father was Station Staff Officer of the Northamptonshire Regiment in charge of Ranikhet, the Indian hill station in Uttar Pradesh. Returned to England on one of the first convoys through the Suez Canal, attended Haileybury and Imperial Service College and became an articled clerk in the City of London. Served in the Honourable Artillery Company and spent 3 years national service with the Royal Army Pay Corps. Returned to Asia with his wife Sally in 1961; worked with Jardine Waugh for 6 years, then Plessey for 7 years until 1974 when he joined Cerebos and became the group's finance director. Joined the Tanglin Club in 1962, was honorary treasurer, 1973, and vice-president under Joe Grimberg before becoming president and serving again on the general committee, 1980-83. His commitment to the rebuilding of the clubhouse is summed up in his comment: "The project was a true labour of love. We visited the shell of the new complex weekly and saw the concepts become reality: the metamorphosis from drawings to models to construction to the beautiful clubhouse it is today." Also a member of the Singapore Cricket Club. Returned to England in March 1990 and is a member of the Oriental Club, London, and the Honourable Artillery, London.

1980  THAI, Chee Ken, (born 1938, Kuala Lumpur, Malaysia) was educated at the Methodist Boys' School, Kuala Lumpur, and the Anglo-Chinese School and Teachers' Training College, Singapore, then qualified as an accountant in 1963. 'Ken' worked for Arthur Andersen, Ernst & Whinney and, from 1973, Price Waterhouse, where he has been the senior partner since 1987. A fellow of the Institute of Chartered Accountants in Australia and the Institute of Certified Public Accountants of Singapore, and a committee member of numerous accountants' institutes in Singapore. Also a member of various advisory boards including the Mass Rapid Transit Corporation; has been chairman of the National Theatre Trust and the Samaritans of Singapore; was awarded the Public Service Medal in 1987. Joined the Tanglin Club in 1968; also a member of the Singapore Town Club, Tanah Merah Country Club, Jurong Country Club and Raffles Country Club.

1981  BRASLIN, Ian Vincent, (born 1936, Tasmania, Australia) arrived in Singapore in 1967 to work for the National Cash Register Co. (Singapore) Ltd. before joining Diethlem & Co. Joined the club in 1973 and served on various subcommittees; was the honorary treasurer, 1976-80. A member of the Singapore Island Country Club and the Harvard Club of Australia. Now resides in Perth, Australia; a keen golfer and wine collector.

1982 1983  EWING, John, (born 1935, Glasgow, Scotland) arrived in Malaya in July 1957 on the *Dolins*, a Blue Funnel cargo-passenger ship. Worked for Malayan Tin Dredging, south of Ipoh, until 1962 when he joined McAlister & Company, Kuala Lumpur. Spent some time in South Vietnam in 1966, then joined The Borneo Company, now Inchcape Berhad, of which he is director of the property division. After his marriage in Sydney in 1967, spent the next few years in Brunei, then Kuala Lumpur, before coming to Singapore in 1973. Has represented Perak, Selangor and Singapore in rugby and also played soccer and cricket. Was on the Tanglin Club redevelopment subcommittee in 1975 and project manager for the construction of the new clubhouse, 1977-82; during his 9 years on the general committee, served on the staff, newsletter, library, sports and entertainment subcommittees. Also a member of the Singapore Cricket Club and Singapore Island Country Club.

1984   NEWMAN, Peter Howard, (born 1937, Northern Ireland) was educated

at the Royal Belfast Academical Institution and came to Singapore in 1963 to join Charles Williams & Company (later Richard Ellis Pte. Ltd.) as a chartered surveyor. Joined the Tanglin Club in 1971 and was elected to the general committee in 1977; also served on the entertainment, newsletter, library and bridge subcommittees. Fellow of the Royal Institute of Chartered Surveyors; a member of the Singapore Cricket Club, Oriental Club, London, and Royal Overseas League. Retired to London in 1988; enjoys bridge and the theatre.

1985   THEIN, Reggie Myint, (born 1941, Rangoon, Burma) a

chartered accountant, joined Coopers and Lybrand in 1963 and is now a senior partner. Was elected to the Tanglin Club committee in 1979; served as honorary treasurer for 4 years during the redevelopment of the clubhouse. A member of the Singapore Cricket Club and the Singapore Swimming Club; enjoys tennis and reading and is active in community service.

1986   GRINSTED, Edward John, (born 1938, Australia) was educated

at Sydney Grammar School and arrived in Singapore in 1975 to work for Fitzpatrick's Food Supplies (F.E.) Ltd. Subsequently became regional director (Asia) of Nabisco Brands Pte. Ltd. and spent 2 years in Bombay, India, from 1987. In 1990 became president and chief operating officer of Britannia Brands Pte. Ltd., a Singapore multinational company. Joined the Tanglin Club in 1976 and served on the general committee, 1982-85. 'Ted' is treasurer of the *Confrerie de la Chaine des Rotisseurs*; also a member of the Singapore Cricket Club, Singapore Polo Club, British Club, Jurong Country Club, Republic of Singapore Yacht Club and Raffles Marina.

1987 1988   HO, Charles, (born 1940, Singapore) at-

tended Anglo-Chinese School, Singapore, and Geelong Grammar School, Australia, and graduated in architecture from the University of Melbourne, Australia. Established Design International Architects in 1970 as a subsidiary of Iversen Van Sitteren; it is now an independent practice whose projects have included the Singapore Turf Club, Bukit Turf Club, Singapore Island Country Club and the Shaw House/Lido Theatre redevelopment, as well as various projects for Shell Eastern Petroleum (Pulau Bukom) and some conservation projects. Member of the Singapore Island Country Club, Bukit Turf Club and Old Geelong Grammarian Ski Club.

1989 1990   SANDOSHAM, George, (born 1938, India) who came to

Singapore in 1946, read law at the University of Malaya, Singapore. Was admitted to the Bar in 1966, appointed a magistrate, then, in 1969, district court judge before going into private practice in 1971. Joined the Tanglin Club in 1973. Awarded the Public Service Medal for services on the Criminal Law Advisory Committee in 1976, also the year his wife Linda, a senior education officer, was awarded the Efficiency Medal. Played cricket for the Singapore Cricket Club; also a member of the Singapore Island Country Club, Keppel Club, Singapore Town Club, Changi Beach Club, Republic of Singapore Yacht Club and Oriental Club, London, and a life member of the National University of Singapore Society.

Appendices

Reciprocal Clubs

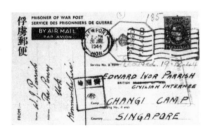

Australia
The Adelaide Club
The Brisbane Club
The Tattersall's Club (Brisbane)
The Australian Club (Melbourne)
Royal Automobile Club of Victoria (Melbourne)
Racv Healesville Country Club
The Tattersall's Club (Sydney)
Union Club (Sydney)
University & Schools Club (Sydney)
The Western Australia Club Inc. (Perth)

Canada
The Vancouver Club
The Glencoe Club (Calgary)

France
Cercle De L'union Inter Alliee (Paris)

Germany
Der Ubersee-club E.v. (Hamburg)

Hong Kong
The Hong Kong Club (Central)
The American Club Hong Kong (Central)
Ladies Recreation Club

India
Royal Bombay Yacht Club

Indonesia
International Sports Club of Indonesia (Jakarta)

Ireland
Kildare Street & University Club (Dublin)

Japan
Kobe Regatta & Athletic Club

Korea
Seoul Club

Malaysia
Kelab Gymkhana Miri
Kelab Diraja Ipoh — Royal Ipoh Club
Kelab Taman Perdana — Lake Club (Kuala Lumpur)
Royal Selangor Club (Kuala Lumpur)
The Malacca Club
The New Club (Taiping)
Penang Club
Port Dickson Club & Yacht Club

The Sarawak Club (Kuching)
The Sarawak Club (Kuching)
Sungei Ujong Club (Seremban)

Monaco
Le Yacht Club of Monaco (Monte Carlo)

New Zealand
The Northern Club (Auckland)
The Auckland Club
The Wellesley Club (Wellington)
The Christchurch Club
The Dunedin Club

Papua New Guinea
Papua Club Inc. (Port Moresby)

Philippines
Baguio Country Club
Manila Club (Makati)

Sri Lanka
The Hill Club (Nuwara Eliya)

Sweden
The Sallskapet Club (Stockholm)

Thailand
The British Club (Bangkok)

United Kingdom
Royal Northern & University Club (Aberdeen)
The New Club (Edinburgh)
The Royal Scottish Automobile Club (Glasgow)
The Western Club (Glasgow)
The Caledonian Club (London)
The Hurlingham Club (London)
The Oriental Club (London)
United Oxford & Cambridge University Club
(London)
Carlton Club (London)
East India Club (London)

United States of America
Harvard Club of Boston
The Georgetown Club (Washington D.C.)
The Pacific Club (Honolulu)
The University Club of Chicago
The Graduates Club Association (New Haven,
Connecticut)
University Club of San Francisco
The University Club (Pittsburgh, Pennsylvania)

Acknowledgements and Credits

This historical review was researched and compiled by the Tanglin Club 125th anniversary editorial committee. GRAHAM BELL, who sailed from Australia to Singapore on his honeymoon in 1964, is a chartered accountant by qualification and a bottle-top maker by profession: he is chairman of the Crown Cork and Seal Co. Inc. group in the Asia Pacific region. He is an honorary life member of the Singapore Australia Business Council and a founder of the Australian Art Award (Singapore). Graham joined the club in 1965 and is a dedicated committee member. An ardent collector of books, Graham has always fancied producing his own book which is why he bravely volunteered to get a commemorative publication off the ground; he is now contemplating a book based on information about members of the Tanglin Club that was, on legal advice, omitted from this one, and is hopeful that the contributions towards it not being published will finance his early retirement in the Algarve. Sydney-born JAN BELL trained at Wagga Wagga Teachers' College, N.S.W., Australia, and came to Singapore with her husband Graham on his three-year posting with Evatt & Co. (Price Waterhouse). Since then she has raised three children and dedicated 25 years to teaching, first at Raeburn Park School (the Singapore Harbour Board School) then at Tanglin School. Jan very much enjoyed her task of burrowing through a wide range of sources and materials which brought its own rewards, including fond friendships with many of those who helped in her investigations and a deeper understanding of the history of the region. Convent-educated BARBARA ANN WALSH, began her travels as a foreign student before continuing in the family tradition, graduating with an LL.B. from Victoria University, Wellington, New Zealand. Since 1970 when she married Frank Walsh, an Australian trade commissioner and Tanglin Club member, she has helped to move him and their three outstanding daughters to Suva, Nairobi, Lagos, Tehran, Vienna, Warsaw, Sydney (where she completed a degree in French), Chicago and Singapore. She has also worked for law firms in New Zealand, Fiji, Australia and the U.S.A., and is currently a legal consultant to the Office of the United Nations High Commissioner for Refugees in Singapore. Barbara has sometimes enjoyed her task of writing this story; a resident of the Claymore district, she regrets the transformation of the area from nutmeg-garden to nut-house.

The editorial committee would like to acknowledge the efforts of all those individuals and members of the club in Singapore and overseas who helped bring this story to life, gave their time and knowledge in different ways and contributed various materials. The committee is especially grateful to Michael Khoo for his contribution on the early legal development of the club as discerned from the documents. Andrew Jordan researched property matters relating to the club. Many other club members made specific contributions. Credit is due to James Ferrie for the caricatures of club presidents and research on the architecture of the original clubhouse. John Ewing traced the developments and renovations of the old clubhouse. Peter Tomkins provided invaluable details of club life and of the construction of the new clubhouse. Peter von Selkey provided architectural details of the new clubhouse. Paul Wright has photographed the club since 1977 and his professional services were used in reproducing many of the materials in the book. Bob Booker traced the diary of Rowland Allen and donated a copy for research. Harry and Sonia Dyne assisted in the search for Straits Directories in the Donald & Burkinshaw library and also obtained the 1904 Tanglin Club smoking concert programme.

Club members, past and present, who shared their recollections and memorabilia of pre-war and postwar times through correspondence and interviews, offered advice on sourcing information, or provided some assistance include: Neill Aitken, Mickey Bain, Betty Bell, Len Bell, Roy Bennett, Peter Bird, Ian Braslin, Hazel Booker, Derek and Jennifer Brown, B.C.J. 'Buck' Buckeridge, Della Butcher, Dr. Robert and Majorie Calderwood, Pat Caldicott, Erica Canning, Francis Chan, Chan Ket Teck, Prof. Yahya Cohen, G.M. 'Tiger' Coltart, Margaret Cowe, John Craig, John Curran, Jo Essery, Ian Ferguson, Isabel Ferrie, Donald Fergusson, Col. L.T. Firbank, Jean Fraser, Harold Godwin Jr., Mike Gorrie, Ken Gould, Joe Grimberg, Vivien Gwee, Kay Hatfield, Frances Henton, Pamela Hickley, Desmond Hill, Charles Ho, Anthony and Phyllis Hopkins, James Houghton,

Lt. Col. H.M.J. Jensen, Lady Patricia Griffith-Jones, Peter Keys, Dr. Koh Eng Yam, Yvonne Lawton, S.F.T.B. 'Joe' Lever, Roger Marshall, Christina Mason, Liz Middleton, Dorothy Oates, John Parker, Ray Parker, Renée Parrish, Gwen Pickering, G.D. Prockter, Len and Lulin Reutens, Rae Rigg, 'Roper' and Pamela Roper-Caldbeck, Mike Rushworth, Nan Sandford, Laurette Shearman, Malcolm Smithson, Harold Smyth, Dr. Raymond Tan, Thai Chee Ken, Reggie Thein, Arnold and Sue Thorne, 'Teddy' Tokeley, Charles Tresise, Anne Tweedie, George Verrall, 'Wal' Waller, Dr. Charles Wilson, 'Pom' Whittington, Katie Witham, Mabel Wong, and Graham Zacharias.

Tanglin Club staff members who were of assistance include: Nizar Ahamed, for his infallible memory of members and events; Savitri Devi, for reminiscences of her father and uncle and her typing assistance; Mary Shotam, for her invaluable assistance in locating information and records; George Zuzarte, for relevant information on the club's sporting and other recreational activities; and many others who answered queries and searched for details, especially T.M.S. Devan, James Koh Meng Seng, Alijah Mahat and Assa Randhawa. Former staff Koh Siang Mong and Jimmy Scheerder were forthcoming with details of yesteryear.

Many individuals have been especially helpful with historical source materials. Michael Sweet of Antiques of the Orient, gave willingly of his time in helping to identify photographs and generously loaned material from his collection for reproduction. Andrew Tan Kim Guan was of considerable help with historical detail and graciously provided maps, postcards and reference material from his private collection. Colonel K. Mellor assisted in the accuracy of military details. Others who kindly expedited the search for materials in various ways include: George Bogaars, Michael Burnett, Terry Curran (British High Commission), Bishop Emeritus Dr. T.R. Doraisamy (Methodist House), Julia Griffith-Jones, Rev. (Dr.) Anne Johnson, Isabella Lau, Prof. Edwin Lee, Lee Kip Lin, Captain Philip J. Rivers, William Tailyour, Mick Tyers and Roger Yue.

Much gratitude is owed to various individuals who willingly lent a hand with research at various libraries and other institutions which kindly allowed access to and reproductions of relevant materials — Hasnah Haron, Lim Kek Hwa, Absah Mingan, V. Perumbulavil, Azizah Sidek, and Wong Heng at the National Library of Singapore; T. Kannu at the Maritime Museum Singapore; Pauline Northey at the British Association, Singapore; Philip Reed at the Imperial War Museum, London, U.K.; Mrs J. Herring at the Library and Records Commission, Foreign Commonwealth Office, London, U.K.; Annabel Teh Gallop at the British Library, London, U.K. (in appreciation, the Tanglin Club has 'adopted' some editions of the Singapore Directory held by the British Museum and contributed to their rebinding); Isabel Yeo and Tay Sok Cheng at Times House. Archival information and publications were also obtained from the National Museum and Archives, Singapore; National University of Singapore library; Public Affairs Department of the Singapore Police Force; Singapore Botanic Gardens; Bukit Turf Club, Singapore; Malaysian National Archives, Kuala Lumpur, Malaysia; Bousteadco Singapore; Commercial Union Assurance; the East India Company archives; Guthrie & Company; Inchcape Berhad; Standard Chartered Bank; Hongkong and Shanghai Bank.

Invaluable support in preparing the draft manuscript was provided by the professional services of Roger Prior Associates, in particular Han-Ong Bee Cheng who bore the task of endlessly keying in amendments to a handwritten text with unfailing good humour, and Christianne Lee (Crown Cork & Seal Co. (S) Ltd.). Finally, true appreciation goes to the professional support of Wordmaker Design Pte. Ltd., especially Loretta Reilly-Chan, Norani M. Ali, Chew Kheng Chuan and Lee Yew Ho, who were most generous in their efforts to assist enthusiastic amateurs to produce a book which, under the patient editorial direction of Vani S., resulted in this story begun by forty 'good men and true' in the island of Singapore.

Sources and Further Readings

Abbreviations used in pictorial credits

A.O. — *Antiques of the Orient Pte. Ltd., Singapore*
N.A. — *National Archives, Singapore*
N.M. — *National Museum, Singapore*
N.L. — *National Library, Singapore*
T.C. — *Tanglin Club*

Allen, Charles, (ed.) in association with **Mason, Michael**, *Tales from the South China Seas: Images of the British in South East Asia in the Twentieth Century*. Futura Publications, London, 1984.

Allen, Rowland, *Experiences During a Voyage to Singapore, Notes On and Description of The Town.* Unpublished diary, 8 May-18 June, 1895.

Archives & Oral History Department, *Road to Nationhood: Singapore 1819-1980*. The Government of Singapore, Singapore, 1984.

Archives & Oral History Department, *The Land Transport of Singapore, from early times to the present*. Educational Publications Bureau Pte. Ltd., Singapore, 1981; revised 1984.

Archives & Oral History Department, *Singapore Retrospect Through Postcards 1900-1930*. Sin Chew Jit Poh (S) Ltd., Singapore, 1982.

Archives & Oral History Department and Department of Civil Aviation, *Singapore Fly-Past, A pictorial review of civil aviation in Singapore, 1911-1981*. Singapore, 1982.

Archives & Oral History Department, *The Japanese Occupation 1942-1945*. Singapore, 1985.

Attiwill, Kenneth, *The Singapore Story*. Frederick Muller Ltd., London, 1959.

Augustin, Andreas, *The Raffles Treasury, Secrets of a Grand Old Lady*. Singapore, 1st printed 1987; reprinted 1987, 1988, 1989.

Augustin, Andreas, *The Singapore Treasury, Secrets of the Garden City*. Treasury Publishing Pte. Ltd., Singapore, 1st edition 1988; 2nd expanded edition 1990.

Backhouse, Sally, *Singapore — The Islands Series*. Newton Abbot, David & Charles Pub. Ltd., Great Britain, 1972.

Barber, Noel, *Sinister Twilight, The Fall and Rise Again of Singapore*. Collins, London, 1968.

Barber, Noel, *The Singapore Story: From Raffles to Lee Kuan Yew*. Fontana, London, 1978.

Bickmore, Albert Smith, *Travels in the East Indian Archipelago*. John Murray, London, 1868.

Bird, Isabella L., *The Golden Chersonese and The Way Thither*. John Murray, London, 1883.

Bleackley, H.M., *A Tour in Southern Asia (Indo-China, Malaya, Java, Sumatra and Ceylon, 1925-1926)*. John Lane The Bodley Head Ltd., London, 1928.

Bloodworth, Dennis, *The Tiger and the Trojan Horse*. Times Books International, Singapore, 1986.

Bloom, Freddy, *Dear Philip, A Diary of Captivity, Changi 1942-45*. The Bodley Head Ltd., London, 1980.

Bogaars, George, 'The Tanjong Pagar Dock Company, 1864-1905', *Memoirs of the Raffles Museum, No. 3.*, Singapore, December 1956.

Bowden, Tim, *Changi Photographer, George Aspinall's Record of Captivity*. ABC Enterprises & William Collins Pty. Ltd. (for the Australian Broadcasting Corporation) Sydney, 1984.

Braddell, Roland St. J., *The Lights of Singapore*. Methuen & Co. Ltd., London, 1934; reprinted Oxford University Press, Malaysia, 1982.

Brown, E.A., *Indiscreet Memories*. Kelly & Walsh, London, 1935.

Buckley, Charles Burton, *An Anecdotal History of Old Times in Singapore 1819-1867*, (2 vol.). Fraser & Neave Ltd., Singapore, 1902.

Burns, P.L., (ed.) *The Journals of J.W.W. Birch, First British Resident to Perak 1874-1875*. Oxford University Press, Kuala Lumpur, 1976.

Butcher, John G., *The British in Malaya 1880- 1941: The Social History of a European community in Colonial South-East Asia*. Oxford University Press, Kuala Lumpur, 1979.

Caffrey, Kate, *Out in the Midday Sun: Singapore 1941-45*. André Deutsch Ltd., London, 1974.

Cameron, J., *Our Tropical Possessions in Malayan India*. Elder Smith, U.K., 1865; reprinted Oxford University Press, Kuala Lumpur 1965.

Chase Manhattan Bank N.A., *Jurong Singapore*. Singapore, 1973.

Chin Kee Onn, *Malaya Upside Down*. Federal Publications, Singapore, 3rd edition 1976.

Chua Beng Huat, *The Golden Shoe: Building Singapore's Financial District*. Urban Redevelopment Authority, Singapore, 1989.

Cook, J.A.B., *Sunny Singapore*. E. Stock, London, 1907.

Corner, E.J.H., *The Marquis: A Tale of Syonan-to*. Heinemann Asia, Singapore, 1981.

Corner, E.J.H., *Wayside Trees of Malaya*. Malayan Nature Society, Singapore, 3rd edition 1988.

Cunyngham-Brown, Sjovald, *The Traders*. Newman Neame Ltd. (for Guthrie & Co. U.K, Ltd.), London, 1971.

Dalton, John N., *The Cruise of Her Majesty's Ship "Bacchante" 1879-1882* [compiled from the private journals, letters, and notebooks of Prince Albert Victor and Prince George of Wales]. Macmillan & Co., London, 1886.

Davies, Donald, *More Old Singapore*. Donald Moore, Singapore, 1956.

Davies, Donald, *Old Singapore*. Donald Moore, Singapore, 1954.

Dennys, N.B., *A Descriptive Dictionary of British Malaya*. "LONDON AND CHINA TELEGRAPH" OFFICE, London, 1894.

Doggett, Marjorie, *Characters of Light, Early Buildings of Singapore*. Donald Moore, Singapore, 1957; reprinted Times Books International, Singapore, 1985.

Drysdale, John, *Singapore: Struggle for Success*. Times Books International, Singapore, 1984.

Durai, Raja-Singam S., *Malayan Street Names*. The Mercantile Press, Ipoh, 1939.

Dutton, Geoffrey, *Impressions of Singapore*. Times Books International, Singapore, 1981.

D'Aranjo, B.E., *The Stranger's Guide to Singapore*.'Sirangoon' Press, Singapore, 1890.

Edwards, Norman and **Keys, Peter**, *Singapore, a Guide to Buildings, Streets, Places*. Times Books International, Singapore, 1988.

Falconer, John, *A Vision of the Past: A History of Early Photography in Singapore and Malaya: The Photographs of G.R. Lambert & Co., 1880-1910*. Times Editions, Singapore, 1987.

Flower, Raymond, *Meet You at Raffles*. Times Books International (for the Raffles Hotel), Singapore, 1985; revised and reprinted Eastern Universities Press Sdn. Bhd., Singapore, 1987.

Flower, Raymond, *Raffles The Story of Singapore*. Eastern Universities Press Sdn. Bhd., Singapore, 1984.

Foster, H., *A Beachcomber in the Orient*. John Lane, The Bodley Head Ltd., London, 1923.

George, T.J.S., *Lee Kuan Yew's Singapore*. André Deutsch Ltd., London, 1973; reprinted Eastern Universities Press, Singapore, 1984.

German, R.L., *Handbook to British Malaya*. The Malay States Information Agency, London, 1935.

Gibson, Ashley, *The Malay Peninsula and Archipelago*. J.M. Dent & Sons Ltd., London, 1928.

Gibson-Hill, C.A., "Singapore Old Strait & New Harbour 1800-1870", *Memoirs of the Raffles Museum No. 3.*, Singapore, December 1956.

Gilmour, Andrew, *An Eastern Cadet's Anecdotage*. University Education Press, Singapore, 1974.

Gilmour, Andrew, *My Role in the Rehabilitation of Singapore, 1946-1953*. Institute of South East Asian Studies (Oral History Pilot Study), Singapore, 1973.

Glaskin, G.M., *A Lion in the Sun*. Barrie & Rockcliff, Great Britain, 1960; reprinted Panther, London, 1963, 1965.

Goh Poh Seng, *If We Dream Too Long*. Island Press, Singapore, 1972.

Goodwood Park Hotel, *The Goodwood Heritage 1900-1980*. Singapore, 1980.

Griffith-Jones, Lionel, *That's My Lot*. Vantage Press Inc., New York, 1984.

Hancock, T.H.H., *Coleman's Singapore*. The Malaysian Branch of the Royal Asiatic Society in association with Pelanduk Publications, Kuala Lumpur, 1986.

Harper, R.W.E. and **Miller, Harry**, *Singapore Mutiny*. Oxford University Press, Singapore, 1984.

Harrison, Cuthbert W., *An Illustrated Guide to the Federated Malay States*. The Malay States Information Agency, London, 1910; 4th edition 1923.

Hill, Anthony, *Diversion in Malaya*. Collins, London, 1948.

Hogan, Norman S., *50 Years with Donaldson & Burkinshaw*. Donaldson & Burkinshaw, Singapore, 1971.

Hon, Joan, *100 Years of the Singapore Fire Service*. Times Books International (for the Singapore Fire Service), Singapore, 1988.

Howarth, David and **Stephen**, *The Story of P & O, The Peninsular and Oriental Steam Navigation Company*. Weidenfeld & Nicolson, London, 1986.

Hubback, Theodore R., *Elephant and Seladang Hunting in the Federated Malay States*. Rowland Ward Ltd., London, 1905.

Jennings, E.L.S., *Mansfields: Transport & Distribution in South-East Asia*. Meridian Communications (SEA) Pte. Ltd., Singapore, 1973.

Jessy, Joginder Singh, *History of Malaya 1400-1959*. United Publishers & Peninsular Publications, Penang, 1961; reprinted 1962, 1963, 1964, 1965.

Josey, Alex, *David Marshall's Political Interlude*. Eastern Universities Press, Singapore, 1982.

Josey, Alex, *Lee Kuan Yew* (2 vol.). Times Books International, Singapore, 1980.

Josey, Alex, *Lee Kuan Yew: The Struggle for Singapore*. Angus & Robertson, Sydney, 1974.

Jurong Town Corporation, *Twenty Years On Jurong Town Corporation (1968-1988*. Singapore, 1988.

Kelly & Walsh Ltd., *Singapore Centenary, A Souvenir Volume*. Singapore, 1919.

Kennedy, Joseph, *When Singapore Fell, Evacuations and Escapees 1941-42*. Macmillan, London, 1989.

Kirkup, James, *Tropic Temper: A Memoir of Malaya*. Collins, London, 1963.

Lattimer, Pamela, *A Family of Ginger Griffins*. Regency Press, London, 1987.

Lau, Isabelle, *Memoirs of Cynthia Koek*. Unpublished, Singapore, 1990.

Lee Kip Lin, *The Singapore House 1819-1942*. Times Editions, Singapore, 1988.

Lewis T.P.M., *Changi, The Lost Years — A Malayan Diary 1941-1945*. The Malaysian Historical Society, Kuala Lumpur, 1984.

Liu, Gretchen, *One Hundred Years of the National Museum: Singapore 1887-1987*. National Museum, Singapore, 1987.

Liu, Gretchen, (ed.) *Singapore Historical Postcards From the National Archives Collection*. Times Editions, Singapore, 1986.

Lockhart, R.H. Bruce, *Return to Malaya*. G.P. Putnam's Sons, New York, 1936.

Makepeace, Walter; Braddell, Roland St. J., and Brooke, Dr. Gilbert E., (eds.) *One Hundred Years of Singapore* (2 vols.). John Murray, London, 1921.

Marks, Violet, 'Pen Pictures of Long Ago', *British Malaya*, London, February 1949.

McKie, Ronald, *Malaysia in Focus*. Angus & Robertson, Sydney, 1963.

McKie, Ronald, *This Was Singapore*. Angus & Robertson, Sydney, 1942.

Minchin, James, *No Man Is An Island, A Study of Singapore's Lee Kuan Yew*. Allen & Unwin, Sydney, Boston, 1986.

Ministry of Culture, *Singapore in Pictures 1819-1945*. Sin Chew Poh (S) Ltd., Singapore, 1981.

Ministry of Defence, *Singapore Artillery, 100th Anniversary*. Singapore, 1988.

Moore, Donald and Joanna, *The First 150 Years of Singapore*. Donald Moore Press Ltd. (in association with the Singapore International Chamber of Commerce), Singapore, 1969.

Moore, Donald, (ed.) *Where Monsoons Meet*. George G. Harrap & Co. Ltd., London, 1956.

Morrison, Ian, *Malayan Postcript*. Faber & Faber Ltd., London, 1942.

Norman, Diana, *Road from Singapore*. Hodder & Stoughton, London, 1970.

Norman, Sir H., *The Peoples and Politics of the Far East*. T. Fisher Unwin, London, 1895.

Paik Choo, (et al.) *The Original Singapore Sling Book*. Landmark Books Pte. Ltd., Singapore, 1986.

Pearson, H.F., *Singapore, A Popular History 1819-1960*. Eastern Universities Press, Singapore, 1961; republished Times Books International, Singapore, 1985.

Peet, George L., *Rickshaw Reporter*. Eastern Universities Press Sdn. Bhd., Singapore, 1985.

Playfair, Giles, *Singapore Goes off the Air*. Jarrods, London, 1944.

Port of Singapore Authority, *Singapore: Portrait of a Port*. Singapore, 1984.

Ramachandra, S., *Singapore Landmarks Past and Present*. Donald Moore (for Eastern Universities Press Ltd.), Singapore, 1961.

Rao, A.N., and Wee Yeow Chin, *Singapore Trees*. Singapore Institute of Biology, Singapore, 1989.

Read, W.H.M., *Play and Politics: Recollections of Malaya by An Old Resident*. Wells Gardner Darton & Co., London, 1901.

Reith, G.M., *Handbook to Singapore*. Fraser & Neave Ltd., Singapore, 1892; 2nd edition 1907.

Rennie, J.S.M., *Musings of J.S.M.R. Mostly Malayan*. Malayan Publishing House Ltd. Singapore, 1933.

Robertson, E.J., *Straits Memories Being Recollections of Incidents, People and Lives in Singapore and the Straits a Generation Ago*. Methodist Publishing House, Singapore, 1910.

Robson, J.H.M., *Records and Recollections 1889-1934*. Kyle, Palmer & Co. Ltd., Kuala Lumpur, 1934.

The Rotary Club and Municipal Commissioners of the Town of Singapore, *A Handbook of Information*. Singapore, 1933.

Russell-Roberts, Denis, *Spotlight on Singapore*. Tandem Books, London, 1966.

Santry, Denis, *Salubrious Singapore by Santry & Claude*. Kelly and Walsh, Singapore, 1920.

Sharp, Ilsa, *The Singapore Cricket Club 1852-1985*. The Singapore Cricket Club, Singapore, 1985.

Sharp, Ilsa, *There is Only One Raffles, The Story of a Grand Hotel*. Souvenir Press (for Times Publishing Bhd.), London, 1981; reprinted 1982, 1983.

Sheppard, Tan Sri Dato' Mubin, (ed.) *Singapore 150 Years*. Times Books International (for the Malaysian Branch of the Royal Asiatic Society), Singapore, 1982.

Singapore Heritage Society, *Pages from Yesteryear: A look at the printed works of Singapore 1819-1959*. Singapore, 1989.

Singapore International Chamber of Commerce, *From Early Days*. Singapore, 1979.

Singh, Daljit and Arasu, V.T., (eds.) *Singapore, An Illustrated History 1941-1984*. Information Division, Ministry of Culture, Singapore, 1984; 2nd and 3rd reprints 1985.

Song Ong Siang, *One Hundred Years' History of the Chinese in Singapore*. John Murray, London, 1923; reprinted University of Malaya Press, 1967, 1984.

Stein, R. Conrad, *World at War, Fall of Singapore*. Children's Press, Chicago, 1982.

Stirling, W.G., *Shadows of a Malayan Screen*. Kelly & Walsh Ltd., Singapore, 1910; 2nd impression 1926.

Swettenham, Frank, *Malay Sketches*. John Lane The Bodley Head Ltd., London, 1895.

Swettenham, Sir Frank, *British Malaya, An account of the origin and progress of British influence in Malaya 1850-1946*. John Lane The Bodley Head, London, 1907; reprinted 1948, 1955.

Swettenham, Sir Frank, *Footprints in Malaya*. Hutchinson & Co., London, 1942.

Tan Bee Choo, *Street Names in Selected Areas of Singapore*. Unpublished B.A. Hons. academic exercise, Dept. of Geography, University of Singapore, 1977.

Tan Keng Kang, (project director) *Social and Economic History of Singapore* (2 vol.). Longman Publishing Pte. Ltd., Singapore, 1985; Vol. 1 reprinted 1985, 1986; Vol. 2 reprinted 1986.

Tate, D.J.M., *Straits Affairs, The Malay World and Singapore*. John Nicholson Ltd., Hong Kong, 1989.

Tate, D.J.M., *The Lake Club 1890-1990*. Oxford University Press, Singapore, 1990.

Taylor, William, *With the Cambridgeshires at Singapore*. Trevor Allen Bevis, U.K., 1971.

Thomas, Mary, *In the Shadow of the Rising Sun*. Maruzen Asia, Singapore, 1983.

Thomson, J.T., *Glimpses into Life in Malayan Lands* (with an introduction and annotations by John Hall-Jones). Oxford University Press, Singapore, 1984; reprinted Kuala Lumpur, 1985.

Tinsley, Bonnie, *Singapore Green*. Times Books International, Singapore, 1953.

Tsuji, Col. Masanobu, *Singapore 1941-1942: The Japanese Version of the Malayan Campaign of World War II*. Ure Smith Pty. Ltd., Sydney, 1960; reprinted Oxford University Press, Singapore, 1988.

Turnbull, C.M., *A History of Singapore 1819-1988*. Oxford University Press, Singapore; second edition 1989.

Turnbull, C.M., *The Straits Settlements, 1826-1867, Indian Presidency to Crown Colony*. University of London, The Athlone Press, 1972 edition.

Tyers, Ray, *Singapore Then and Now* (2 vol.). University Education Press, Singapore, 1976.

Van Cuylenburg, J.B., *Singapore — Through Sunshine and Shadow*. Heinemann Asia, Singapore, 1982.

Warren, James Francis, *Rickshaw Coolie, A People's History of Singapore 1880-1940*. Oxford University Press, Singapore, 1986.

Williams, Hilary, *Arthur Scrimgeour, The Beginnings of Glaxo in China, A Life — Recollected by Helen Scrimgeour*. Glaxo China Enterprises Ltd., Hong Kong, 1990.

Wilson, Dick, *East Meets West: Singapore*. Times Printers Sdn. Bhd., Singapore, 1971; revised second edition 1975.

Winsley, Capt T.M., *A History of the Singapore Volunteer Corps 1854-1937*. Govt. Printing Office, Singapore, 1938.

Winstedt, Sir R.O., 'Singapore, Past and Present', *British Malaya*. London, March 1938.

Winstedt, R.O., and Wilkinson, R.J., 'A History of Perak', *Journal of the Malayan Branch of the Royal Asiatic Society* (Vol. XII). Singapore, 1934.

Wise, Michael and **Mun Him**, *Travellers' Tales of Old Singapore*. Times Books International, Singapore, 1985.

Woodcock, George, *The British in the Far East*. Weidenfeld & Nicolson, London, 1969.

Wright, Arnold and **Cartwright, H.A.**, *Twentieth Century Impressions of British Malaya*. Lloyd's Great Britain Publishing Co. Ltd., London, 1908; reprinted Graham Brash, Singapore, 1990.

Wright, A. and **Reid, T.H.**, *The Malay Peninsula: Record of British Progress in the Middle East*. T.F. Unwin, London, 1912.

Wurtzburg, C.E., 'Singapore, Past and Present', *British Malaya*. London, December 1940.

Ziegele, Otto, *Singapore Diary 1886-1890*. Unpublished, Rhodes House Library, Oxford, U.K.

Advertisers

The early development and membership of the Tanglin Club was inextricably linked with the growth of British business concerns in the island colony and the Far East. Thus, when this commemorative history was first conceived, it was decided to invite advertisements from those companies that have been in continuous operation since the club was founded 125 years ago and the following establishments responded to our invitation.

The Borneo Company was established on July 31, 1856, having its genesis in W.R. Paterson & Company (1846) which later became McEwan & Company (1852); it is now a subsidiary of Inchcape Berhad. In 1865, on the founding committee of the Tanglin Club, the vice-president Herbert Buchanan, the honorary secretary Joseph Webster, and a committee member William Mulholland were all with The Borneo Company. In 1866 a clerk of The Borneo Company, John Crum, loaned the club 5000 Spanish dollars to build its first clubhouse. Four club presidents and many committee members have been with the company.

Bousteadco Singapore was first established as Boustead & Company in 1828 then became Boustead & Schwabe & Company in 1834 and carried on business near Elgin Bridge in what was called the seven-and-twenty pillar house. In 1849 the firm reverted to the name Boustead & Company and has since continued business in shipping and trading. Since 1865 nine club presidents and many of its committee members have been with Bousteads.

John Little & Company was originally founded in 1845 as Little, Cursetjee & Company. In 1853 when this partnership dissolved John Little was joined by Matthew Little and the business has continued to the present as John Little & Company; since 1955 it has been a wholly owned subsidiary of Robinson & Company. In 1876 Matthew Little loaned the Tanglin Club $3,500 when it was in serious financial difficulty.

Robinson & Company was established in 1859 after the partnership of Spicer & Robinson, a new family warehouse set up by Philip Robinson and James Spicer at Nos. 9 and 10 Raffles Place in 1858, was dissolved. Initially located at the corner of Coleman Street and North Bridge Road, in the 1860's it opened at No. 1 Raffles Place and advertised as: 'wholesale and family wharehouseman; wine ale and spirit merchants; oilmen and general provisioners; drapers milliners and haberdashers; clothier and outfitters'.

Royal International was established in London in 1845 as Royal Insurance and in 1846 appointed Middleton Harrison & Company as its agents in Singapore. In 1865 the London & Lancashire and The Liverpool & London Fire Insurance Company, both now members of the Royal Group, were represented respectively by Middleton Harrison & Company and Syme & Company.

Standard Chartered Bank was established at the north corner of Raffles Place in 1859 as the Chartered Bank of India, Australia & China, and was known as the Chartered (to distinguish it from the Chartered Mercantile Bank of India, London & China which was situated at D'Almeida's offices at the south end of the square). A number of presidents and treasurers of the Tanglin Club have been with the Chartered, including the first honorary treasurer L. C. Masfen in 1865.

Sun Alliance Insurance was first established in London in 1710 as the Sun Fire Office which in 1845 appointed Maclaine Fraser & Company as its first agents in Singapore. In 1865 they were represented by John Purvis & Company offering a comprehensive cover against fire, goods, merchandise and other property. Phoenix Assurance, a member of the Sun Alliance Group, was also doing business in Singapore in 1865, represented by Reme, Leveson & Company.

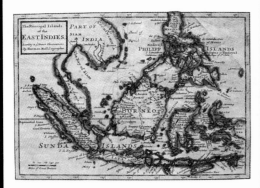

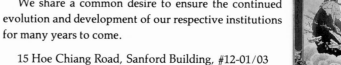
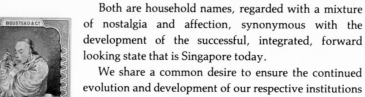

Alexr Duff
Hon. Secretary

Registra
This

Received of and from the
James Davidson, David Ro
Jonas Daniel Vaughan th
Six hundred being the co